Monetary Authorities

Monetary

ALLAN E. S. LUMBA

Authorities

Capitalism and

Decolonization

in the

American Colonial

Philippines

DUKE UNIVERSITY PRESS   Durham and London   2022

Designed by A. Mattson Gallagher
Typeset in Whitman, Letter Gothic Std, and Engravers LT Std
by Westchester Publishing Services
Printed and bound by CPI Group (UK) Ltd, Croydon, CR0 4YY
Library of Congress Cataloging-in-Publication Data
Names: Lumba, Allan E. S., [date] author.
Title: Monetary authorities : capitalism and decolonization in the
American colonial Philippines / Allan E. S. Lumba.
Description: Durham : Duke University Press, 2022. |
Includes bibliographical references and index.
Identifiers: LCCN 2021031833 (print)
LCCN 2021031834 (ebook)
ISBN 9781478015550 (hardcover)
ISBN 9781478018186 (paperback)
ISBN 9781478022794 (ebook)
ISBN 9781478092582 (ebook other)
Subjects: LCSH: Capitalism—Philippines. | Decolonization—Philippines. |
Anti-imperialist movements—Philippines. | Colonization—Economic
aspects—History—19th century. | Philippines—History—1898– |
Philippines—Politics and government—1898–1935. | Philippines—
Economic conditions. | Philippines—Foreign economic relations—
United States. | United States—Foreign economic relations—Philippines. |
BISAC: HISTORY / United States / General | HISTORY / Asia / Southeast Asia
Classification: LCC DS685 .L86 2022 (print) | LCC DS685 (ebook) |
DDC 330.12/2v—dc23/eng/20211012
LC record available at https://lccn.loc.gov/2021031833
LC ebook record available at https://lccn.loc.gov/2021031834

This book is freely available in an open access edition thanks to
TOME (Toward an Open Monograph Ecosystem)—a collaboration of the Association of American Universities, the Association
of University Presses, and the Association of Research Librar-
ies—and the generous support of Virginia Tech. Learn more at
the TOME website, available at: openmonographs.org.

To Chris, and his love for *merdeka*.
To the ancestors, whose struggles guide our struggles.

1 _____

2 _____

3 _____

4 _____

5 _____

Contents

Acknowledgments

I am filled with deep sadness as I write these acknowledgments. It has been over a year since the official beginning of the COVID-19 global pandemic. Around the world, so many have suffered incalculable losses. Yet, these losses have been felt unevenly, structured by histories of racial capitalism and interlocking colonialisms. The writing of this section is thus not simply one of celebrating a completion of a journey, but also a weary recognition of survival. Still, although bringing this book to publication has been a long, and sometimes frustrating experience, it has also been a journey marked by countless moments of genuine joy, made only possible through the immense kindness of kin, comrades, colleagues, and strangers.

I want to first thank all the archivists and librarians that helped guide my research in both the Philippines and the United States. I was fortunate enough to receive research funding from the University of Michigan's Bentley Library and the Newberry Library in Chicago. I was also privileged enough to gain affiliation with the Third World Studies Center at the University of the Philippines, which provided a temporary base as I visited archives throughout metro Manila. I thank them for all the generous support they provided.

This project could not have been possible if not for the material support of several grants and fellowships. I was lucky enough to receive multiple FLAS and department grants from the Southeast Asian Center and the Department of History at the University of Washington throughout my graduate career. I was also fortunate to receive a Fulbright Hays Dissertation Grant, which enabled me to conduct research in the Philippines for a year. After obtaining my doctorate, I again was privileged to have received two generous postdoctoral fellowships. The first was the Global American Studies Postdoctoral Fellowship from Harvard University's Charles Warren Center. The second was the Society of Fellows Postdoctoral Fellowship at the University of Michigan. I am especially thankful to Arthur Patton-Hock and Larissa Kennedy at Harvard University, and Donald Lopez and Linda Turner at the University of Michigan, for all the immeasurable aid and guidance during my fellowships. Finally, this book greatly benefited from the TOME (Toward an Open Monograph Ecosystem) grant. My gratitude to Peter Potter at Virginia Tech for all the help working with Duke to have my book be part of the TOME initiative.

In completing the manuscript, I received numerous forms of support from the History Department and the College of Liberal Arts and Human Sciences at Virginia Tech. Thank you to my colleagues, the students, and the staff in the History Department, who have been nothing but welcoming and encouraging. I thank my formal mentors in the department, Helen Schneider and Carmen Gitre. And my thanks to Dennis Halpin, Melanie Kiechle, Brett Shadle, and Danna Agmon for sharing their experiences and advice with me on the book publishing process. In addition, my genuine appreciation to abolitionist organizers I have closely worked with at Tech, especially Bikrum Gil, Ginny Pannabecker, and Jack Leff. I especially thank Edward Polanco, Dominique Polanco, and Zaida Polanco for gifting my family with nourishing sociality during this era of social distancing.

I am grateful to everyone at Duke University Press for making this seemingly intimidating process into one filled with kindness and patience. I especially thank Ken Wissoker, Kate Herman, Ben Kossak, the members of the Board, and other staff that kindly put their labor into this book project from the beginning stages to the end. Thank you also to Westchester Publishing Services and Ideas on Fire for the indispensable copyediting and indexing services. I am also immensely thankful for the invaluable feedback and thoughtful suggestions from the two anonymous reviewers. Their generous comments were crucial in reshaping this book into, what I believe, to be a more concise and convincing text. Finally, my gratitude to Elizabeth Ault, who guided this book through tumultuous waters. There were a lot of personal life changes and global material upheavals that occurred during this whole process, but she remained reassuring and generous throughout the entirety. For that I am incalculably grateful.

Monetary Authorities would not have been possible if not for the inspiring work of scholars that came before. The works of Peter Hudson, Yoshiko Nagano, and Emily Rosenberg, in particular, were crucial for my thinking. It was their scholarship on money and banking in the colonial world that I would constantly return to as I grappled with this history. I thank them and their works sincerely. Parts of chapters 1 and 2 were initially published in *A Cultural History of Money and Credit* and *Diplomatic History*. I thank Chia Yin Hsu, Thomas Luckett, Erika Vause, and the editors of *Diplomatic History* for giving me the opportunity to rehearse some ideas that would eventually end up in this book.

Throughout the formation of this book, I have had the great fortune to learn from and receive advice from numerous scholars. San Francisco, Seattle, Manila, Cambridge, Ann Arbor, and Blacksburg: intellectual communities in all these places fundamentally shaped the manuscript, even before it was a book. I have learned from and had the pleasure to converse with amazing junior and senior scholars, students, organizers, and just really good folks. I am indebted to so many relations as a result. Sometimes these would be brief yet meaningful conversations or feedback. Sometimes these were a long series of mentorship, intellectual exchange, and collaborations. Some were people I wrote alongside with and tried out ideas with. And some were friends for nourishment, playing music together, watching films, or grabbing drinks and breaking bread. For all these reasons I thank the following.

From my time as a master's student at San Francisco State University, I thank Trevor Getz, Ari Cushner, Rebecca Hodges, and Dawn Mabalon. It saddens me that I will not be able to share a copy of this book with Dawn, who passed away in 2018. I still remember the house party she invited me to in Oakland back in 2005, where I got to listen to a once-in-a-lifetime reunion of a Bay Area punk band I loved so much. And I thank (or I blame) Chris Chekuri especially for planting the idea of pursuing a PhD in my head.

From my time as a doctoral student at the University of Washington, I thank Celia Lowe, Christoph Giebel, Sara Van Fleet, Kiko Benitez, Christina Sunardi, Jed Domigpe, Micaela Campbell, Chandan Reddy, Ileana

Rodriguez-Silva, Cheryll Alipio, Will Arighi, McKaye Caruthers, Evi Su-
trisno, Julie Myers, Hoang Ngo, Mike Viola, along with many others. Some
of my most meaningful friendships were forged during my dissertation research. I think back fondly to my friendships—mainly nonacademic—with
those in Seattle, Portland, and Manila. A lot of liquor consumed and a lot
of bad ideas were subsequently hatched. In Manila, I thank especially John
Torres, Shireen Seno, Kathy Gener, Selena Davis, Mike Benedicto, Mick
Benedicto, Shinji Manlangit, Francis Cabal, Fabian Mangahas, Vinny Tagle,
and Erwin Hilao. In Portland, Ryan Barber, Colin Hulbert, Jonah Nolde, Eli
Nolde, and Tommy Paluck. In Seattle, I thank especially Joe Guanlao, Car-
mel Laurino, Roger Habon, Amalia Aquino, Meg Viera, Michael Castaneda,
and Sue Shon. I am lucky to have been part of a cohort with Jon Olivera,
Marites Mendoza, Matthew Nicdao, Joe Bernardo (the best roommate),
and Chris Grorud. I still cannot fully comprehend a world without Chris,
and I hope I do some honor to his life with this book. I deeply respect the
Grorud family for keeping his memory alive.

Finally, incalculable gratitude goes to my dissertation committee.
Thank you to Rick Bonus for being a model of generosity. Thank you to
Laurie Sears for gifting me so many opportunities to grow as an ethical
scholar. Thank you to Moon-Ho Jung for always reminding me to affirm my
commitment to intertwining radical traditions. Finally, thank you to Vince
Rafael, whose encouragement and support of this book project has never
wavered. His enthusiasm to critically look at the making and unmaking of
worlds has always pushed me to rethink things whenever I felt intellectually stuck. I owe a great debt of gratitude to his mentorship.

From my time in Cambridge, I thank especially Ju Yon Kim, Vincent
Brown, Holger Droessler, Sven Beckert, Erez Manela, Ben Weber, William
Chiriguayo, Liz Mesok, Alex Orquiza, Vivek Bald, Chris Capozzola, Jordan
Camp, Christina Heatherton, S. Ani Mukherji, Lorgia García Peña, along
with many others. I am especially thankful to Genevieve Clutario for the
treasured friendship and Walter Johnson for being an immense intellectual
and ethical influence.

From my time in Ann Arbor, I thank especially Geoff Eley, Jay Cook,
Kathleen Canning, Amanda Armstrong, Alice Goff, Jay Cephas, Maximillian
Alvarez, Meryem Kamil, Martha Jones, Howard Brick, Matthew Country-
man, Amanda Alexander, Anne Berg, Ana Vinea, Zhiying Ma, Aniket Aga,
Katie Lennard, Hiroaki Matsusaka, Kevin Ko, along with many others. I am
especially grateful to Manan Desai, Charlotte Albrecht, Victor Mendoza, and
Deirdre de la Cruz for the genuine mentorship and invaluable friendship.

Throughout the writing of this book, I have had the benefit of being inspired by, and gained feedback from, so many scholars, teachers, comrades, and fellow travelers. I thank Neferti Tadiar, Caroline Hau, Leloy Claudio, Paul Kramer, Jojo Abinales, Pheng Cheah, Josh Gedacht, Bobby Benedicto, Thea Tagle, Noah Theriault, Karen Miller, Colleen Woods, John Munro, Daniel Doeppers, Ruth Mabanglo, Teresita Ramos, Sheila Zamar, Christa Wirth, Julie Greene, R. J. Lozada, Chris Nichols, Nancy Unger, Raul Hinojosa-Ojeda, Cesar Ayala, Kimberly Kay Hoang, Michael Ralph, Alyosha Goldstein, Ananya Roy, Simeon Man, Adrian De Leon, Bradley Camp, Emily Hue, Shelley Lee, along with many others. Thank you to Naoko Shimisawa, Patrick Chung, Heather Lee, and Anthony Pratcher for reading parts of my book and giving me vital feedback as I was about to send it off to Duke. At a later stage of the publication of this book, I got to know a bunch of Filipinx scholars through FWIP, which gave me energy to keep pushing forward. I thank all of them for constellating new intellectual geographies. Special shout out to Destin Jenkins and Justin Leroy for inviting me to study and dialogue with Shauna Sweeney, K-Sue Park, Pedro Regalado, Ryan Jobson, and Manu Karuka. I learned (and unlearned) so much from our conversations about racial capitalism. Finally, throughout this process, Rick Baldoz has been a great friend, mentor, and an inexhaustible source of good music suggestions.

To all my kin I owe immense gratitude. Throughout the long journey of this book, I was able to inherit a larger family. I thank Jasprit Singh, Amrit Kaur, Amrita Singh, Nirmal Kaur, Meher Singh, Baljinder Singh, Neil Bilolikar, Inderroop Singh, Meher Singh, Sheena Singh, Simran Bilolikar, and Darshan Bilolikar, for generously welcoming me into their lives. Thank you to Ariel Lumba, Amado Lumba Jr., Anais Fawcett, Abigail Lumba, J. C. Fawcett, Alyssa Lumba, Ashley Lumba, Anjah Fawcett, Amele Fawcett, Akean Fawcett, Avian Reyes, and Oliver Reyes. My siblings have always sincerely supported my strange and scattered endeavors, even if it might diverge from their own thinking, and for that I am forever grateful. I am especially thankful and astounded by my nieces and nephews for their limitless curiosity, awareness for justice, and genuine affirmation that other, more compassionate and abundant worlds are possible. To my parents, Amado Lumba and Ester Lumba, my everlasting appreciation. The horizons I followed might not have been what they had predicted, nonetheless, they always eventually wholeheartedly supported my idiosyncratic pursuits.

When the seeds for this book began to germinate, I never fathomed that I would experience a life so euphoric. I am fortunate to have found two people that have made me strive to be more kind, generous, and caring. At the same time, I am fortunate to have found two people that have affirmed and intensified my commitments to struggle for and work toward collective liberation. I cherish Amaru for consistently punctuating my life with tiny, yet immeasurable, thrills. I am truly rapturous. And Balbir, thank you for enduring my often caustic and pessimistic personality. Your patience, wisdom, humor, aesthetics, and brilliance make the quotidian always feel exceptional; the sublime presence that constantly pulls me toward the future, without doubt, full of love.

Introduction: Monetary Authority

Manuel Roxas was exhausted. He had traveled to Washington, DC, from Manila at the end of 1931 to make his routine plea for Philippine independence. It was now late January 1932. For months he had been arguing that the Philippines, after over three decades of U.S. colonial rule, was secure enough to be an independent nation-state. The multiple-term Speaker of the Philippine House of Representatives, along with other prominent Filipino decision-makers, had been making similar arguments for decades. Every two or so years since the first Philippine Independence Mission in 1918, a group of Filipino statesmen would journey to the U.S. settler metropole to make their case for Philippine sovereignty. Although previous attempts had ended in the familiar refrain of American lawmakers decreeing "not yet," 1932 felt different. After all, the United States was deeply feeling the devastating effects of the Great Depression. Other imperial powers, such as Japan and Germany, had been making rapid extraterritorial grabs, disturbing the international status quo. The world order seemed increasingly threatened by intensifying calls for decolonization by the "darker nations."[1] In addition, fears of the "rising tide of color against white supremacy" ate away at the minds of majoritarian publics, who for decades had ignored the prescient warnings of W. E. B. Du Bois: that the upheavals of the twentieth century would be caused by the "problem of the color line."[2]

Global publics believed that these world-spanning insecurities were a direct consequence of capitalist crisis, particularly the failures of an interimperial monetary, banking, and financial order based on the gold standard. For Roxas, the security of the Philippine monetary system would serve as a crucial component in convincing Americans that the Philippines was secure enough for independence. In his historical narrative of Philippine currency, Roxas emphasized its establishment by American economic experts as a kind of colonial experiment. This historical narrative was not meant to shame Americans about colonialism, but instead to praise the work of U.S. Empire. Roxas flattered Congress by underscoring the novelty of tethering the colony to the U.S. gold-standard monetary system. He reminded lawmakers that the large-scale systemic transformation witnessed in the Philippines had "never been attempted elsewhere."[3] This narrative of a successful and secure colonial monetary system was meant to not only remind Congress of American imperial achievements, but to simultaneously assuage the fears of Americans weary of the fate of capitalist security after Philippine independence. This narrative thus operated as a promise, a guarantee by Roxas that American capitalism would remain secure in the Philippines, even in a postcolonial future.

Currency, because of its material and meaning-making functions, was essential to this promise of postcolonial capitalist security. Indeed, Roxas would boast greatly of the Philippine currency's durability under crisis. "Those who founded our currency system believe that unless our reserves are tampered with in the United States our currency is going to survive any crisis. As a matter of fact our currency has not been under any strain during this period of economic depression when currencies of other countries have tottered or actually depreciated."[4] The security of the Philippine monetary system could thus symbolize a postcolonial world in which the security of global racial capitalism and U.S. Empire was guaranteed. As Roxas argued, "our currency system will not fail if the United States currency does not fail, and I believe that will never happen, but if it ever happens, I suppose the end of the world would be near."[5]

Roxas's supposition that the failure of U.S. currency would mean the end of the world is striking, and provokes me to ask several questions. How did Roxas perceive his current world? How would his world look after the Philippines gained its independence? Why was money so important to both achieving independence and securing against the end of the world? Roxas was a colonized subject who had inherited a world forged by colonizers historically committed to the intertwining logics of racial capitalism and counter-decolonization. By using the term *counter-decolonization*, I emphasize how U.S. authorities were obsessed with eradicating or domesticating ongoing movements for decolonization, not insurgencies or rebellions. Thus *counter-decolonization* centers decolonization as the key analytic for comprehending Filipino struggles for liberation.

I also use *counter-decolonization* to illuminate how the violent suppression of Philippine decolonization was part of a longer American tradition of reactionary logic. Indeed, U.S. counter-decolonization was deeply shaped by its origins as a settler colony, white supremacist society, and capitalist empire.[6] Taking this perspective, I build off Manu Karuka's concept of countersovereignty: "a position of reaction to distinct Indigenous protocols governing life in the spaces the United States claims as its national interior."[7] By situating U.S. Empire first as a settler colony, I diverge from scholarship that argues that Americans only met anticolonial resistance to their economic and territorial expansion as it spatially moved farther away from the borders of their supposedly settled nation-state. By emphasizing that decolonization was anterior to expansion, I recast U.S. Empire as fundamentally a historical force of counter-decolonization.[8] This is especially clear in the first half of the nineteenth century. During this period, U.S. Empire first expanded through "frontier" wars with Indigenous and Mexican peoples, and second, through the establishment of the Monroe Doctrine (and later the Tyler Doctrine), which sought to crowd out other capitalist empires throughout the Western hemisphere, placing liberated Indigenous or other decolonizing peoples under U.S. formal or informal dominion.[9] In the last decades of the nineteenth century, U.S. Empire was unapologetic as it pursued counter-decolonization across vast bodies of water in the settler colony of Hawai'i, the former Spanish colonies, Cuba, Puerto Rico, the Mariana Islands, Guam, and the focus of this study, the Philippines in 1898.[10]

This book examines how and why, from the late nineteenth century to the 1930s, monetary authority was essential to strategies of counter-decolonization in the Philippine colony. I define monetary authority as an ensemble of authoritarian and authoritative decision-making powers over a capitalist monetary system. Drawn from both sovereign power as well as what I call market knowledge, monetary authority aimed to securitize territory and populations. I examine how, for over three decades, monetary authority shaped and ordered multiple dimensions of Philippine colonial life including infrastructure, logistics, and the economic activities, habits, and practices of colonized subjects. Operating at the level of the mundane and quotidian, those who wielded monetary authority constantly attempted to refract its interventions through its promises of maintaining racial order and capitalist security. This book traces these variegated formations of monetary authority through colonial bureaucratic institutions and imperial economic policies decades before the establishment of the Central Bank of the Philippines.

In the contemporary, the central bank is the preeminent figure of monetary authority, managing and intervening in multiple areas of economic life including currency, debt, banking, and even fiscal and labor matters. Indeed, monetary authorities, or central banks, are considered a necessary and normative institution for almost all sovereign nation-states. For over four decades of U.S. colonial rule in the Philippines, Americans claimed that Native Filipinos were a race that lacked monetary authority and thus were unprepared for decolonization. I scrutinize the multipronged ways Filipino decision-makers attempted to gain sovereign powers by proving their racial capacity for monetary authority. The struggle over monetary authority in the Philippine colony allows me to think through the material histories of global racial capitalism and interlocking transpacific colonialisms. With this in mind, I follow Neferti Tadiar's assertion that the Philippines can be considered an "important theoretical place" from which to comment on and think through "the larger world within which it is situated."[11]

In the Philippine colony, monetary authority could only be possible through the policymaking of economic experts. Composed mainly of academics, bankers, and businessmen (and they almost always identified as men), many were drawn to U.S. Empire's new colonial frontier for several intertwining reasons. These included proving white supremacist economic and racial theories, advancing their careers, personally profiting from colonial investments, or seeing it as their paternalistic duty to uplift savage peoples.[12] Most significantly, I chart how American economic experts were deeply committed to normalizing monetary authority as essential to colonial governance. Experts argued that American colonial sovereignty could only be legitimized if the state guaranteed the security of capitalist accumulation by adhering to the laws of the capitalist market.

The last decades of the nineteenth century witnessed a critical mass of these economic experts, who claimed intimate knowledge over the natural laws and raw data of the capitalist market. In the case of the Philippine colony, experts claimed that the analysis of accumulated economic data, for instance, currency circulation or exchange and interest rates, would more efficiently enable American authorities to maintain racial, colonial, and capitalist orders. By focusing on the archives of experts—from scholarly articles, to official reports, to private correspondences, and to public debates—I illustrate how market knowledge naturalized the laws of capitalism and simultaneously intervened in social and political realms in the name of these naturalized laws. Oftentimes, experts would collaborate with, and work within, the colonial state and the banking and business community. At other times, however, experts would butt heads with state agents, bankers, merchants, and capitalists. I build on the insightful scholarship on institutional and political histories of Philippine monetary and banking systems and trace the many techniques adopted by experts to resolve these tensions in the interests of counter-decolonization.[13]

Monetary authority, moreover, rested on the notion that the securitization of capitalism could only be achieved through the securitization of racial hierarchies. Pathbreaking scholarly work on racial capitalism asserts that racism and colonialism are not epiphenomena of capitalism, but instead materially ground the very logic and practices of capitalist accumulation, dispossession, and exploitation.[14] This specific study of the Philippine colony examines how and why, on one hand, race organizes, exploits, and extracts value from colonized peoples to accumulate capital, and, on the other hand, race securitizes tensions and antagonisms within capitalist relations in the colonies. I focus especially on how monetary authority operates through the logic of racial hierarchies and justifies colonial policies through what Warwick Anderson calls a "flexible, and sometimes unstable" categorization of populations according to their racial capacities.[15] Racial capacities worked both ways in the Philippine colony. White Americans, on one hand, hoped to prove their capacity to lead in a racial capitalist world system through monetary authority. Nonwhite peoples, on the other hand, had to constantly prove their racial capacity for monetary authority while remaining under colonial sovereignty.

This study additionally examines how racial capitalism is fundamentally intertwined with the colonial. As Frantz Fanon asserts, "in the colonies the economic infrastructure is also a superstructure."[16] Comparative world historians and world-systems theoreticians have also demonstrated how capitalism is utterly dependent on colonial extraction and peripheral economies.[17] Through circuits laid down by U.S. Empire, economic experts traveled to colonies and demarcated which races were considered modern, civilized, and, most significantly, sovereign. Colonial expertise determined which people possessed the racial capacity to soundly make decisions over large-scale capital, and which people did not. Natives in the Philippines were determined racially incapable of monetary authority. Thus, until those abilities developed, they would have to remain colonial wards of U.S. Empire, under the racial paternalist supervision of what Vicente Rafael calls "white love."[18] I trace this wardship through the Philippine monetary system, which was forcefully bound to the U.S. dollar. Colonizing the Philippine monetary system benefited the United States by housing reserves in U.S. banks, boosting its economic prestige among other capitalist empires, providing a site to test out economic theories of racial capitalism, and offering up a fantasy of white paternalist success. In addition to the monetary system, experts found other ways to gauge the racial capacity of Natives. The capacity to save, the capacity to manage debt, the capacity to endure economic crisis: these and other abilities were used to determine whether Natives were capable of sovereignty.

U.S. imperial monetary authority was essential to combat and delay movements for liberation in the Philippine colony, a multipronged doctrine that I refer to as counter-decolonization. I explore how monetary authority adopted multiple techniques to pay for both military and civil colonial state projects and the securitization of capitalist endeavors in the colony. Indeed, profits from the establishment and maintenance of an American colonial currency system—seigniorage, currency funds, reserves, foreign exchange—not only contributed fluid assets to the U.S. imperial financial and banking system, but, more significantly, the profits generated revenue to sustain the American colonial state. The colonial monetary and banking system was additionally essential for the logistics of military occupation. Funds were needed to remunerate troops and colonized workers and for the acquisition and transportation of weapons and supplies. Colonial currency reserve funds maintained the stable and consistent flow of money between the settler metropole and overseas colony, and eventually other parts of Asia that the U.S. military occupied. Profits from establishing and maintaining the colonial monetary system, therefore, would routinely fund military operations that violently suppressed and drowned out Native resistance throughout the Philippine archipelago and the wider region.

Counter-decolonization strategies also relied on infrastructural projects. The monetary and banking system made available credit and loans for the colonial construction of roads, irrigation systems, interisland shipping, and railroads. Profits from seigniorage, currency reserve funds, and banking reserves were also deployed to finance private enterprises in plantations, mining, and real estate. At the same time, the monetary and banking system was itself infrastructural. Currency and banks were crucial components of the built world of colonial society and structured the quotidian social life of colonizer and colonized alike.

Monetary authority entailed policing economic activities, habits, and practices of colonial society to ensure the securitization of racial capitalism. In this I build from Tadiar's observation that "economic prosperity and political security" remained paramount to American and Filipino authorities anxious over a future postcolonial Philippines.[19] Economic experts were especially obsessed with ensuring that economic norms—based on the norms of an idealized white American capitalist society—were reproduced in the Philippines. Often these economic norms were conjoined to other sorts of norms, reinforcing interlocking and intersecting structures of power.[20] I focus on how monetary authority seemed obsessed with conceiving of economic norms through race and how the process of racialization was, at different times, attempts to regulate economic activities that unsettled normative categories of gender, religion, ability, and sexuality.[21]

The policing of economic activities was applied unevenly according to race. On one hand, various racialized publics had to be assuaged. Bankers, mainly white Americans and Europeans, wanted to feel secure by being free of economic regulations such as taxes and laws. American colonizers, such as soldiers and civil servants, wanted to feel secure with stable exchange rates, access to savings, and remittances for their salaries. Wealthy Mestizos wanted to feel secure with access to lucrative credit and loans. On the other hand, various subjugated populations were heavily surveilled and punished. Some wealthy Natives were cast as corrupt and chronic defaulters. Chinese merchants and retailers were figured as smugglers, cheats, usurers, or potential economic adversaries. Native laborers and peasants were perceived as hoarders, counterfeiters, and idlers. In the eyes of economic experts, it was this final group, the laborers and peasants, that posed the biggest threat to capitalist security. The refusal of laborers and peasants to recognize U.S. monetary authority could quickly transform into a mass refusal to recognize American sovereignty and perhaps even become a revolutionary movement for decolonization.

Monetary authority was also a terrain of antagonism. I probe monetary authority as part of what Paul Kramer calls "the politics of recognition," a contested (though potentially inclusive) field of imperial and racial capitalist power.[22] I thus contribute to ongoing discussions about the profound ways that struggles over political power in the Philippine colony had deep and lasting ramifications on the societies and institutions of both the Philippines and the United States.[23] At first, American colonizers claimed to possess something the colonized were racially incapable of possessing. Until the colonized could prove they could possess monetary authority, American authorities reasoned, Filipino sovereignty would never be recognized. Many elite and powerful Filipinos thus desired monetary authority, for it offered a path toward gaining more sovereign power within colonial society. By the interwar period, as most of the political realm of the American colonial state underwent Filipinization,[24] monetary authority remained firmly under American control. Eventually, however, market knowledge was claimed by Filipino economic experts in the late 1920s and early 1930s, leading to knowledge-based challenges to American authorities during the Great Depression. By arguing that Filipino economic experts were more racially intimate with a local market knowledge that Americans could never comprehend, Filipino authorities asserted that they had finally achieved monetary authority and thus should be granted more sovereign power.

At the same time, however, what haunted both American and Filipino claims to sovereignty were the anarchic disruptions of unconditional decolonization.[25] Disorderly flare-ups of unconditional decolonization would rupture the tenure of U.S. colonial rule. As I define it, *unconditional decolonization* was a liberatory movement toward a more just world, without the racial and colonial structures of capitalism and empire. The desire for unconditional decolonization was a desire for new disorderly forms of collective life that were unrecognizable to the orders of colonialism, capitalism, imperialism, and nationalism. It is this possibility of the disordering of the world as they knew it that drove the anxieties and panic of monetary authorities, in particular, and colonial authority in general.

The chapters in this book chart a series of economic crises and social upheavals in the Philippine colony from the 1870s to the 1930s. Each chapter examines how and why monetary authority emerged as an assemblage of power sought by different colonial state and capitalist agents to domesticate threats to racial capitalism and colonial sovereignty and secure their world against the possibility of unconditional decolonization.

Chapter 1, "The Wealth of Colonies," focuses on the twilight of Spanish colonial rule in the Philippines and the eruption of a sustained organized movement for unconditional decolonization. In the last three decades of the nineteenth century, the Spanish Empire was unsettled by a series of political and economic crises in its Philippine colony. During these unsettling times, loyalist Spanish economic intellectuals publicly lamented the lack of government effectiveness in managing economic crises, on one hand, and a racialized hierarchical order, on the other. Philippine liberal reformers appropriated the economic language of Spanish economic intellectuals, asserting that a new political entity—the nation—should instead be in control. The chapter then turns to the role of money from the beginning of the 1896 Revolution through the short life of the first Philippine national government, the Malolos Republic. Founded in 1899, the Malolos Republic attempted to appropriate the economic apparatuses of the Spanish colonial state by courting foreign capital, maintaining systems of taxation and wages that benefitted the wealthy, and reconfiguring extant debt-credit relations. The Republic would also violently suppress unconditional decolonization by upholding Spanish forms of racial and class hierarchies. The economic policies and governing logic of the Malolos Republic would go on to shape Filipino strategies for conditional decolonization during most of the American colonial period.

The next two chapters shift perspective, charting the formation of American monetary authority during the long Philippine American War. After defeating Spain in 1898, the United States disavowed ongoing movements for Philippine decolonization by purchasing the Philippines for twenty million dollars and declaring sovereignty over the archipelago. Chapter 2, "Mongrel Currencies," frames U.S. imperial expansion into the Philippines as a twofold operation of counter-decolonization and the securitization of global racial capitalism. First, imperial agents were confronted with the conditions of a wartime market, in particular the fiscal disorder and the violent fluctuations of what authorities considered a byzantine bimetallic monetary system. At the same time, by following public and private disagreements between military and government officials, academics, and intellectuals, I map out the confusion of colonial decision-makers as they grappled with American, Chinese, and Filipino racial capacities to handle money. Second, American economic experts used market knowledge to push the establishment of the gold standard beyond settler colonial territories, but also extractive colonies such as the Philippines. Experts, furthermore, hoped that instituting a gold-based colonial monetary system in the Philippine colony would signal to other empires that white Americans held the racial capacity to be global leaders in a racial capitalist world.

Chapter 3, "Bad Money," explores how American anxieties over unconditional decolonization fundamentally shaped colonial economic policies and institutions. It focuses particularly on the concrete attempts by economic experts to administer a new monetary and banking system, grounded in notions of U.S. racial and capitalist historical development. The new monetary system would play a critical role in financing the counter-decolonization logistics and infrastructure of a protracted war. Banks, and in particular the culture of banking and bankers, also became a primary concern for counter-decolonization infrastructure. At the same time, economic experts were obsessed with domesticating the ongoing insecurities caused by the wayward economic practices of Chinese and Native subjects. In the interests of securing capital accumulation and racial orders, American experts would develop diverse modes of policing, including harassment, surveillance, and even public punishment. By shaping the economic habits of racialized subjects, moreover, experts hoped to normalize the necessity of market knowledge, justify white paternalism, delay desires for decolonization, and celebrate narratives of American economic success in the archipelago.

Narratives of success in the Philippines, however, would rapidly unravel from the mid-1910s through the 1920s. Chapter 4, "An Orgy of Mismanagement," examines the struggles over decolonization through the spectacular rise and fall of the Philippine National Bank (PNB). The PNB was the first major government-backed investment bank and caretaker of currency reserves and fiscal funds in the American colonial Philippines. The United States' growing dominance as a creditor empire in the capitalist world system, the wartime price boom for Philippine agricultural commodities, and the increased Filipinization of the political realm: all these global and local contingencies shaped the establishment of the PNB in 1916. By the end of the 1910s, a new incoming American colonial regime intended to reverse Filipino political gains by promoting a narrative of imperial and white redemption in the colony. The new colonial regime quickly latched onto the PNB, and its eventual failure, to signify the general failure of Filipinization. During the first half of the 1920s, battles over the PNB leadership and management would become highly public and would come to represent broader hostilities over Filipino racial capacities. On one side of these hostilities were Filipino decision-makers who desired sovereign power and access to large-scale capital by gaining control of the PNB. On the other side were American authorities, who were deeply invested in making a spectacle of counter-decolonization by situating themselves as simultaneous victims and saviors of Filipinos. By the end of the decade, U.S. and Philippine publics would eventually lose interest, and the PNB would cease to be a spectacle of controversy. Nevertheless, Filipino authorities learned much from this experience, inheriting new modes of critiquing and challenging American monetary authority for decades to come.

Chapter 5, "Under Common Wealth," examines the Philippine colony during the Great Depression. In the beginning of the 1930s, the racial capitalist world seemed on the brink of catastrophe. Global movements for decolonization coincided with the growing popularity of reactionary political ideologies such as isolationist nationalism, militarism, and fascism. U.S. imperial decision-makers would attempt to resolve the contradictions of racial capitalist crisis by jettisoning the Philippines and Filipinos, colonial possessions they now considered to be more burden than asset. Consequently, money would be a terrain through which struggles over Philippine decolonization would unfold. Filipino statesmen, capitalists, and exports utilized the success of the monetary system during the Depression, to critique U.S. sovereignty and demand increased autonomy. In 1935, these demands would bear fruit as the Philippines' colonial status shifted from U.S. insular possession to U.S. commonwealth. At the same time, with new-found autonomy came a deluge of insecurities. The Philippine Commonwealth era was a time of upheaval, when norms were regularly unsettled and new revolutionary worlds were being imagined. This chapter maps how peasant and worker organizations imagined revolutionary new worlds and how they made collective demands for unconditional decolonization.

The book concludes with a brief reflection on the profound legacies of colonial monetary authority, even after the Philippines' nominal independence. I think about how the end of American colonialism in the Philippines did not signal the end of the racial capitalist and interimperial world. Indeed, the contemporary Philippine nation-state has inherited many of the unresolved antagonisms that unfolded during the formal U.S. colonization of the Philippines. The continued dependency on the U.S. dollar and military, the valorization of capitalist markets and fantasies of capitalist security, the simultaneous exploitation and devaluation of peasant and worker lives, the adoption of counter-decolonization strategies by the postcolonial state: these are just some of the material and ideological legacies that have shaped the Philippines during the long "American Century." At the same time, I also think about the legacies of the Philippine radical tradition (if we can call it that) and how it continues to haunt our contemporary world with demands for an unconditional decolonization that has yet to arrive. This book echoes with these sorrowful, yet resolute, calls.

The Wealth of Colonies

1

In 1893, Spanish economic observer F. Aguilar y Biosca published the entire record of Spanish monetary legislation in the Philippine colony. Biosca explained that his inspiration for writing the *Legislación Sobre Moneda Filipina* had been to aid a Spanish imperial public perplexed by the "constantly changing market" and government "proclamations, orders, decrees, resolutions, and circulars of all kinds and provisions." To the typical Spaniard, the value of currency in the Philippine colony seemed to rely more on the arbitrary "mark of the die" rather than on the reality of the "weight and the law."[1] Whether migrant or settler, private merchant or state bureaucrat, no one could escape the byzantine and costly process of remitting or transferring funds between the colonial archipelago and the metropolitan peninsula. For Biosca, and many other Spanish economic observers, all were pulled into the chaotic commercial culture of fluctuating exchange rates that encouraged disorder, demoralized all those involved, and left in its wake "the exuberant growth of evil."[2]

On one hand, Biosca's text, which recounted laws established as far back as the sixteenth century, was a challenge to Spanish imperial decision-makers. The Philippine colonial monetary system was dangerously insecure, severely limiting capital accumulation in, and ultimately the value of, the Spanish colony. On the other hand, economic insecurity threatened to lead to social and political insecurities, an unsettling possibility for proponents of Spanish colonial authority in the archipelago. Biosca's text, therefore, served as a warning to a Spanish Empire that had been overtaken by other European capitalist empires. If a solution to the monetary problem was not quickly found, then unwanted evils would rapidly surface. In the eyes of Spanish authorities, the most terrifying evil was decolonization.

This chapter explores how money, and the foreign capitalist markets that it represented, constantly threatened to erode Spanish colonial sovereignty in the Philippines. The figure of the foreign—emerging in various economic guises—would operate as a primary source of anxiety to Spanish authorities. From the sixteenth century to the nineteenth century, the Spanish colonial state had failed to establish a unified hegemonic currency in the Philippine Archipelago. Instead, the colonial monetary system was oftentimes ruled by a de facto system composed of different foreign currencies. Foreign markets and money, at the same time, operated as a power that Spanish authorities wished to possess. Foreign capitalist markets, after all, provided potential wealth and security for the colonial state. However, because the Spanish colonial state could not contain the effect of foreign currencies, it would instead target specific races that it believed to be alienated from the norms of colonial society.

Under Spanish rule, social life in the archipelago was hierarchically ordered according to race. The stratification of Europeans, Criollos, Mestizos, Indios, and Chinese, was reproduced through racial capitalist practices and logic. Monetary policies, therefore, and more generally state decisions over capital accumulation, were deeply shaped by racial and colonial norms. Money was a terrain on which Spanish colonial authority and white (and Christian) supremacy was, on one hand, enforced by colonizers, and on the other hand, challenged in various ways by those colonized. During the monetary crises of the late nineteenth century, there emerged multiple voices critical of Spanish authority. Some sought reform, to bring the colony closer to the imperial metropole, while gaining more political recognition for Mestizos and Indios. Others saw monetary crises as evidence of the failure of Spanish imperial authority and demanded more sovereign power granted to the nation. This desire of a nation-state to take the place of the colonial state without fundamentally disturbing the structures of racial capitalism is what I call the desire for conditional decolonization.

Nationalism, however, did not always aim for conditional decolonization. Movements for unconditional decolonization would also surface at this time. A revolution would erupt in 1896, led by Indios and Mestizos who sought to overthrow the Spanish colonial state. Although defeated by a superior trained and equipped Spanish colonial military, the energies of revolution refused to disappear. Movements for decolonization would again emerge in 1898, this time against American colonial occupation. Money, and more broadly capital, would continue to be a terrain of struggle during this era of political and social upheavals. Proponents for decolonization would be split according to their relation to money as capital. On one side were proponents of conditional decolonization, a sort of maintenance of racial and economic norms while attaining political sovereignty for the nation. On the other side were those who desired unconditional decolonization, a remaking of the world, in which colonialism and racial capitalism would have no future.

The Undomesticated Past of Philippine Currencies

Despite claiming sovereignty over the archipelago since 1521, it would not be until the nineteenth century that the Spanish colonial state would seriously attempt to establish a uniform and standardized monetary system in the Philippine colony. For centuries of Spanish rule, therefore, various forms of money circulated throughout the archipelago, a consequence of numerous accretions of different precolonial trade networks, sometimes overlapping and sometimes in conflict. Although there are few surviving formal records of Philippine economic life before the Iberian colonial encounter, scholars have uncovered evidence of the archipelago's Native inhabitants circulating throughout Northeast and Southeast Asia since the eleventh century. During this period, Natives were usually laborers of traveling merchant ships.[3] Consequently, both transoceanic laborers and traders most likely spread Malay coins, later locally known as *salapi*, throughout various parts of the archipelago.[4] The fourteenth century introduction of Islam to the southern islands of the archipelago further enmeshed Natives into the circuits of the Asian-centered economic world system long before the arrival of Iberian colonizers.[5] The southern island of Sulu, beginning in the sixteenth century maintained a significant connection for centuries to the lucrative Indian Ocean trade. Trade with Arab, Chinese, Portuguese, and eventually British merchants would prompt the Sulu sultanate to mint its own coins from the fifteenth century into the first half of the nineteenth century. In the mid-eighteenth century, the British Empire would steadily encroach into the archipelago, eventually occupying Manila from 1762 to 1764 during the Seven Years War. Although brief, British economic presence would continue well into the nineteenth century, infusing local markets in the islands with currencies from places under imperial rule, such as India and China.

From the mid-sixteenth century into the eighteenth century the Spanish Empire would slowly intensify formal colonization of the archipelago. During this period, however, most of the Philippines would be treated mainly as an economic afterthought by the Spanish Empire. To Spain, capital accumulation in the Philippines was minor, especially in comparison to more lucrative colonies in the Americas and the Caribbean. Instead, the colony, and specifically the port city of Manila, would mainly serve as a crucial entrepot in the Spanish Galleon Trade (from Manila to Acapulco), a profitable trade route that connected Asian commodities and markets to the Americas. It was during this period that the Philippine colony became forever intertwined with other historical processes in both the Old and New Worlds. As a primary node through which currencies of the Americas and commodities of Asia would flow through, the Philippine colony became further entangled with settler colonialisms throughout the Americas and the Pacific, the racial slave trade that circulated masses of African peoples across the Atlantic, and the capitalist markets of Western Europe.[6] Through the Galleon Trade, therefore, the global historical role of the Philippine colony was far from minor. Money would reflect the relation between the Galleon Trade and the Philippines, as money from New Spain, now known as Mexico, would circulate throughout the world. The "Mexican dollar" as it would later be known, would become the de facto circulating currency in Manila and thus the basis of the monetary system of the entire Philippine colony.

Mexican independence in 1815 marked the end of the Galleon Trade, however, creating uncertainty over the place of the Philippine colony within the Spanish imperial economy. As a result, the crown intensified its focus on its remaining colonies in the Pacific and the Caribbean. Anxious to catch up to more industrialized empires in the increasingly crowded global competition of capital accumulation, the trading ports throughout the Philippine colony were officially opened up to foreign capitalist powers such as the British, American, German, and French. The intensified exposure of the colony to world markets rapidly, though unevenly, accelerated transformations of local economies. For the majority of colonized subjects—Indios, Mestizos, and Chinese especially—this led to radical changes in social life. One stark example was the transformation of subsistence farming to export cash crops such as tobacco, sugar, and coffee. As a result, from the 1820s to the 1870s, Philippine commerce and agriculture became further entangled in the webs of the global capitalist system, deeply shaping the quotidian day to day of colonial society.[7]

Colonial authorities were weary of the Philippine colony's exposure to foreign capital. This weariness was captured in the words of a Spanish economic observer. "Sad is that Spanish land. If one looks at its currency, Mexico appears. If one looks at the most prominent influence on the indigenous masses, China appears. If one looks at its most valuable commercial trade, England, Germany and North America appear."[8] The different circulating coins was evidence of Spain's powerlessness to foreign economic forces. The dominating Mexican peso, Latin American coins, taels from China, rupees from British India, the yen from Japan, the florin from the Dutch East Indies, and the salapi brought in through the Malay trade: all these conventionally operated as currency within the colonial monetary system.[9] Additionally, other forms of nonstate currencies continued to circulate, especially in the non-Christian "frontiers" of Spanish authority. In the Igorot-controlled mountains of Northern Luzon, copper coins were circulated, and in the Muslim dominated areas, Sulu currency was especially widespread and circulated. Alien and alienated currencies seemed to threaten Spanish colonial sovereignty from both without and within.

An additional threat arrived in the coins of former Spanish colonies. In the first half of the nineteenth century a wave of Spanish colonial possessions in Latin America fought for, and gained, independence. Liberation movements in the Americas would greatly affect currencies across the capitalist world system more broadly and the Philippine colony specifically. For much of the life of the colony, currencies from other colonies such as Mexico and Argentina had freely circulated throughout the archipelago. After independence, coins from the Americas now possessed a meaning that exceeded the economic. In its attempt to ward off the spread of national liberation across the Pacific, the Spanish colonial state would counterstamp coins of former colonies, attempting to censor any evidence of decolonization.[10]

The scramble to counterstamp the influx of formerly colonized currencies exposed the long durée of imperial failures in addressing monetary insecurities. For instance, throughout the eighteenth century, there had been previous imperial experiments in minting smaller denominational coins for the colony. The minting of barilla copper coins (this is where the Tagalog word for *barya* or small change comes from) or the silver *cuartillas* and *reales*. Imperial support for colonial currency was short-lived, however. Consequently, colonial authorities would attempt to manufacture coins locally, sometime contracting out the work to Chinese craftspeople. Much to the chagrin of colonial authorities, locally minted coins proved to be crudely made and inconsistent. Moreover, with most makers unfamiliar with the Spanish language and culture, coins would contain frequent misspellings and skewed iconography. Regular discrepancies with the look and feel of locally manufactured coins left Spanish currency vulnerable to rampant counterfeiting and suspicion over authenticity.[11] Colonial officials feared that doubt over money's legitimacy could translate to doubt over the legitimacy of colonial authority more broadly. To combat these recurring threats to colonial sovereignty, the Spanish imperial government finally decided to create a completely localized Philippine colonial monetary system.

In 1861 the Spanish colonial state introduced a monetary system made up of both silver and gold coins, otherwise known as a bimetallic system. The Casa de Moneda de Manila was founded with the responsibility of reconfiguring Spanish American gold coins, commonly called *onzas*, into Philippine-specific gold coins, simply called *pesos*. The peso's design marked the first time the word *Filipinas* appeared on an official Spanish coin. The gold coins, however, did not solve the problem of small denomination coin scarcity. The following year, the Casa de Moneda minted silver small denomination coins, known as *centimos de pesos*. Over the next decade or so, as different monarchical regimes came to power on the Iberian Peninsula, the minting of coins would change to reflect each administration's preference.[12] Despite these cosmetic changes of the currency, the bimetallic monetary system held relatively stable for almost fifteen years.

By the late 1870s, however, a majority of the imperial North Atlantic states had shifted to a monometallic currency system based on the gold standard, destabilizing the global rate of exchange between silver and gold currencies.[13] As a result, the market value of the gold coins circulating in the Philippines was much more than the official state-sanctioned value. Mexican silver currency, still dominant in Asian trade and commerce, and therefore in abundant supply in places such as Amoy, Hong Kong, and much of Southeast Asia, was subsequently trafficked into the colony to purchase the more valuable gold coins. By 1877, the rapid exportation of gold coins finally prompted the Spanish government to ban future importation of Mexican coins. All this would be in vain, however, since by 1884 all gold coins had disappeared from the islands.[14] To add to the frustrations of authorities, throughout the rest of the 1880s the market price of silver routinely underwent wild fluctuations, making the de facto silver currency in the Philippines unstable.[15]

In addition to an anarchic monetary system, Spanish colonial sovereignty was threatened by other disorderly facets of foreign capital. In particular, during the last three decades of the nineteenth century, foreign banking and commercial institutions seemed to constantly impede Spanish economic development in the colony. For instance, despite the establishment of the Banco Español Filipino (Bank of the Philippine Islands) in 1851, over the next several decades British institutions such as the Chartered Bank of India, Australia, and China and the Hongkong and Shanghai Banking Corporation had gained dominance. As a consequence, most financial firms, traded and exchanged according to rates posted by London, not Madrid. The only other major Spanish bank of note was the Monte de Piedad (Mount of Piety). The Monte de Piedad, however, was formally a savings bank aimed toward charity rather than a commercial bank and would have little effect outside of Manila.[16] The Spanish colonial state was also alarmed by the commercial power of British, Chinese, and Mestizos in the islands.[17] The reaction of the colonial state to the dearth of Spanish commercial presence led to mass deregulation and the privatization of major cash crop industries, such as tobacco and sugar.[18] In addition, fiscal policies and tariff legislation were reconfigured to attract more peninsular capital investment and increase Spanish trade in the colony.[19]

State attempts to increase Spanish economic presence would largely fail to attract peninsular capital. By the 1890s, the Spanish economic future in the colony looked dire, with the monetary system receiving much of the blame. Under the pressure of increasing material insecurities, many economic observers of the time applied pressure on imperial decision-makers to make drastic changes to the colony's economic structures. Despite these calls for reforming the economy, these demands would frequently fail to gain serious recognition from the peninsula. Indeed, it would be a Native uprising that would force Spain to finally pay attention to the precarious material conditions of the Philippine colony.

Imperial Insecurities and Fantasies
of Reform

The year 1872 sent shock waves throughout the Spanish colonial Philippines. An insurgency had exploded in the province of Cavite just south of Manila, the center of colonial state power. Colonial authorities at the time called it a mutiny. Three secular and nonwhite priests were executed for supposedly spreading radical ideas to Natives.[20] Since class and racial antagonisms infused all parts of colonial society, the fears of a peasant rebellion intensified. Unconditional decolonization appeared imminent. Enter the *Ilustrados*. Self-named after the European Enlightenment movement in philosophy, politics, and science, the "enlightened" ones would soon coalesce as a self-conscious group of mainly Mestizo and Criollo intellectuals with the goal of reforming the colonial system.

For Ilustrados, reforms meant recognition as equal subjects within the Spanish Empire, separated no longer by the racial hierarchy between the peninsula and the colonies. Instead of seemingly irrational and antiquated racial hierarchy, reformers called for a reasonable distribution of sovereign power in which the colonies would have increased representation in political decision-making. Eventually, many reformers would call for the peaceful transfer of sovereign power. The Ilustrado vision of decolonization was indebted mainly to liberal European political and moral philosophy, which emphasized political concepts of individual liberties and rights. At the same time liberties and rights were structured by a particular normative notion of society as a capitalist society, one that functioned and was bound together through capitalist logics of exchange, property, and contracts. It was a vision of the future in which the transfer of governmental powers would occur, like a contract between property owners, from the Spanish colonizer to the most capable colonized subjects. From the Ilustrado viewpoint, the colony should be politically represented by the economically successful and the most educated individuals from the islands.

Racial capitalism would not be radically disturbed in the Ilustrado vision of decolonization. Some reformers offered a critique of capitalism—particularly the way its distribution and management by the Spanish colonial state offered little to no benefit to the vast colonized masses and instead generated class and racial antagonisms. Critiques of capitalism in the Philippines were often not meant as challenges to the logic of capitalism. Instead, critiques of capitalism were deployed as criticism of colonial and imperial economic policies. Ilustrados offered no vision of an economic or social system radically different from the world structured by colonial and racial capitalism. If there were socialist or anarchist influences, they were relatively marginalized. Most famously, in the case of Jose Rizal's novel *El Filibusterismo*, anarchism—the violent destruction of the colonial state and the property of the wealthy elite—was presented as a potentially tragic alternative if an enlightened and liberal kind of decolonization remained rejected by the Spanish Crown.[21] Moreover, the Indio, the racial majority of the colonial population, were presented as a source of terror, particularly if economic security became threatened. Indeed, authorities feared that if economic insecurities continued, Indios would become more unruly and antagonistic, leading to violent insurrection. Ilustrados and reformers would focus in on money as a possible entry point for regaining economic security and repairing relations between colony and metropole.

Some, however, did not want reform, but instead wished to fortify the imperial asymmetry between the colony and metropole. The major public opponents to the Ilustrados were loyalists, those against liberal reforms and deeply committed to the Spanish Empire. The major organ of loyalists was *La Politica de España en Filipinas*, a promonarchic journal printed in Madrid. For the founders of *La Politica*, brothers Jose and Pablo Feced, and Wenceslao Retana, the monetary system in the Philippine colony was an increasingly important site where political arguments over sovereignty, recognition, and representation unfolded. Concerns over the monetary system articulated by loyalists in *La Politica* could be seen as indicative of the overall Spanish anxiety over the precarious future of the Philippine colony.

The central focus of monetary discourse was the matter of currency standard. There were three primary points of view.[22] First were the gold-backers who were against the continuation of the silver Mexican coin, as well as any other type of silver-based currency. They argued that any type of silver currency would simultaneously disturb the exchange rate between the colony and the peninsula and generally devalue the peninsula's currency.[23] Second were bimetallic supporters, who advocated for silver currency to be used on a local scale and gold currency to be used for foreign transactions. Strongly supported by Criollos and some Mestizos in the Manila business community, bimetallic supporters argued that the adoption of both gold and silver would bring the colony's markets closer to the peninsula's own official bimetallic system.[24] This proposed unity of the monetary system was also interpreted as formally bringing the Philippine colony further within the fold of the Spanish Empire. Bimetallism generated the most public controversy as it implied severe political consequences, such as the official recognition of the Philippines as a province of Spain.[25]

In opposition to both gold-backers and bimetallists were the silver-backers. Silver-backers asserted that by establishing a strictly silver-based currency specific to the Philippine colony, the crown could reestablish the hierarchical relation between peninsula and colony. This process, moreover, would cost little to the Spanish colonial state. Proponents argued that the state could simply take the already existing Mexican silver coins from circulation, melt it down, and remint the silver bullion into a currency more similar to the Spanish duro.[26] La Política was one of the main public proponents of the silver currency strategy. In particular, they were vehemently against any type of monetary unification between the colony and the peninsula, especially if it led to the possibility of raising the political and racial status of the Philippines. Furthermore, they feared that monetary unification could eventually lead to political equality and subsequently the end of a recognizable Spanish Empire.[27]

Despite the complex and contradictory makeup of these differing camps, there remained a consensus that the primary source of monetary crisis in the Philippine colony was the Mexican silver coin. Indeed, the most common word associated with the Mexican coin was extranjero, which meant foreigner or stranger. The Mexican coin was thus seen as an undomesticated foreign presence. Clearly, Mexican currency was foreign to the colony because the stamp on the coin belonged to a nation-state independent from, and thus foreign to, the Spanish Empire. Many observers obsessed over iconography and frequently referred to the eagle adorning the face of the Mexican coin. In the minds of loyalists, the predatory eagle came to signify all the illegal activities and social disorders tethered to the foreign.[28] Soon, however, another foreign figure was attached to the estranged Mexican coin: the Chinese.[29]

The casting of the Chinese as both a figure of the foreign and the market was not necessarily limited to the late nineteenth century Spanish Philippines.[30] Chinese traders had traveled throughout the Philippine Archipelago long before European imperial exploration in Southeast Asia. However, by the Spanish colonial era, various racist and violent state policies limited the growth of the Chinese population in the colony. Despite legalized racial exclusion, colonial capital depended on Chinese labor and commerce, subsequently increasing the Chinese and Chinese-Indio Mestizo population.[31] As their communities became more visibly present, the colonial state began to soften its stance on the Chinese. Chinese migrants rapidly and unexpectedly filled the role of broker and creditor within the commercial system of the archipelago. This new role was a consequence of two pressing needs of capital formation in the Spanish Philippines: the lack of currency supply outside of Manila and the lack of credit networks in outlying provinces. Through the establishment of credit networks, the Chinese soon dominated the movement of money and commodities back and forth between foreign merchant houses and agricultural producers throughout the surrounding provinces.[32] Moreover, through this system Chinese agents opened up general merchandise stores and offered small credit to peasants and workers far from urban centers.[33] The success of Chinese as mediators of capital helped grow the population from about eight thousand in the 1880s to about forty thousand by 1900, with over half living in Manila.[34] Chinese merchants, therefore, due to the combination of various commercial and political restrictions and the increase of local and regional commercial needs, inevitably became the corporeal embodiment of money and debt in the colony.

However, as the most visible representation of the capitalist system in colonial society, the Chinese unfairly became the face of all economic insecurities. As Caroline Hau observes, the Chinese merchant represented "the point at which money appears and disappears in the presence of ordinary people."[35] The Chinese were thus blamed for profiting off economic insecurity, including price fluctuations, hoarding of necessary goods, price gouging, and predatory lending.[36] This public imagining rendered the Chinese merchant as mere parasite to the division of labor necessary in the capitalist mode of production. Moreover, Chinese merchants, stresses Hau, were the daily reminder to Natives of the alienation of their labor from the product of labor.[37] The Chinese, therefore, were both an alien and alienating presence in colonial society.

During the second half of the nineteenth century, the racialized and classed figure of the Chinese merchant was normatively attached to monetary and market insecurities. Jose Rizal's El Filibusterismo, for instance, highlighted the manner in which Quiroga, the wealthy Chinese merchant and aspiring colonial consul, accumulated money as well as political power through his access and control of the Manila ports. The Manila ports, in this case, represented the threshold between colony and foreign markets. Rizal emphasized Quiroga's position as mediating gatekeeper by mentioning the Chinese merchant's involvement in the "Mexican peso affair" and his notorious talent for smuggling through customs anything he wished, including illegal Mexican coins.[38] During this period, the Chinese were also suspected of counterfeiting Mexican currency. The lower silver content of the counterfeit coins allowed traders to purchase goods, including Spanish gold and silver coins, for much less than the bullion value of the counterfeit.[39] Thus, the Chinese were seen as not only mediators at the borders between legal and illegal or foreign and domestic. Through their perceived attachment to smuggling and counterfeiting, they were also the figures of the border between the domestic and the foreign itself and the undomesticated uncanny that fundamentally structured borders.

In addition to Sinophobia, other racial and class antagonisms would continuously haunt attempts to reform the asymmetrical monetary relations between colony and metropole. The clearest example of this can be found in the works of monetary reformer, Francisco Godinez, a lawyer and former president of the Banco Español Filipino.[40] Frequently cited by both reformers and loyalists, Godinez eventually became a polarizing figure for his advocacy of monetary unification.[41] In one article, Godinez laid out a multistage policy that would bring about monetary unification without causing, as he argued, any "strong shocks" to the political and economic order.[42] The most controversial stage in this process entailed the temporary replacement of all circulating foreign coins (primarily Mexican silver currency) with paper money. Resolving racial and class antagonisms were crucial in defending the feasibility of this plan.

In the article, Godinez highlighted the historic fear of paper money in Western societies, acknowledging how the introduction of paper money stoked public paranoia over the government's capacity to maintain order and security.[43] The turn to paper money signaled in the eyes of the public both the weakening and desperate abuse of state authority.[44] More specific to Spanish concerns, however, was the fear of how monetary unity could potentially disturb an imperial order founded on racial hierarchy and ability. From the imperial perspective, the currency system aggregated and hierarchized colonial populations according to intersecting axes of race, class, and ability. The braiding of race, class, and ability was starkly evident in Godinez's analysis of the figure of the Indio and the Indio's capacity to handle paper money.

"The Indio," Godinez asserted, "has the qualities and defects of youth or childhood that characterizes not only the age of the individual but of the people."[45] The Indio's undeveloped state could be observed through various racial "defects of the people," including frivolity, slothfulness, volatility, idleness, and impulsivity. In other words, Indios, like children, had yet to learn to control their base desires. Predictably, Godinez did not deviate from the transimperial discourse of Indigenous-as-children deployed by other colonial authorities concerned with asserting a clear hierarchical dichotomy between the savage Indio and the civilized colonizer.[46] At the same time, however, through the metaphor of the child, Godinez implied that this difference could be overcome through the accumulation of time and knowledge. The savage, therefore, could eventually be civilized. Like a child, the Indio was "trusting, credulous and of good faith, is respectful of all authority, and has the ease of adapting to all situations and novelties."[47] The Indio, therefore, could still be molded into a responsible modern economic subject, the kind of subject who could soundly manage money and respect authority.

Godinez recognized this potential in the more educated and refined Indio, a racialized class that exhibited comprehension and ingenuity "equal to the most intelligent people of any race."[48] Indeed, in regard to this class of wealthy Indigenous, specifically those enlightened and educated, Godinez remarked: "judging by their knowledge of reading and writing—they are not behind many other peoples in Europe."[49] Here Godinez made a distinction between this class of Indio and what he termed the "more crude" Indio, a social distinction that also denoted a racial designation within the Philippine colonial context. The educated and refined class, from the perspective of both loyalists and reformers, was primarily defined by its Mestizoness. The hybridity and mixture implied by Mestizoness, in this case, did not necessarily mean the "race-mixing" of Spanish and Indio. Instead, the racial category of the Mestizo came to stand-in for any kind of non-Indigenous colonized figure: for example, those whose ancestors were Chinese and Indio. In the context of the last decade of the nineteenth century, however, the Mestizo was a racial and economic figure that was shaped by its proximity to Western thought, art, and ideas. Unlike the Indio, to be Mestizo meant that one was more intellectually and culturally intimate with Europe and thus more distant from savagery.[50]

The vast majority of Indios, according to Godinez, had yet to develop the cognitive capacity to handle the intricacies of paper money. After all, paper money entailed treating the notes as though they were authentic containers of value, a monopoly held in Western societies by metal coins. Moreover, paper money involved understanding and interpreting the printed symbols and figures on the face of the note and simultaneously recognizing it as an accurate representative of exchange-value in the capitalist market. However, paper notes were meant to replace higher denomination coins and not the lower denomination coins, which were the kinds of currency with which the vast majority of colonial society—namely Indio peasants and workers—interacted. Godinez thus argued that the more educated and wealthy Indios were not only intellectually capable but were also ideal racial subjects for such experimentation.

Godinez justified this evaluation by arguing that the wealthy Indio was "respectful of all authority" and as such was racially capable to handle paper money. He cited the *cedula* tax as evidence of this racial capacity.[51] According to Godinez, the colonial state's routine of documenting the proof of payment of personal taxes for the cedula, prepared the Indio to properly recognize the fiduciary symbols of a paper currency. The key to paper currency's future success, therefore, resided in the relationship between the Indio and the colonial state. Godinez underscored this particular relationship by citing the Indio's seemingly unquestioned recognition of the authenticity of the documentation received as proof of personal service rendered or days worked for the cedula.[52] In other words, much like a state document was a representation of the services or labor value of the paid cedula, the state's paper currency would be a representation of concrete exchange value within a capitalist market.

The Indio's historical relation to colonial state authority within a racial order was crucial to Godinez's confidence in not only the success of currency reforms, but also the stabilization of the colonial monetary system as a whole. This type of authority arrived not from the Indio's understanding of the valuation of the market, but rather from the sovereign power of the state to monopolize the colony's currency market. It was the recognition of, and obedience to, the sovereign power of the Spanish colonial state by the Indio that constituted this authority. Unlike modern societies from the North Atlantic that had historically been suspicious of authority if state-issued currency did not appear to hold inherent value, according to Godinez, the more educated—in other words the more Mestizo—Indio was racially prone to submit to the imperial sovereign's assignment of value to materially worthless pieces of paper. However, Godinez argued that despite this historic fear, in this instance, paper money could repair the damage done by Mexican currency in the archipelago and potentially in other parts of the Spanish Empire. Moreover, the Philippine experiment could have profound imperial consequences, especially for other Spanish colonies.[53]

Another unanticipated consequence of Godinez's articles was their appropriation by more politically confrontational writers. A significant example of this can be found in the writings of Marcelo del Pilar. The editor of *La*

Solidaridad, the propaganda organ of the Ilustrado reformers, del Pilar used Godinez's analysis to critique Spanish monetary policy, and more broadly the backwardness of imperial rule and the colonial order. After praising Godinez's work as "elegantly written" and "clear," del Pilar summarized the contents of the report.[54] Agreeing with Godinez on the complexity of the situation in the archipelago and the heterogeneous market forces at play, del Pilar nonetheless drew attention to the powerful economic impact of the church in the "remittance market." Del Pilar would go on to highlight the extraction of "material wealth" by the politically powerful Spanish friars of the colony and the subsequent transmittal of this wealth to church coffers in the peninsula. These remittances, moreover, occurred with little, if any, state regulation or "financial reciprocity of any kind." However, what del Pilar emphasized was not the particular actions of certain authorities such as the church or the government, but rather the incapacity of such agents to adequately comprehend the "abnormal situation in the Philippines." In contradistinction to these traditional authorities, del Pilar argued that only economic experts such as Godinez could correctly understand the crisis, and only experts such as Godinez knew how to study the "natural laws of economics" for solutions to the "erroneous policies of the government."[55]

Praising Godinez's work as "truly scientific," del Pilar underscored the naturalness of the movement of money, characterizing "the financial life of the Philippines" as subject to natural laws outside the colonial state's authority.[56] Del Pilar took the idea of natural laws further, making use of analogies to the organic body in describing the circulation of money in the Spanish Philippines.[57] Likening Spanish imperial state authorities to an untrained doctor, the colonial society to an ailing body, and monetary policy to medical surgery, del Pilar asserted: "In talking of government intervention, we tremble as the sick would tremble at the hands of an inexperienced surgeon. The mistakes in this matter cannot be corrected with flowery words that are usually the remedy given by our government officials."[58] Money, according to del Pilar, was vitally necessary to the social body of the Philippines. But in times of crisis, money could also make the body sick or fatally injured. Balancing the necessity and danger of money, in del Pilar's view, demanded expert intervention. Yet, del Pilar argued, Spanish imperial authorities were not only too hasty and recklessly invasive in making policies, but they were also inexperienced and untrained. Unlike more modern governments that valued the scientific knowledge of economic experts, the Spanish Crown remained content to either disavow or obscure the ailment of a monetary crisis through flowery words.

Turning to global monetary relations, del Pilar highlighted the Spanish Empire's inability to "extricate" not only the Philippine colony, but also the Spanish metropole itself, from the "commercial dictatorship of Great Britain."[59] By doing so, del Pilar located the ultimate threat to Philippine society not in the Spanish Crown, but in the foreign figure of Britain, the financial center of the global capitalist market. Immensely skeptical of the Spanish state's ability to protect the social body of the Philippine colony from the disorderly effects of the international capitalist market, del Pilar seemed to call for an alternative authority to the Spanish state, one that could wield the force of capitalism for the benefit of the colony. In other words, using the metaphor of surgery and emphasizing the necessity of manipulating the market by scientific methods, del Pilar appeared to wish for an authority that could domesticate the capitalist market. This was an endeavor he believed the Philippine colonial state was incapable of accomplishing and the political form of the Spanish Empire would never permit. As an alternative to both empire and the colonial state, del Pilar might well have envisioned the nation as this ideal authority. But for such a nation to obtain the kind of authority over money imagined by del Pilar as necessary, it would require not only state power, but also the capacity to implement modern monetary policies crafted by economic experts. In del Pilar's view, therefore, authority over money could not be grounded purely in the political authority of the state but required expert knowledge of the capitalist market.

Godinez's analysis of colonial monetary policy reveals the crucial ways liberal notions of citizenship, authority, and sovereignty were imagined as possible state solutions to the intersecting antagonisms within a colonial order. Even with del Pilar's critique of the Spanish authority and British financial power, the normativity of a state capable—through economic expertise—of ensuring capital accumulation was left undisturbed. However, colonial, racial, and class antagonisms could never be fully resolved by making the colonial state more knowledgeable or liberal. Even the promise of nationalism that del Pilar seemed to invoke could never fully ward off these intersecting structural antagonisms. Instead, nationalism merely attempted to displace colonial, racial, and class antagonisms, recoding desires for unconditional decolonization as individual desires for wealth, citizenship, and sovereignty. This fundamental antagonism between unconditional decolonization and conditional decolonization was especially evident from the very beginning of the 1896 Revolution.

In August 1896, Spanish authorities raided an underground printing room in Manila, confirming suspicions of the clandestine nationalist society called the Katipunan.[60] A heavy police crackdown ensued throughout the city. Once exposed, the Katipunan instigated a rebellion in the impoverished parts of Manila, a rebellion that would spread across myriad barrios and surrounding provinces. Significantly the Katipunan urban rebellion in 1896 began by tearing up cedulas, a government document necessary for identification and taxation. To Natives, the cedulas reified the colonial and racial hierarchies of quotidian life under the Spanish. Tearing up the cedulas was thus a violent refusal of not only unjust state expropriation through taxes, but also a collective and spectacular challenge to colonial authority and state surveillance.[61] Local Katipunan chapters were soon spontaneously formed, swelling the revolutionary ranks through the attraction of tens of thousands of small landholders and peasants.[62] In contradistinction to the Ilustrado-led Propaganda reform movement, the Katipunan Revolution challenged colonial sovereignty by amplifying the desires of those not considered educated or Mestizo: the Indio peasantry and urban poor.[63] By December 1897, out-armed and exhausted, revolutionary morale rapidly declined. Afraid of ending the revolutionary war without gaining any concessions, Katipunan leaders decided to sign a pact with the Spanish, voluntarily going into exile to Hong Kong in exchange for amnesty and P800,000 Mexican pesos. The Spanish on their end would regain order in the colony by disarming revolutionaries and removing nationalist leadership. For both Spanish and Katipunan leaders, the 1896 Revolution had seemingly been crushed. Soon, however, global events would unsettle Spanish colonial sovereignty, releasing, once again, revolutionary desires for decolonization.

On March 1898, Spain was challenged for its Caribbean colonies by an ever-increasingly aggressive U.S. Empire. This was instigated by the sinking of a U.S. warship outside of Havana a few months earlier, which was, at the time, blamed on the Spanish military. American public demands for war with Spain intensified, aided immensely by "yellow journalism" and a longer history of increased U.S. corporate investments in the Caribbean and Latin America.[64] Soon, U.S. Navy warships circled Manila Bay. Accompanying the United States were exiled Katipunan leaders, such as Emilio Aguinaldo, who had allied themselves under the understanding that they would gain an independent government, free from Spanish rule. Many surviving Filipino revolutionaries would side with U.S. imperial forces during the

Spanish American War. The war would end fairly quickly, officially lasting less than four months. Spain had lost its remaining major Caribbean (Cuba and Puerto Rico) and Pacific (Guam, Mariana Islands, Philippines) colonies. Most significantly the Spanish had ceded sovereignty to the United States, not to those it had colonized. Despite what Katipunan leaders such as Aguinaldo fantasized, the United States did not grant independence to the Philippines.

Filipino leaders, thus, faced a new occupying colonial presence, the U.S. military. In response, Aguinaldo and other elites invoked revolutionary rhetoric, this time declaring war against American colonial occupation in 1899. A major strategy adopted by Filipino leaders was the establishment of a rival state months earlier, one that claimed to be the legitimate sovereign in the Philippine Archipelago. In a church in Malolos, Bulacan, the first Philippine republic was constituted on September 15, 1898. Hoping to beat the United States to the punch, Filipino leaders attempted to transition the Katipunan revolutionary government into a "civil" government. This transition entailed the establishment of a congress and the drafting of a constitution.

The founding of the Malolos Republic would ideally serve two purposes. First, leaders wished to gain recognition of their capacity for self-government from foreign empires. Second, they sought to gain recognition domestically, from the Philippine population. In adopting this strategy, the Malolos government pursued a path of conditional decolonization, one that would remove the colonizers from the colony, without necessarily undoing colonial structures and norms. The Malolos government thus envisioned a recognizable modern Philippines, one in which state formation and capital accumulation would continue, albeit replacing a colonial sovereign with a national one. The institution and administration of currency, banking, and taxation systems was crucial to gaining this recognition. Thus, for leaders, the Republic needed to ensure the securitization of capitalism in the Philippines. Any disturbance to capitalist structures or disorder to capitalist society would mean the end of recognition. For the Malolos government, therefore, achieving decolonization meant the securitization and stability of economic and social orders and norms.

War against U.S. colonial occupation and imperial claims to sovereignty forced the Malolos Republic to pursue the appearance of order and normativity. Much to the dismay of Malolos authorities, however, the economic realm during wartime was one of disorder and unruliness. Indeed, less than a week after the outbreak of the 1899 Philippine American War, Baldomero Aguinaldo sent an anxious correspondence to the secretary of the interior.

Observing the market in Manila, the Malolos minister of war was shocked to find runaway prices, rampant speculation, and widespread hoarding. In addition, there were reports of increasingly antagonistic retail transactions between merchants and consumers over the true value of currency. The fluctuating value of coins made no discrimination as it victimized soldiers and civilians alike. There was talk of people refusing coins, preferring instead to barter. Some other areas chose to create their own types of currency out of wooden tokens. Exploding market prices put necessary commodities out of reach and the uncertain value of money made collecting taxes for the young government a frequently violent encounter.[65]

In addition to local markets, fiscal matters remained insecure. From its very beginning, the Republic found itself scrambling to obtain fiscal revenue. The collection of taxes would fail to cover the enormous costs of founding a government, especially since most of the population paid in kind rather than in cash. To finance its administrative operations and ultimately its war against U.S. Empire, therefore, the Republic continuously sought out loans. First it looked to domestic sources and as the situation became more desperate, from foreign creditors. Approved and announced in October 1898, the first plan for a twenty-million peso national loan involved the collection of "spontaneous and voluntary" monetary contributions from local propertied individuals. In exchange for these contributions, the government would exchange bonds redeemable in forty years. Guaranteeing this loan was "all the property belonging to the republic," which included "all estates which the people have recovered or may recover in the future."[66] By presenting the market as a scene of unruliness the minister of war hoped to appeal to the patriotism of merchants to tame "the spirit of profit" that was inflicting such harm on the nation.[67]

A month after its initial proclamation, Emilio Aguinaldo felt compelled to publicly justify the need for a national loan. Much of his rhetoric was based on the necessity for external recognition as a legitimate sovereign with a functioning and self-sustaining government. Recognition from the "outer world" entailed not only demonstrating that Filipinos had "reached the age of manhood" and had the "capacity necessary in order to establish an independent government directed by themselves." Recognition also relied on giving "incontrovertible proof" that the nation-state had "more than sufficient revenues" to sustain an independent government.[68] Yet the national loan's function was not limited to foreign recognition. Despite being looked at with "repugnance and even with horror" by even the most patriotic, "contributions of war" toward the national loan were warranted by the Republic's "unavoidable duty of protecting" the "welfare" and "interests" of "its people." As a result, the nationalized people were obligated to invest in the "business of the revolution," not only for the government's welfare, but also for their own.[69]

Through the national loan, Aguinaldo hoped to establish that the Malolos government was a responsible debtor. Hoping to demonstrate that there was no bad faith in soliciting credit from the people, Aguinaldo guaranteed the loan's "more or less remote restitution" through the issuance of bonds. These bonds would signify not only a debt to be paid by the government to the bondholders, but also a debt paid with interest. The nation, thus, was to convert its present wealth into a form of credit, credit that was subsequently guaranteed with interest by its own future capacity to generate and accumulate surplus capital. By promising to capture the nation's surplus capital of the future, the Republic attempted to capture, through the loan, the nation's wealth in the present.[70] Thus, this collective wealth of the present, accumulated mainly through coerced or exploited labor, would provide the revenues for the new nation. To be clear, appropriating and generating revenues of a society's collective wealth through financial techniques of bonds and loans was not a backward idea, but in reality, it demonstrated the Malolos Republic's capacity to govern like the supposedly more modern capitalist empires of the North Atlantic.

The Republic, however, failed to sell enough bonds before war broke out with the United States in February 1899. As a result, Prime Minister Apolinario Mabini and the secretary of the treasury issued a decree in April, soliciting the nation to purchase bonds in order to ward off the government's "imminent bankruptcy." Like Aguinaldo before him, Mabini justified this specific call for a national loan by highlighting the "extraordinary needs . . . which cannot be secured by ordinary taxation." War with the United States, however, made it even more necessary that the government seek "an extraordinary source of revenue." The guarantee of bonds, moreover, had changed. In addition to the abstract promise of future national property and land invoked earlier in Aguinaldo's pronouncement, this new version now indebted "the income from mining concessions; operation of railways and lines of communication and other natural resources of the archipelago which may be applied to industries: such as waterfalls and others of a like nature; and the special taxes on forestry products."[71] Capital accumulated from future infrastructure, rents, taxes, tariffs, energy, and extractive industries were now brought forth into the present through the magic capture of state-issued bonds.

Over two months later, overwhelmed by the immense military and economic resources of the United States and unable to raise enough revenue through domestic sources, the Malolos Republic looked to foreign creditors. Announced in July 1899, the Foreign Loan Act attempted to borrow twenty million pesos in gold through the issuance of bonds to foreign creditors. The bonds would be redeemable two decades after recognition of independence, with a yearly interest of five percent. Felipe Agoncillo was chosen as the representative of the Malolos Republic abroad, invested with full power of the government. Agoncillo was, furthermore, empowered to pledge not only "all the property and revenues of the national treasury" but also the "revenues of the Manila Customs house." Not only were state resources put up as security but so too were all future national resources. By subscribing to the loan, foreign creditors would "also enjoy preference over other bidders with regard to the sale of privileges of agricultural exploitation, railways and mines."[72] Thus, an independent Philippines—and all its current and future natural resources and fixed capital—would be partitioned, privatized, and auctioned off to foreign investors. The desperation of the Malolos Republic to sell off its sovereign control over the nation's resources and infrastructure to foreign capital in order to exist as a state demonstrates again the contradictions of conditional decolonization. The desire for sovereignty meant that the nation-state would actively participate in the exploitative and extractive process of capital accumulation. This would paradoxically render the nation-state ultimately unsovereign.

The dependence on capital for the sake of sovereignty can be further explored in the Republic's attempt to establish a national currency. Tied to the November 1898 act to establish a national loan, the Malolos Congress passed a measure to issue three million pesos worth of paper notes.[73] In June 1899, a presidential decree supplemented the initial congressional act by establishing several practical details, which included the denomination of the notes to be issued and the legal limitations of its circulation. Like the national loan, the Republic's currency was guaranteed in detail by the nascent nation-state's debts, primarily the properties and resources of the government. Unlike the bonds, however, the notes would earn no interest, but they would be redeemed and recognized by the Republic for the payment of taxes and other government obligations. Thus, like other modern states, the adoption of Republic money was fundamentally dependent on coercive techniques of expropriating wealth from the population under their control.

A month later, a financial body was created in order to manage this new state apparatus.[74] Similar to other governments, the Republic would attempt to establish further measures to both legitimize and give physical form to their currency. Even though in 1899 the Constitution of the Malolos Republic empowered the president to coin money, it was Aguinaldo's dictatorial powers that brought about the minting and production of the Republic's money.[75] Due to the constraints of the war only the two-centimo denominations were ever coined. Two different versions of the coins survived the war. No exact mintage figures, however, are known, and there is little evidence of actual circulation.[76] Paper currency, however, most likely because of the ease in printing in comparison to minting, did manage to briefly circulate in several Luzon provinces.[77] On June 30, 1899, a presidential decree in Tarlac stated that the secretary of finance was to issue notes immediately in small and large denominations. After the November 1899 shift to guerrilla warfare, however, few currency notes and coins were ever able to be manufactured, much less circulated. Still, these measures reveal the desire of the Malolos Republic to hold authority over money, an authority that officials believed would help lead to gaining sovereign power over the Philippines.

The Limits of Conditional Decolonization

The Malolos Republic's intention to appropriate and wield state authority over different dimensions of the Philippine economy quickly ran into difficulties, especially in the realm of taxation and wages. Despite attempts by the Republic to create a legitimate taxation system, efforts to collect taxes never went as intended. Taxes were especially dubious to Natives because of the manner in which taxation normalized colonial and racial hierarchies. In 1881, the Ilustrado Gregorio Sancianco, for instance, explained how the colonial state reinforced racial hierarchies in and through taxation. He would argue that, on one hand, the "ruling race composed of the pure Peninsular Spaniards" and "those of Spanish or European lineage, the Mestizos," were "exempt from the tribute." On the other hand, those without European lineage, the Indios, Chinese, and the Chinese Mestizo, would pay the heaviest toll to fund the Spanish colonial state.[78]

Expropriation of wealth according to racial categorization would be adopted and reinforced by the Malolos Republic. During the Philippine American War, the Malolos government instituted what it called a war tax system. The war tax system was additionally meant to replace the cedula form of identification with a "certificate of citizenship."[79] At the same time, however, the certificate of citizenship exposed the Republic's obsession with categorizing and managing race through additional or specialized taxes. Some aspects remained bound to Spanish colonial and racial orders. For instance, the additional tax faced by those racialized as Chinese contributed not only to the conceptualization of Chinese as a figure of the market, but at the same time excluded those marked as Chinese (as opposed to Chinese-Mestizo) from the national and political body.[80]

In addition to the legacies of racial hierarchies, correspondences between the Republic and local authorities and various citizens reveal how taxation was a frequent source of suspicion and conflict. There was widespread suspicion on the part of the public regarding imposters and false collectors.[81] The Malolos president soon felt compelled to respond to the flurry of reports that those "without proper authority" were soliciting war taxes and committing "excesses and abuses of all kinds."[82] By December 1898, the Republic had created an official form, to be carried by those authorized as tax collectors.[83] Unfortunately for the Malolos government, suspicion over false collectors had spread to suspicion over collections in general. Thus, the figure of the imposter had migrated from unknown and unidentifiable individual collectors and attached itself to the collecting operations of the government itself.

Suspicion had intensified to such a point that it elicited a long circular from Aguinaldo and Arcadio del Rosario (Secretary of Treasury) in March 1899. The circular justified taxes due to the ongoing state of war. "We are engaged in a war," argued the circular, "it is known by all that one of the most important factors in sustaining war undoubtedly consists in money." The circular promised that the tax would only be in force as long as the war continued and argued that the government had not "forgotten the worthiness of those who fight for the country."[84] Akin to the national loans and bonds, therefore, patriotic discourse was deployed by Malolos officials to convince the broader public that there was no bad faith in the collection of taxes. Indeed, Malolos leaders wanted taxes to be publicly seen as an investment in the future of national independence rather than mass expropriation.[85]

The Republic's most prolific tax evaders, however, would be Filipino capitalists. In one correspondence, a wealthy landowner described his devout patriotism and loyalty to the Republic, accounting for various contributions to the national loan. In this instance, the government cast doubt on the truth of the letter writer, asserting that all were suffering under an "anomalous" wartime market.[86] The response of the government to those who concealed their ability to pay taxes was to cast them as traitors. "He who voluntarily conceals the means with which he can contribute," as one government official declared, was not only a traitor to the Republic, but also a "traitor to his conscience."[87] Thus, when one was dishonest to the nation-state, one was dishonest to oneself. Perhaps this sentiment drove some concerned citizens to act on the part of the government, by taking it on themselves to spy on suspicious locals and provide the government with lists of names of who they thought were concealing their true assets.[88]

Despite the Republic's attempt to apply pressure on the wealthy to pay their fair share, however, the burden of taxes nevertheless disproportionately fell on the poor. This was likely because those authorized to collect taxes were simultaneously the wealthiest individuals of a locality. It is thus not too surprising that popular reaction to local authorities ranged from militant protest to armed conflict. Milagros Guerrero's *Luzon at War* recounts myriad historical episodes of organized and disorganized dissent against the Republic's taxation. One example was in Nueva Vizcaya, where townspeople held an armed protest at the provincial capital. They not only questioned the legitimacy of war taxes, but they also suspected that the current local officials conducted themselves "far worse than the Spanish authorities" by making false decrees in the name of the Republic.[89] Another striking instance of popular suspicion occurred in Laguna, where townspeople argued that the Republic's war tax was simply another ruse for corrupt local officials to extract more money from the lower classes.[90]

Like the realm of taxation, the Republic would also meet resistance from workers over the unequal power between labor and capital. Within the Republic's writings, struggles to end wealth inequality or labor exploitation were not as prioritized as demands over sovereignty, liberty, and fraternity. The establishment of the Malolos Republic could therefore be seen less as the culmination of the revolution and more as an attempt to domesticate unconditional decolonization. In the interests of attaining national sovereignty, the Republic never openly challenged the structures of racial capitalism. This is especially apparent when considering wage disputes and labor rights. Indeed, not only were the concerns of labor justice oftentimes deferred by Republic leaders, it was eventually perceived as a threat to conditional decolonization.

One salient example of this was a strike led by railroad workers in the Luzon provinces of Pangasinan and Pampanga, areas just north of Manila. In a letter dated September 23, 1898, President Aguinaldo addressed the railroad workers. In the letter, Aguinaldo mentioned his dismay that workers refused to report to work due to their desires for increased wages. Aguinaldo immediately labeled the strike an unproductive action, for it would not only fail in gaining the workers what they demanded, but it would subsequently put a halt to commercial activities. The disruption of commerce, in turn, threatened the very future of the nation, for the "necessities of life will be scarce and we shall be starved."[91] Aguinaldo then emphasized that the workers misrecognized the meaning of the word "union" by differentiating between a union grounded in labor versus a union of people under the nation. "Our union does not lie in what you have done—refusing to go to work with the railroad company. There should be a union in hailing the sacred liberty of our native land and in defending the same from being again taken from us by the Spaniards or by any other foreign nation. Our union should not consist in small things, as what you have done, i.e., refusing to go to work, which discredits you and all of us in the eyes of other nations who are now contemplating us."[92] A national union thus trumped the desires of "small things" such as economic equity. Instead, a national union enabled the pursuit of larger values, such as liberty and sovereignty. Thus, the value of political sovereignty must be held higher than any type of fair valuation of labor. Aguinaldo clearly obsessed over how the outside world would interpret the strikes.[93] After all, the global politics of recognition entailed that Aguinaldo be forever mindful of how the "eyes of other nations" contemplated and criticized the political authority of the Republic.

Additionally, Aguinaldo's anxieties over the labor strikes were not simply about foreign recognition. Rather, Aguinaldo was nervous over the spontaneously organized decision to strike on the part of those workers who he saw as ignorant and unenlightened. "I do not censure your present attitude, as it shows our union which is the fountain and strength of our present struggle against the Spaniards . . . but, what I expect you to do is to consult me before doing anything, for I am always at your service, ready to listen to your complaints and give wholesome advice as to what should be done."[94] The problem therefore was not the action of striking against a foreign corporation, for it displayed to Aguinaldo a type of bravery and vigor undergirded by nationalist sentiments. Instead, the problem lay in that the railroad workers not only spontaneously organized, but also collectively decided to strike, without looking to the proper authority: Aguinaldo and the Republic. In other words, from his perspective, the strikers made a collective decision autonomous of the sovereign. Through this decision, the workers expressed their own sovereign power, threatening the claims of sovereignty made by the Republic. Unlike the economic, social, and political hierarchies offered by the Republic, Aguinaldo was uncertain as to what lay behind the decision-making power expressed by organized labor. As a result, he attempted to disavow this possibility of a Native challenge to the Republic's authority by shifting the blame to more known enemies, such as "foreigners" that "always desire" the Republic's "disgrace and misfortune."[95]

News of the railroad strike, however, inspired many more strikes throughout Luzon, leading to a myriad of militant labor actions even in Manila. September through October of 1898 was an especially busy period of strikes and work stoppages by labor in a wide array of sectors including, but not limited to retail, cattle brokerage, domestic service, tobacco manufacturing, tram operations, shipping, and the railway. Provincial Governor Ambrosio Flores mentioned all these strikes, echoing Aguinaldo's letter above, by first asking: "Are these strikers justified in their action? Are the grounds alleged well founded?" The question of justice goes conspicuously unexplored as Flores dismissed these as the wrong sorts of questions.[96]

Flores asserted that questions of economic justice damaged the image of the nation in the eyes of the world. He chastised the strikers for bringing undue foreign concerns over whether Filipinos "possess the requisite ability and culture for self-government." On one hand, the sentiment of Flores indicated a concern over the global politics of recognition. After all, Manila at the end of the Spanish American War was under the jurisdiction of the U.S. military. In this liminal period, where sovereignty over the archipelago was still unsettled, every potential blemish to the capacity of Filipino self-government was anguished over by Filipino authorities. Out of fear of being seen as unable to govern their own citizens, Flores asked the Native workers if they had thought about how striking "may give rise to false impressions concerning the depth of our national character?" On the other hand, however, was Flores's understanding that events of striking and work stoppages appeared as symptoms of uncertain political authority. The stability of political authority was inextricably linked to the state's capacity to attract capital to the archipelago. It was not surprising, therefore, when Flores anxiously mentioned how labor actions called into question the Republic's ability to "sufficiently guarantee order" for "protected foreign interests."[97] Similar to Aguinaldo, he evoked the possibility of foreign minds behind the workers' actions. Moreover, Flores disavowed the capacity of laborers to organize and politically challenge authority autonomously from more educated and wealthier political leaders. He speculated "outside influences" were "working unceasingly to disparage the virile and powerful Philippine race."[98]

In the last section of his letter, Flores implored strikers to return to "honored work, which is the source of all prosperity," and encouraged them to ignore "the nationality of your employers" and to only "seek redress through legal and prudent methods." Only after the workers "have exhausted every means of conciliation" will labor be "justified, individually or collectively, in resorting to passive resistance." In a last-ditch attempt, he warned the workers that "in no case should you resort to violence or cause disorders which only serve to belie your naturally pacific, docile and honorable character, which even our very enemies and exploiters could not but acknowledge at all times."[99] One could read the inherent qualities of the Filipino as "naturally pacific, docile, and honorable," as yet another example of a racialized politics of recognition. Of note, however, is a sudden shift in tone from the earlier sections of the letter, which utilized the rhetoric of persuasion, to an authoritative command, banishing the potential of violence or disorder: "in no case should you resort to violence or cause disorders." This tonal shift to command reveals some other type of fear. No doubt this fear was rooted in the potential for violence and disorder, but what form of violence and disorder in particular?

Perhaps Flores was fearful of a type of violence in which previous orders, systems, institutions, and authorities became unrecognizable. In Flores's words, there was a clear distinction between the conditional decolonization espoused by the Malolos Republic and the possibility of unconditional decolonization opened up by striking workers. As Frantz Fanon writes, decolonization "is always a violent event." In arguing this, Fanon was not romanticizing armed revolution but instead considered decolonization an "agenda for total disorder" in which the very structures and norms of the colonial status quo was violently undone and unconditionally replaced by a new world and new forms of life. Furthermore, Fanon stressed, "what is singularly important is that it (decolonization) starts from the very first day with the basic claims of the colonized."[100] In other words, unconditional decolonization's necessary origins emerge from the unrepressed and spontaneous desires of the colonized. In the case of the Philippine strikes, the violence of workers struck at the violent foundations of the world as they knew it: the daily labor exploitation of colonial and racial capitalism. The radicalness of this violence was a foundational violence, for it held the possibility of creating new forms of life, full of novel kinds of intimacies and solidarities. Perhaps most frightening, therefore, to Republic leaders, was not merely the potential violence of labor strikes against the state or the deceleration of capitalist accumulation in the islands, but instead a future in which law and authority had been completely abolished and replaced by a more just and caring world.

On March 23, 1902, Emilio Aguinaldo was captured by the U.S. military and eventually coerced into pledging allegiance to the United States. After Aguinaldo's call for all Filipinos to surrender to the United States, the Malolos Republic was dissolved. The United States would subsequently declare the war over. For countless Filipinos, however, war was far from over. Indeed, the Philippine American War would endure well into the 1910s. Over the next decade and a half, both U.S. military and civil colonial formations would continue to be violently unsettled by monetary insecurities inherited from the Spanish colonial era. On one hand, despite the United States being a foreign and occupying presence, concerns over foreign currencies, foreign banks, and foreign figures (such as the Chinese), would weigh heavily on the minds of American colonial authorities. On the other hand, Native desires for both conditional and unconditional decolonization would continue to plague American claims to colonial sovereignty. In reaction, the United States would instigate a series of multipronged strategies of counter-decolonization. The following chapters examine how monetary authority operated as a key component of U.S. counter-decolonization.

Mongrel Currencies

2

In her memoirs titled *A Woman's Impressions of the Philippines*, Mary H. Fee recalled the feelings of frustration that swept over her every time she received her wages. A white American schoolteacher during the Philippine American War, Fee made the journey across the Pacific on the uss *Thomas* during the initial years of U.S. colonial occupation. Fee described her 1901 travels across the Pacific like a sightseeing trip, witnessing exotic lands she had only imagined through various works of literature. Once within the cycle of work, however, the romantic scales fell from her eyes, as she had to confront the realities of earning a living. It is from this mundane experience of receiving her paycheck that "one of the most irritating... features of life" in the Philippines germinated.[1] When Fee arrived in the Philippines, all the local banks and financial institutions throughout the islands operated within a de facto silver currency system in place since the twilight of Spanish governance. In considering a currency system that was dominated by the Mexican dollar and some other coins of unknowable foreign origins, Fee lamented that only the "experts of the Government could tell where it all came from."[2]

From the end of the nineteenth century onward, many of the North Atlantic capitalist empires had adopted the gold standard for their respective monetary systems. This monetary status quo would cause the value of silver currencies—the monetary basis of supposedly less developed peoples across the planet—to regularly undergo violent fluctuations. Based on a de facto silver system, the Philippine economic world appeared like a nightmare to those employed by the U.S. colonial government. During such quotidian activities of cashing a check, depositing funds in a bank, or sending remittances back to the United States, colonial workers and managers had to first convert their wages paid in gold into the local silver value. Fee explained that for over two years she, along with the rest of the Americans living in the Philippine colony, would remain victim to the "evils of a fluctuating currency."[3] There was "tremendous protest," she claimed, concerning the currency, but also the "extortion which grew out of it."[4]

This chapter examines how and why establishing a new U.S. colonial monetary system in the Philippines was considered fundamentally necessary by colonial authorities, not only to securitize colonial occupation but to simultaneously ward off the possibility of decolonization. Myriad U.S. colonial authorities identified currency insecurity as a central obstacle to winning the ongoing Philippine American War. For authorities, currency represented several imminent insecurities. The frictions between the capitalist market and imperial state decision-makers, the quotidian frustrations of dealing with local moneychangers and retailers, and the unruliness of racialized workers are all contingencies that sowed insecurities in the effectiveness of American colonial occupation. U.S. imperial officials would turn to Charles Conant, an economic expert who claimed to possess the necessary market knowledge to fix these insecurities. This chapter explores the justifications and consequences of a colonial monetary system designed by American economic experts such as Conant. It pays special attention to, on one hand, the desires of economic experts to prove the racial capacity of white Americans to be a leading capitalist imperial force within a racial capitalist system, and on the other hand, to prove that market knowledge could be deployed to racially uplift Filipino Natives out of savagery and insecurity.

During the last three decades of the nineteenth century, U.S. racial capitalism was deeply shaped by the tension between the logic of the capitalist market and the sovereignty of the imperial state. This is most evident in the violent money debates of the post-Reconstruction era, an era in which economic experts would try to arrange the world into particular logics that served both U.S. capital and the imperial state. Yet this dual allegiance would often create contradictions that would in turn create more need for expert fixing. A self-serving cycle would be formed and expanded, as the increasing authority of the hardening discipline of economics would gain more power within both capitalist and banking classes and state and government realms.

U.S. imperial experts sent to fix the Philippines were especially shaped by debates over currency, banking, and capital during the 1890s. Framed mainly by the banking panics and the subsequent Long Depression from the previous decades, the public debates of the "money question" coalesced into two opposing sides. On one side, so-called populist currency reformers argued for a bimetallic system of gold and silver currency and on the other side were procapitalist gold-standard supporters. Reformers argued that having more silver-based currency would decrease the U.S. market's dependence on international forces and increase the economic power of U.S. agricultural producers. Populists specifically blamed Northeastern bankers' and capitalists' ties to the London-dominated international financial system. The "free silver" movement, as it would eventually be known, envisioned a monetary system that would focus less on international exchange and instead cultivate domestic production through increased agricultural credit and loans. Racial anxieties over Black populists would trump class solidarity as the presidential election of 1896 loomed ever closer.[5] The major white populist organizations would eventually assimilate into the counter-Reconstruction Democratic Party led by William Jennings Bryan.[6] His stump speech played to the money question especially, warning against America's crucifixion on a "Cross of Gold." The struggle over monetary reform symbolically culminated in the presidential election of 1896, which saw the defeat of Bryan to the corporate, finance, and the rhetorically pro-empire favorite, Republican William McKinley.[7]

The steady series of gold-backer political victories was both a product and producer of an ideological ensemble that positioned money and the market as a natural phenomenon dictated by its own internal laws. Although far from reaching a consensus and always brimming with tensions and contradictions, these historic struggles constructed a normative notion of money and the capitalist market in the public. The money debates helped congeal public acceptance that the capitalist market, despite being produced and sustained by people, was not wholly of the people. This is what I refer to as the *logic of market knowledge*. Through this logic, the capitalist market was conceptualized as separate from both state and society and, though artificial, operated with its actions dictated by laws natural to itself.[8]

One of the primary agents in popularizing the concept of market knowledge was the economic expert. Within both academic and public realms, the expert would produce knowledge about an object called the capitalist market and through this production would naturalize the market as an object autonomous from state and society. At the turn of the twentieth century, the U.S. imperial state would increase its recognition of expert authority over market knowledge, especially regarding colonial policymaking. The symbiotic and complex bond between the economic expert and the state was expressed in the Yale University president's 1899 presidential address, which stated that the experts' ultimate future "lies not in theories but in practice, not with students but with statesmen, not in the education of individual citizens . . . but in the leadership of an organized body politic."[9] It is in and through this ideologically shaped desire for collaboration in colonial policymaking that economic experts would be driven to formulate new theories about money, the market, and the racial destiny of the United States in a world grounded in an interimperial system.

One such expert was Charles Conant, a self-taught intellectual who made his name in the banking community through a decade of writing editorials and articles in various journals, mainly covering and commenting on issues of commerce and finance. Conant would eventually become one of the most visible and well-traveled members of the U.S. Commission of International Exchange (CIE), a diplomatic apparatus tasked in creating an American-led global financial system based on the gold standard.[10] Although never quite achieving the promised foreign relations outcomes, the CIE would rehearse how U.S. economic imperialism would unfold in the first half of the twentieth century. Rather than rely on diplomats employed by the U.S. government, the imperial state would encourage the deployment of individuals from the private sector on behalf of U.S. global interests. Many of these experts and bankers would attempt to outmaneuver other rival capitalist empires by locking colonial or semicolonial governments into loans based on the U.S. dollar or convince developing nations to institute monetary reforms in which the new currency would be based on U.S. dollars as reserves.[11]

A staunch gold-standard supporter, Conant made a splash at the Indianapolis Monetary Convention of 1898, eventually gaining the attention of several prominent figures intimate with the McKinley administration. He would be known especially for railing against the "limping standard" of bimetallism and for the bright future of a global capitalist system based on gold.[12] In addition, however, many of his published works were dedicated to understanding why, despite the efficient and satiated productivity of American industry, financial markets would periodically collapse and go into crisis. Perhaps more importantly, these texts reflected Conant's inquiry into how American business and the U.S. government could effectively resolve the devastating effects of economic crisis.[13]

For instance, published just a month into the Spanish American War, Conant's article "The Economic Basis of 'Imperialism'" situated U.S. transpacific expansion as a consequence of the "natural law" that guided both "economic and race development."[14] Assuming that the growth of capitalism was synonymous with the progress of Western civilization, Conant positioned capitalist crisis as a natural consequence of industrialism and the advancement of the white Anglo-American race.[15] Specifically, capitalist markets of the United States and Europe had become heavily stagnated by an overproduction of supply and the lack of capital investment. The last three decades, which were marked by recurrent crises, were the results of this stagnation. For Conant, therefore, rather than stifle economic and racial growth by retreating within the already domesticated borders of the United States, imperial expansion enabled capital and the white Anglo-American race to flourish.[16] Transpacific colonization would fix racial capitalist stagnation in two ways. First, since savage and darker peoples had failed to properly develop their lands, U.S. colonization would turn these territories into more productive sites for capital investment. Second, colonization would racially uplift Natives to white and Western civilizational standards, creating new modern consumers of American commodities and finance. As Conant stated: "I am a strong believer in 'Imperialism' in the sense that the advanced powers should open the undeveloped countries to civilization and introduce among them the machinery of modern production, commerce, and finance."[17]

Conant believed economic experts were necessary to manage capitalist crisis through the creation of sound imperial financial and monetary policies. The strategy of economic imperialism, according to Conant, entailed going beyond both the old "decaying countries" of Europe and the American continental territory, to pursue the "equipment of new countries of production and exchange."[18] To go beyond the U.S. settler colonial space of North America, U.S. capitalists had to turn their gaze toward the countries of Asia and Africa, which had "not felt the pulse of modern progress." U.S. capital would be invested in not only the extraction of natural resources or labor through the construction of buildings and machinery, but also in public infrastructure, such as roads, dams, irrigation, and sewage systems.[19] Following the pattern of other North Atlantic capitalist empires, U.S. capital accumulation in its nonsettler colonies, such as the Philippines, would occur through the development of colonial infrastructure.

For Conant, U.S. Empire, and in particular its military apparatus, was necessary to clear the way for the unchecked spatial flow of capital to where it could profit. He differentiated this Anglo-American style of empire from, in his view, less rational types of empires. Those of the Slavic or Latin races, for instance, were wedded to colonization for "sentimental reasons" and kept their colonial markets closed. The old-world imperial policy of closing off markets exacerbated the existing problems of overaccumulation, consequently destroying "the purchasing power of one's purchasers" by putting up a protected wall and intensifying "contest against each other before the same body of consumers." These kinds of colonial economic policies went against the "natural laws of trade" and were outmoded by the Anglo-American sort of economic imperialism that touted the opening up of undeveloped economies to the "free market" for the benefit of the global capitalist system in general.[20]

Conant's writings make clear his belief that white Anglo-Americans were the proper inheritors of capitalist and Western civilization. As such, they were burdened with an enormous world-shaping obligation to advance and spread capital and civilization to the world's so-called darker peoples. Yet, Conant also believed in the immense racial capacity of white Anglo-Americans to innovate and find new ways to break out of stagnation. Transpacific expansion would allow white Anglo-Americans to overcome spatial limitations and colonizing the Philippines would prove their racial capacity to potentially lead a world of capitalist empires.[21] This meant that U.S. Empire had to create secure conditions in these new areas for the stable investment of capital. In other words, colonial territories or "half savage lands" as Conant put it, had to be disciplined into orderly and secure spaces, not only in the present but also for the long-term future.[22] The problem, however, was that the Philippine colony remained plagued by economic and military insecurities. A primary source of these insecurities was money.

Money at War and the Desire
for Monetary Authority

In 1898, the most pressing logistical concerns of U.S. military occupation consisted of purchasing supplies, paying wages for colonial labor, and disbursing paychecks to soldiers: all these arrangements necessitated a stable supply of cash.[23] In less than two years, military ranks would swell to an estimated seventy thousand troops, who all required cash to be clothed, fed, and remunerated. Moreover, because the U.S. military was now an occupying population filled with soldiers involved in a protracted war against Native *insurectos*, the stabilization of day-to-day banking services and commercial and retail transactions became even more important to maintain a sense of normalcy and morale.[24] It is within this situation that the security of money became a pressing concern of imperial decision-makers, economic experts, and military leaders. And it is within the mundane activity of managing logistics that concerns over monetary insecurities revealed multiple frictions between different colonial agents.

For example, the disbursement of wages provided one of the largest headaches for the military colonial state. Every department seemed to have their own system of distributing paychecks and often, local paymasters, when frustrated, would shift to different systems from month to month.[25] As one paymaster complained, it was "practically impossible to transfer" necessary funds.[26] These feelings were especially due to the discrepancy between the form of payment and the local currency conditions in which soldiers found themselves. At first, soldiers were paid in a combination of U.S. silver and gold coins. As the money supply dwindled for the ever-growing military population, paymasters switched to issuing U.S. Treasury notes. Many paymasters were convinced that local banks and exchange shops would accept the notes at the same value as gold-based U.S. dollars.[27]

For many American soldiers who were being paid in gold-based notes, however, the silver-based commercial world of the Philippine colony would appear predatory and criminal. One newspaper article warned that "American Money [was] Discredited," causing "perversities, complexities, difficulties, and impossibilities." Soldiers, without adequate leadership, thus encountered an unsettling and threatening colonial world in which "all the natural cursedness of the climate and all the artificial eccentricities of the place and people [we]re concentrated in the currency."[28] Printed in a pro-American newspaper, this article appeared to panic over the disrespect given to U.S. currency. Eventually this article, and other similar critiques, would make the rounds across the desks of the War Department, prompting action from decision-makers.

Frictions would occur between high-ranking authorities, frustrated by the contradictory ad hoc methods being applied on-the-ground in the archipelago.[29] "The rates of exchange should be established," one colonial official complained, "in orders similar to those issued to exchange in Cuba and Porto [sic] Rico."[30] In comparison to ongoing U.S. colonialisms elsewhere, the economic occupation of the Philippine Islands seemed to go awry. Empire forced many American colonial occupiers to confront a social life completely foreign to one they had ever experienced. Occupation entailed the consumption of Native commodities and services, things from which soldiers felt alienated. For example, since most retail transactions involved silver-based currency and most soldiers were paid in gold-based currency, soldiers had to first convert their paycheck from gold to silver. The military government, however, did not have the capacity or resources to provide silver currency. To convert gold into silver, therefore, soldiers had to go to an agent external to the military government, primarily foreign-owned banks or local moneychangers who would regularly charge an inflated service fee or commission. Moreover, based off the ebbs and flows of international market valuations, local banks and moneychangers would change local exchange rates daily.

There was also prevailing suspicion within the military ranks of illicit collaboration between banks and moneychangers. As one paymaster in 1899 asserted, "the two English banks of Manila seem to be in collusion, and charge exorbitantly for all business transacted over their counters." The paymaster went on to detail how exchange rates would even detrimentally affect the value of money in a soldier's savings account. "When an officer or enlisted man goes to deposit his gold with them it is credited to his account in silver, at the current rate—for this is a silver country—and if he want gold for any purpose they charge him never less than 5 per cent for it." In addition to the predatory withdrawal fee, the paymaster suspected that banks manipulated the exchange rates, especially when "pay day approaches" to "make a greater profit from these soldiers."[31] Bankers defended their banking practices, blaming the "frequent misunderstandings and misrepresentations" of currency values on the general lack of knowledge of Americans soldiers.[32]

In addition to friction with bankers, soldiers frequently came into conflict with Native retailers and moneychangers. This made sense. Natives, after all, were especially suspicious of U.S. currency. According to a special report made just after the Spanish American War by Edward W. Harden to the Treasury Department in November 30, 1898, Natives illogically demanded the less valuable Mexican coin over U.S. money. "The native will take the Mexican dollar, worth less than 50 cents gold, in preference to the United States dollar, worth 100 cents. Any change in the coinage will require time for the natives to become accustomed to it before it will be accepted readily." The Native's suspicion of U.S. currency, however, according to Harden, was not malicious. Rather, suspicion of U.S. currency came from the Native's lack of knowledge, a sort of illiteracy of currency. To Harden, the problem was that "a very small proportion of the inhabitants understand English." Illiteracy in English made it especially hard for Natives to "decipher the inscription on a coin" unless it was written in Spanish. He would go on to reason that if the Philippine Islands were to be converted to a gold-standard system, Natives would have to be slowly and patiently "educated to the value of the new currency."[33]

Although Harden correctly anticipated the long-term U.S. colonization of the Philippines, he seemed to neglect that illiteracy went both ways. After converting their wages into local currency, many U.S. soldiers most likely felt as if they were at a clear disadvantage due to their lack of knowledge of the extremely complex Philippine monetary system and their unfamiliarity with non-English languages. In one account, Charter Bank representative G. Bruce Webster cataloged the myriad types of coins circulating as currency in Manila: "(a) Spanish Filipino silver peso, (b) Mexican dollar, (c) Filipino silver half dollar (debased), (d) Filipino silver peseta of 20/100 dollar (debased), (e) Filipino silver half peseta of 10/100 dollar (debased), (f) Filipino copper cuartos and centavos."[34] Of most concern for the typical soldier, particularly for smaller-scale daily commercial and retail transactions, was what Webster categorized as Filipino copper cuartos and centavos. Despite the Spanish colonial state's attempt to overhaul the Philippine currency supply during the last three decades of the nineteenth century, small denomination coins continued to be scarce, disproportionately affecting the working and poorer classes.[35] For most of the colonial population, interaction with, and access to, any type of money was limited to small denomination coins. Therefore, for most of the population, to conceive of money was to envision not gold or silver but copper.

The local small denomination currency, however, was especially troubling to Webster, who described the copper coins as "dilapidated pieces of metal, on many of which it is difficult to discern any image or superscription." The inability to "discern any image or superscription" placed the American customer in a precarious position, for in a retail transaction, the customer had to defer to "the ruling of the Chinese or Filipino small dealers." Thus, due to the American's illiteracy or lack of knowledge of local currency, he or she necessarily depended on the knowledge of Chinese or Native retailers. This scenario troubled Webster, not only because the colonized held authority over the prices of commodities, but also because American customers had to "accept the ruling" of Chinese and Native retailers concerning the value and authenticity of coins.[36]

Seen in this light, decisions over the value and authenticity of coins were seemingly formed autonomously of any state authority. Deferment to the authority of Chinese and Native retailers was ultimately the result of the American consumer's illiteracy in the language of local money. Because Chinese and Native retailers could read what Americans found "difficult to discern" they had access to knowledge Americans did not. As a result, Chinese and Natives held authority over money and over American consumers through their ability to discern or, put another way, to mediate, knowledge of the local, day-to-day, retail market. Equally troubling was the concern that authority over money arrived autonomously of the colonial state. Webster's account, after all, presented a world where colonizing consumers had to "accept the ruling" of colonized retailers. In this world, then, the Chinese and Natives' seeming arbitrary decisions over valuation and authenticity had the upsetting public appearance of being sovereign of any state authority. The seeming autonomy of money and the market was not, however, limited to smaller-scale retail transactions. Uncertainty over the unruliness and illegibility of money and the market could be located in larger-scale instances.

In July 1900, fluctuating rates between gold and silver were severely affecting the military government's large-scale purchases of war supplies. This global fluctuation was due in large part to the vast quantities of money invested in troops and war supplies by collaborating imperial forces attempting to suppress the Boxer Rebellion in China.[37] In a cablegram dated August 3, 1900, General Arthur MacArthur accused banks in the Philippines of exploiting the U.S. military government during this moment of wild fluctuations. MacArthur, like many of the troops serving below him, believed the Boxer Rebellion, or what he referred to as the "Chinese War" was simply "made pretext by local banks for profitable speculation in United States currency." Illustrating the precarious situation of American imperial sovereignty in the Philippines, MacArthur cast suspicion on the local "foreign banks" that controlled the money supply and set rates of exchange "in opposition to the interests of the United States." As a temporary solution to these predatory practices, MacArthur suggested artificially setting the rate of exchange between silver and gold at "two for one."[38]

From MacArthur's perspective, the powerful banks in Manila had been taking advantage of wartime economic insecurities to artificially set exchange rates. One newspaper article corroborated this notion of collusion between the banks that had "arbitrarily reduced the rate of exchange on American gold" and encouraged MacArthur to "take measures to guard against the action of the banks."[39] In another correspondence, MacArthur recalled the previous promise made in 1898 by the three major banks in the Philippines—the British-owned Hongkong and Shanghai Banking Corporation; the Chartered Bank of India, Australia, and China; and the Spanish-Filipino-owned Banco Español Filipino. According to MacArthur, all three banks assured that if allowed to reestablish the duty-free import of Mexican silver dollars they would maintain a parity of exchange "at not less than two Mexican dollars for one gold dollar."[40]

The importation of Mexican silver coins had been banned by the Spanish colonial state in 1877 in the Philippine colony partly due to rampant accusations of predatory bank practices.[41] Despite being suspected of immoral practices, over the next two years, the banks did indeed keep their part of the bargain, maintaining an exchange rate at, or below, a two-to-one ratio. However, after the outbreak of the Chinese Boxer Rebellion and the subsequent rapid escalation of silver prices in global markets beginning August 1900, representatives of the banks claimed that they could no longer maintain this rate of exchange without risking great losses. As a result, local moneychangers and banks began varying the rates at 1.75-, 1.70-, 1.60-, or 1.50-to-1 U.S. dollar. These drastic changes in ratio consequently transferred the supposed losses of banks to those whose wages were paid in U.S. dollars, specifically laborers and troops employed by the U.S. military.[42] By suggesting to artificially reinstate the originally agreed upon ratio, MacArthur asserted the legitimacy of the state to determine what he believed to be a more reasonable exchange rate between gold and silver. In addition, he essentially argued that the state had the legitimate power to bypass any claims that the capitalist market was the ultimate judge of value.

MacArthur's suggestion of the state as the legitimate decider of value sparked off a series of criticisms from the probanking community.[43] One of the most hostile responses came from U.S. Secretary of Treasury Lyman J. Gage. As a powerful proponent of laissez-faire policies in the McKinley administration and banking community, Gage was willing to publicly attack any sort of perceived government intervention in the economy. The treasury secretary defended the action of the banks and scoffed at MacArthur's notion that exchange rates could be fixed by the military government. "In considering the subject-matter in the light thrown upon it by General MacArthur's letter," Gage stated, "I am first struck with the thought that the quartermaster's rate of exchange is itself arbitrary and unnatural—one that there would always be difficulty in maintaining, at least upon the present principle."[44] For the treasurer, a government fixed rate would not only be an expression of arbitrary government rule, but would also go against the very nature of capitalist valuation. Gage thus invoked the logic that only the capitalist market's "law of demand and supply" could determine the true and natural value of currency. As he pointed out, unintentionally echoing Marx's insight of the always-existing dual value of a commodity, the "value of the bullion" of the coin should be considered separate from the "commercial value" of currency.[45]

The heated exchange between MacArthur and Gage revealed the strange paradox within the capitalist logic of valuation. MacArthur seemed to believe that the bullion content of a coin contained a natural value. Yet, he also believed that this natural relation between silver and gold currency values could be set at about two to one, or the conventional exchange rate agreed upon since the 1898 American occupation. Responding to this, Gage argued that this notion of metal having an essential value was in actuality "arbitrary and unnatural." For Gage, there appeared to be an even higher register of nature or truth than the "natural" metal bullion. This more truthful value was intangible and instead determined only in and through local and global markets. From Gage's perspective, and what was the dominant perspective of many economic experts at the time, the "law of demand and supply" was the only true determinant of value.

As a result of this notion of how value was determined and produced, Gage defended the actions of the banks by asserting that every individual, commercial entity, and even every government, ultimately existed under the same rules of the capitalist market. Ignoring the open collusion between major banks to artificially set prices, the treasurer argued that even those who seemed to disproportionately benefit from the market, for instance, banks, could eventually become "necessary victims" to "movements they can not control." To Gage, banks were "obliged to adjust themselves and their actions," and MacArthur was ultimately "subject to the same rule of commercial necessity."[46] Questioning MacArthur's inability to comprehend that he too was "subject to the same rule" as everyone else, Gage simultaneously naturalized and authorized the logic of the market. The market, therefore, no matter what MacArthur or the bankers believed, ruled over not only the production and exchange of values, but it also ruled over any social being or activities connected to the production or exchange of values.

Two seemingly incompatible perspectives of the relation between the capitalist market and the military colonial state in the Philippine colony emerge from this exchange between MacArthur and Gage. From MacArthur's perspective, in order to end the exploitation caused by the capitalist market toward both the military treasury and the wages of the troops, the military government had to reassert its rule by setting parity at two to one. From the perspective of Gage, however, government action without understanding the natural movements of the market would be reckless and ultimately an expression of "arbitrary" and "unnatural" authority. At the same time, despite their seeming incompatible perspectives of the currency problems, Gage and MacArthur in actuality shared a common understanding: the capitalist market operated as if autonomous of both the military government and colonial society.

Apprehending the Racial Capacities of the Colonized

The year 1901 marked the formation of the second Philippine Commission, headed by William Howard Taft. The goal of the commission was to begin the transition from an occupying military government to a civil colonial government in the Philippines.[47] From the perspective of Taft, key to this transition would be establishing a U.S. colonial monetary system. Taft had long been anxious about how the monetary crisis continued to hamper local and global conceptions of U.S. sovereignty in the Philippines. At one point, Taft even considered allowing "English dollars" to circulate as official U.S. legal tender in the islands, preferring it over coins with the "stamp of the Mexican Government."[48] Many of Taft's superiors in the settler metropole would oppose this suggestion and would turn instead to the solutions proposed by economic experts such as Charles Conant.

On July 23, 1901, Conant was appointed as an economic advisor to the commission. Tasked with assessing monetary conditions and subsequently drafting a policy for currency reforms, he would report to the Secretary of Finance and Justice Henry Ide. Notably, Conant was hired upon the recommendation of his friends and colleagues in the McKinley administration,

Secretary of War Elihu Root and Secretary of the Treasury L. J. Gage. Root, who often served as a corporate lawyer, the banker Gage, and Conant traveled within the same prominent banking and business circles and all three were eventually involved in the passing of the U.S. Gold Standard Act of 1900. After his trip to the Philippines, Conant was immediately hired as treasurer of the Morton Trust Company of New York, which subsequently became the bank in charge of the reserve funds of Philippine currency.[49]

Before his appointment to the Philippine Commission, Conant had already formed a schema in his mind for the Philippine currency system.[50] He looked specifically to other colonial monetary policymakers, such as those in the colonies of British India and the Dutch East Indies. Both British and Dutch colonizers implemented a gold-standard monetary system in their colonies, while maintaining a silver currency in local circulation. For both the British and the Dutch, colonial seigniorage was highly profitable for both private and state capital accumulation. However, while British India would run into frequent problems in maintaining its supply of gold within the colony, Dutch Java would instead sell foreign exchange drafts to maintain parity between silver and gold supplies. It would be the Dutch Javanese model that Conant would suggest for the Philippines.[51]

Conant's plans, however, would be drastically changed after encountering the specific racialized relations of power in the Philippine colony. Along with the reports of the U.S. military colonial government, Conant and other experts received most of their information through various non-Native sources, such as Spanish monetary policies and debates from the last two decades.[52] Another valued source for Conant was the highly vocal class of white American and European bankers and capitalists, who had been heavily invested in the Philippines for years.

Interviews of Manila locals conducted by the first Philippine Commission reveal that there were many who opposed the gold standard. Racial ideologies and civilizational discourses grounded anti-gold arguments. For example, one British trader and former bank manager, Charles Ilderton Barnes, defined the Philippines as a "producing country" in which the "wealth of the country, the wealth it produces, is entirely from the soil."[53] The Philippines' only value was to produce raw resources for the industrialized world. A more rudimentary currency, such as silver, would thus suffice. Since Natives were racially conceived of as producers, they were in turn not thought of as consumers. Many reasoned that unlike individual lifestyles in industrialized societies, the Native's naturally impoverished way of life would be incompatible with gold-based currency.

American entrepreneur John T. Mcleod argued that the Native would never be able to afford any of the higher prices that usually accompanied gold-based currency. Unlike individuals in modern industrial societies who understood how to properly save and invest money, the Native would simply "gamble it away."[54] Yet, even if the Native did in fact manage to not waste money through gambling, the Native's way of life did not necessitate consuming higher priced modern commodities that a gold-based market would bring. Asked by the commission whether Natives, once on gold, would consume higher priced commodities produced in the United States such as manufactured clothes, Barnes dismissively answered: "the native does not use a great deal of clothing."[55] For both Mcleod and Barnes, therefore, the savage Native—one who wasted money and had primitive consumption needs—was incapable of the more modern desires that naturally accompanied gold currency.

Perhaps the most prudent rationale for anti-gold arguments, however, especially for American and European capitalists and entrepreneurs, had to do with the effect of gold currency on wages.[56] If the prices for the necessities of life were to increase, wages would have to correspondingly be raised. Increased wages would cause a problem for American capitalists eager to profit from the colonial occupation of the Philippines. Another concern was that Natives could demand more value for their work and thus challenge the authority of their white employers and by extension the authority of the colonizer. This Native challenge to authority, however, would come not from market knowledge, but instead ignorance. Many authorities doubted the Native's racial capacity to comprehend modern value. As the Director of the Banco Español Filipino, Bernacio Balbas, asserted, the Native "can't understand when you give him a small piece of gold that it is worth more than silver. Moreover, they don't care for it, it is too small for them."[57] According to the Criollo banker, Natives' primitive mental capacity would not allow them to comprehend that the smaller gold coin was worth more than the larger Mexican silver coins.[58] Because of this race-based cognitive disability, the Native would not be able to grasp that value was determined not by the aesthetics or the concrete dimensions of the coin but rather by the capitalist market.

Due to Natives' ignorance of the true value of coins, they would in turn demand that they get paid the same numerical amount of coins as before. Put differently, Natives would cast suspicion on the new gold currency and would doubt that the smaller-sized coins and lesser number of coins would be equal in value to their previous wages. This sentiment was echoed when the commission questioned American financial broker William A. Daland on the matter of wages.

Q. You think that if you made a contract with the native to pay him so many dollars you would have to pay him as many gold dollars as you now pay him silver dollars?

A. That would be the native's idea; yes.

Q. In the matter of wages and the price for labor?

A. They would expect the same wages as they get to-day.

Q. The effect would be that we were paying them double?

A. Yes.[59]

The problem was not limited to the individual Native laborer, however. Instead, the problem also involved the local market conditions of the Philippines in which Native retailers would, because of their racial incapacity, refuse to believe that the smaller gold coin was worth more than the more familiar silver Mexican coin. As H. D. C. Jones, the head of British-owned Hongkong and Shanghai Bank complained: "He [the Native] can get more for the silver dollar than he could for the gold, and when he has got the Mexican silver dollars he naturally feels he has more money in hand to spend."[60] The Native, therefore, measured value seemingly outside of either state decree or economic knowledge, rejecting both the state's and the market's determined valuation of money and instead decided the coin's worth by how it "naturally feels." In this imagined scenario, the Native's incapacity to submit to state or market valuation of money, and the simultaneous capacity to make autonomous decisions on the value of the coin, enabled the Native to appear dangerously sovereign from both empire and capital.

In addition to interviews of white bankers and capitalists, Conant also drew from the interviews of a small number of mainly Filipino Mestizo defectors and collaborators. Through their initial collaborations during the war, some of the defectors, namely Pardo de Tavera, Jose de Luzuriaga, and Benito Legarda, would each eventually earn positions as colonial administrators within the founding phase of the civil colonial state. It would be Legarda, however, the self-described capitalist, who would gain the most attention from Philippine Commission interviewers concerning monetary questions.[61] Despite being recognized as an authority due to his racialized identity, Legarda introduced racial and economic notions that simultaneously contradicted and corroborated non-Filipino interviewees.

On one hand, contradicting the American and European interviewees, Legarda argued that the majority of the population of the Philippines not only had the capacity to understand the modern value of money but additionally would welcome the establishment of the gold standard. To prove the cognitive ability of Natives to work, buy, and sell under gold, Legarda reasoned that gold coins were "circulating today" and simultaneously being accepted "at double the price of silver."[62] Legarda additionally asserted that Natives would recognize the authority of the United States in stabilizing the exchange ratio at two to one. On the other hand, despite recognizing the cognitive capacity of the Native to understand value, Legarda nevertheless agreed with Americans and Europeans regarding the racialized habit of Native labor. Establishing that Natives did not need to consume much to reproduce their ways of life and were thus "very lazy by nature," Legarda reasoned that the gold standard would help increase Native productivity by raising wages and creating new wants. Thus, by "creating the necessities that civilization brings with it," the United States and the gold standard would not just racially evolve the Native, but the Native would ultimately desire all the new commodities that they could access through U.S. colonialism.[63] By this logic of racial uplift, the gold standard in the Philippines would mutually benefit the Native, global capital, and American authority.

At the same time, however, Legarda differentiated the Native from various multiracial people in the archipelago, such as the Mestizo and the Español-Filipino.[64] Expectedly, Legarda considered the Español-Filipino (a person of Spanish and Native parentage) to be on equal footing to any American or European. However, his description of the Mestizo (a person of Chinese and Native parentage) as "a very good citizen and a very hard worker" is surprising considering his view of those he considered purely Chinese. Throughout the rest of his interview, Legarda reinforced a broader colonial norm of anti-Chinese racism by arguing that Natives were "terribly against the Chinaman," particularly for the Chinese's ability to "discredit" and "adulterate" the value of commodities and labor.[65]

Legarda's interview gestures to how the Native was not the only racialized subject that attracted attention from those debating currency reforms. The Philippine Commission was obsessed with linking money's unruliness to the figure of the Chinese. Some of those interviewed demanded adopting, in the Philippines, the explicitly anti-Chinese immigration policies of the U.S. settler metropole. In effect for several decades, this federal anti-Asian policy would limit Chinese migration to manual laborers and place a time limit on the residence of Chinese migrants in the colony.[66] The permanent exclusion of Chinese settlement in the Philippine colony would allegedly protect the development of Native capital. At the same time, because of the mass refusal of Natives to work for the U.S. colonial state, some authorities advocated for the recruitment of low-wage Chinese (and "East Indian") "coolie" labor to build much needed infrastructure in the colony.[67]

Many of those interviewed by the Philippine Commission, however, racialized the Chinese migrant as a parasite to local economies. Often these accounts called on the popular narrative of the Chinese as predatory entrepreneurs, fearing that the Chinese would outdo Americans as settler colonists in the Philippines. This narrative was perfectly encapsulated in Edwin H. Warner's statement that "the Chinaman comes here as a coolie; he saves a little money and at once goes into the country and starts a small store." After the establishment of his business, however, the Chinese merchant revealed his true nature of having "no system of morality at all" by "systematically adulterat[ing] everything" and cheating "the Native in bargaining."[68]

Because of this anti-Chinese obsession, some argued that policing the economic role of the Chinese would benefit both the Native and the colonial state. On one hand, as Jones asserted, the Native would benefit because "the Native has a great antipathy to the Chinaman."[69] On the other hand, the colonial state would benefit from anti-Chinese policies because, according to Legarda, the Chinese were "the most demoralizing people" and "use their means in every way to evade the law, to get around the law, to get the better of it."[70] Moreover, to the detriment of Philippine society, the local market, and the colonial state, the Chinese simply "make money and take it away with them."[71] If anti-Chinese policies were pursued, however, the economic role of merchant, retailer, or moneylender would theoretically be left vacant. Consequently, it would not be the racialized Native who was "too lazy to keep store" that would fill the role.[72] Instead, as Daland speculated, once the Chinese were expelled from the retail and middleman position, "the English, the Americans, and civilized nations" would "come here to keep store."[73]

Notably, Conant refused to engage with any direct accounts from Native, Chinese Mestizo, or Chinese interview subjects. This was most likely due to the fact that while interviews were being conducted in Manila, the Philippine American War was far from settled. Officially, there were two governments laying claim to sovereignty in the Philippines after the Spanish American War: on one side were the United States, and on the other, the nascent Native government, the Malolos Republic. On one hand, most elite Natives who would have experience with, and knowledge of, monetary and financial manners held leadership positions in the Republic and were subsequently considered the enemy. On the other hand, Natives who were not officially part of the Republic were, at the same time, not necessarily friendly with the occupying U.S. government. Some, like the Manila shopkeepers and merchants who refused to pay taxes and recognize U.S. control of tariffs in January 1899, were outright antagonistic. Others, like labor union leaders and proindustrialists (those of a particular property-owning class) Isabelo de los Reyes and Dominador Gomez, were deeply nationalistic. Consequently, their ambivalence toward the United States and increasing militant organizing was looked upon with intensifying suspicion by the colonial state.[74]

The combined information of past Spanish monetary debates and policies, local hierarchies, assumed racial capacities and civilizational discourses, and the divergent desires and complicated allegiances of the business and banking community in the Philippines would go on to shape Conant's initial schema for currency reform. Instead of an orthodox gold currency, Conant drafted and submitted his plan for a new coinage, materially consisting of silver bullion but with a value equivalent to a theoretical gold peso.[75] To maintain existing racial orders and stabilize colonial divisions of labor, Conant altered his belief in a world smoothed out by one unified gold standard and instead introduced a plan for a hierarchical gold exchange standard in the Philippines.[76]

Reinforcing Orders through Colonial Currency

In 1901, Conant drafted a currency reform policy, laying out a multistep plan involving such details as restructuring the value of small coins and changing the names of different denominations.[77] After the Philippine Commission interviews on currency reforms, Conant was forced to rethink the applicability of his universal theories to the concrete conditions in the archipelago. Conant had to address many of the arguments of those in favor of maintaining a silver-based currency and as well as those who advocated extending the U.S. dollar into the colony. In response, he argued that maintaining a currency based on silver or bimetallism would be disastrous for the future foreign trade of the country, due to "the fact that the value of silver as expressed in gold" was "subject to constant fluctuations." If silver currency was chosen, therefore, it would have to be maintained by a state fiction that went against "the free play of the laws governing the value of money."[78] Silver, most significantly would be detrimental, according to Conant, to the needs of Natives and the local conditions of Native life.

Unlike his previous works, which saw the colonization of silver countries as a solution for gold-based industrial nations to overcome economic crises caused by overproduction, Conant relied on racialized assumptions of the benefits of gold exchange to transform, in a series of measured stages, the economic life of Natives. Certain to make clear that his conclusions about the benefits of a gold exchange standard to a less developed race was informed by positivist knowledge, he argued that those who desired to simply extend the American system to the colony had not "studied from a scientific point of view the monetary necessities of the Filipino people." If they had, they would have known that utilizing American currency for a race that, on the whole, did not have the capacity to understand the true market value of currencies would lead to "a great confusion in retail prices and in rates of wages."[79]

For Conant, the Native was both suspicious of new objects and far too mentally underdeveloped to comprehend values that they could not determine through bodily sensations—such as by touch or sight. The most consistent example of both this reactionary suspicion and market value illiteracy was the Native's perception that the smaller and unfamiliar U.S. gold dollar was worth less than the larger, more familiar, Mexican silver coin. Informed by this normative perception of the racial incapacities and desires of the Native, Conant created what he believed could stabilize value, make trade and capital investment easier with industrialized countries, and bind the Philippine currency to the American monetary and financial system. The realization of these goals, however, depended on the Native's recognition and acceptance of the new currency.

The new silver coin would be called the Philippine peso, to symbolically distance it from the dollars (American and Mexican) currently in circulation.[80] This would ease the "inconvenience in retail trade" and would protect against any future confusion over "interpretation of contracts." Despite this nominal distinction, believing the Native suspicious and illiterate of modern market value, Conant asserted that there should be no "radical change" in the weight or fineness of the coin.[81] Fighting the urge to drastically reduce the silver content of the token silver peso, Conant argued for a coin that would not disturb the haptic conditions of exchange to which Natives had "long been accustomed."[82] Still, the creation of a token coinage system invited the twinned possible threats of counterfeiting and smuggling. If the silver bullion content contained in the coin was valued higher than the state fiat value, it could initiate desires to extract the silver content from the coins and "drive them to the melting pot." If the silver bullion content was too little, however, it could, according to Conant, "invite distrust and expose the new coin to the same danger of counterfeiting as American silver money."[83] To caution against both smuggling and counterfeiting, the new silver peso would contain just enough silver and be similar enough in size to the previous Mexican silver coin that the Native would recognize it as authentic. At the same time, however, to combat driving the new coins to the "melting pot" of smugglers, the silver bullion content of the coin would be reduced below the set value of the theoretical gold peso.

Conant's plan essentially called for the creation of two new currencies: the token silver peso and the theoretical gold peso. The proposed currency system thus secretly held its true value somewhere else, a ghostly monetary system that physically existed neither in the Philippines nor in the United States. This was a potential contradiction, in which the naturalness claimed by the gold standard came into tension with the artificiality required by creating a theoretical gold dollar. The new token silver coins, moreover, had to be recoded as familiar and authentic to the Native while at the same time secretly reorient its source of valuation toward the foreign monetary and financial system of the United States. Through this technique of secrecy and familiarity, Conant intended to stabilize and render consistent the coin's value. Stabilization and consistency, in this case, was not only intended to help foster commerce but was also necessary to keep colonial labor wages and costs of living low.[84]

Despite these radical changes, the new currency's design and form would be recognizable enough to Natives so as to not raise suspicion. Suspicion of the American colonial state currency, after all, could easily be extended to suspicion of the American colonial state in general. Suspicion, wrought from misrecognition, was a common source of fear for Americans during wartime, particularly for a colonial economy that still could not reliably differentiate between *amigos* (friends) and *insurectos* (insurrectionists). As a result, Conant made certain to argue that the correct plan for currency reforms not only fulfilled economic aims, but were also politically affective enough to ensure the "progress of pacification."[85]

As Conant's plan circulated within government and expert circles, it would contend with preconceived notions of the Native's capacity to comprehend gold currency. These notions were often shaped by racial paternalism. One British banker, A. M. Townsend, compared the Philippines to the currency reforms implemented in other colonies populated by so-called darker races, such as British India. The currency reform success of nonwhite peoples, such as the Japanese, were more of an exception to Townsend. Instead, Townsend paternalistically warned that Natives would bear the brunt of any economic disturbances, stating that "all currency matters" in the Philippincs required a "delicate handling."[86] Others like Webster took paternalist thinking on a different route but arrived at a similar anti-gold conclusion. Philippine trade would benefit from the change to gold, but this would simultaneously create mass hardship to the "provincial and wage earning classes."[87] Finally, the U.S. Army paymaster general would argue that Natives would not only suffer from "great confusion" if gold was to be introduced, but consequently bankers would continue to manipulate exchange rates to prey upon their confusion.[88] He instead supported the notion of a gold standard that was not directly attached to the U.S. gold dollar. The paymaster general believed that Americans, simply by keeping the Philippines colonized and flooding the Philippines with U.S. dollars, could first educate Native capitalists. After influencing the wealthier classes, he reasoned, eventually the "knowledge would spread to the more common people."[89]

In the first months of 1902, after failing to push currency reforms through Congress the previous year, the Bureau of Insular Affairs (BIA) made a concerted effort to sway public opinion before currency reform again went before Congress. The BIA reached out to Conant, once again, to be the public face of Philippine currency reform. Conant drew upon his public intellectual persona and launched an elaborate private and public lobbying campaign for a Congress-approved Philippine currency reform.

On one hand, private lobbying consisted of tapping into intellectual networks of academic and financial journals for favorable articles, intimidating banking community members through the power of the secretary of war, and even wooing various notable American silver-backers.[90] Public lobbying, on the other hand, circulated a more simplified message of currency reforms in the Philippines. For instance, one press release from the War Department attempted to resonate with the broader populace through a nostalgic narrative of white supremacist expansion into North America. "The idea of a special coin for colonial dependencies distinct from those of the realm is by no means new. In fact, it is as old as the colonial system of Great Britain and the now United States of America and apparently originated for use right here on our own soil within about five years of the first prominent foot hold of the white man on the North American Continent."[91] The press release would thus connect the creation of the Philippine colonial currency in America's "Asiatic Archipelago" to the United States' inheritance as a settler colony and its subsequent obligation to spreading white civilization to supposedly savage peoples.

On January 9, 1903, a currency reform bill was reintroduced through the Committee on Insular Affairs. Conant's public campaign looked to have been effective, since a month later, the Conant plan found its way through the Senate.[92] After being sent back through the House, with very little changed, the bill was adopted by a close vote a week after the Senate approval. On March 2, 1903, President Theodore Roosevelt signed the Philippine Coinage Act, granting the civil colonial government the sovereign power to institute lasting currency laws. One of the key sections of the new law was that the power of seigniorage was granted to the Philippine colonial state. The process of seigniorage, which entailed mintage, maintaining parity between the silver peso and gold dollar, the purchasing of bullion, and the transportation of minerals, was also potentially a highly profitable state practice. Although there were limits on what the colonial state could do with the profits from seigniorage, it nevertheless provided the possibility of capital accumulation to be used for ongoing and future counter-decolonization projects.[93] Upon receipt from Congress, the Philippine Commission approved Act 938, otherwise known as the Gold Standard Act. The act established a gold reserve fund in order to maintain parity between the circulating silver peso and the theoretical gold peso. The gold reserve fund would house the profits of seigniorage. Later in July 1903, a silver certificate fund was approved for the purpose of maintaining parity between the Philippine silver peso and the Philippine gold peso. The gold-standard fund, which would be held in New York reserves, would be especially beneficial for both the colonial state and Wall Street banks. Thus, although the Philippines may never have been as commercially profitable for American capital as initially anticipated, the maintenance of the monetary system provided a consistent form of profit for the purpose of at least sustaining the colonial state.

A few years after the passage of the monetary law, the new currency designed by Conant had established, like every successful state-issued currency, a seeming monopoly of the urban Philippine markets. Philippine currency reforms were thus publicly proclaimed as a success by U.S. colonial officials. The truth, however, was that there were still ongoing currency shortages for most in the rural provinces. In addition, anticolonial insurgencies endured long after the war was declared officially over by the U.S. government in 1902, impeding the rollout of currencies in many war zones. Insurgencies unsettled American authority, and the legitimacy of the new colonial currency was analogously uncertain.

Indeed, even the initial introduction of the new "Conants," as they were soon to be popularly called, ran into trouble almost immediately. There were two interrelated causes for this trouble. First, colonial authorities needed to drive out and "dispose" of older currencies. Disposal entailed the removal of silver coins, melting down of metal, and repurposing the silver bullion for the minting of new coins. The problem was that most of the commercial banks in Manila held their reserves in older currencies and, out of fear of incurring great losses, refused to release their money to the colonial government.[94] The second problem was the price of silver in world markets suddenly ballooned. Silver bullion would be scarce at the very moment when Conant currencies needed to be minted in San Francisco. Moreover, much of the minting of the new currency would depend on the silver bullion collected from disposed coins. Yet, because silver had suddenly become more valuable, it was even more difficult to extract the older silver currencies from Philippine circulation. The higher price of silver would rapidly lead to a scarcity of Conants.[95]

In July 1903, Conant reforms would suffer further setbacks. Signs of the "money market tightening" sent Manila bankers and capitalists into panic, with many businesses abandoning the newer currency in favor of the more abundant Mexican currency.[96] The price of silver, in Manila especially, was wildly fluctuating, rendering exchange rates just as unpredictable as during the beginning of the Spanish American War. Moreover, colonial authorities feared that the hoarding of currencies and the smuggling of bullion out of the colony would paralyze economic activities in the islands.[97] In addition to market disturbances, tensions between the War Department and the colonial state were triggered by minor irritants such as the use of the word *Conant* as the nickname for the new currency[98] or the refusal of military officials to accept the new currency for payment of debts.[99] Despite all these frictions and irritations, the monetary system was able to survive this tremulous rollout, but at the cost of public weariness of American economic expertise and state decision-making.

For example, about half a year after the introduction of the new colonial currency, English language newspapers in Manila severely criticized the Conants. Many wrote that the U.S. colonial state had failed to properly educate and prepare the Natives in the new colonial currency. One editorial argued that despite suffering "from the vagaries of the mongrel currency," Natives continued to refuse the new Conant coins. These refusals disrupted the quotidian life of the American colonizer who was fundamentally dependent on Native labor. "A very large part of the expense of the living in the Philippines goes to native help and others who know nothing about the change of monetary standards," the writer complained.[100] Another article featured an interview with an American banker who recounted a story of a Native newspaper delivery boy who refused to accept the new coin. "If the very street gamins want the old coins," the banker grumbled, "do you suppose that the savages in the tobacco plantations of the north and the sugar groves of the south will take the Conant pesos?"[101] From these perspectives the lack of market knowledge by the Native strangely endowed them with the capacity to refuse, decide, desire, and even make demands without consideration or care of American authority. The final thoughts of the editorial remained pessimistic about the success of monetary reform, at least when it came to convincing Natives. "The demand for old money will continue, regardless of explanations and theories," declared the writer.[102]

Other observers were especially skeptical of the ability of American economic experts to change Native capacities and domesticate the unstable effects of the capitalist market. One particularly scathing editorial titled, "Bastard Coins Must Go," argued that "financial experts in the U.S. have little success in adapting their theories to the vastly different conditions in the Orient." The editorial would go on to criticize the "financial kings and experts" who were reduced to "wailing infants" when confronted with the alien and concrete conditions of the "Far East." From this perspective, Natives were not the only ones who lacked market knowledge. Ironically, lacking in knowledge were the infant-like American economic experts. Rather than theories that "looked beautiful upon paper," the editorial touted the knowledge accumulated from experience in the colony. Moreover, the writer warned, expert knowledge pressed on an ignorant people would not lead to the rule of law but the predatory law of the market. As long as naive American experts attempted to force universal theories onto local conditions, it would exacerbate disorders, a situation where "money changers" would be given "full sway to fleece the people."[103]

The ignorance of Natives and the naivety of American experts created a situation in which, according to some newspapers, American colonial authority would be vulnerable to foreign threats. One recurrent foreign threat was the supposedly predatory Chinese moneychanger. The threat from Chinese moneychangers was especially dangerous for those in the provinces, where American authority remained shaky.[104] Another foreign threat was counterfeiters who would "shove" large amounts of "queer" coins into circulation. While previous counterfeiters would concentrate on small denomination coins, the final months of 1904 witnessed the mass appearance of "spurious...Conant money." The authority of the colonial state was destabilized by counterfeit coins, and the public would adopt various means to differentiate between genuine and fake money. Individuals would have to "listen to the coin," as the "only means of discovery was to ring them." American colonial authority was put into question as the coins sounded like "lead but have every appearance of the real thing."[105]

What kind of effect would it have on American sovereignty when one listened to the coin rather than to colonial authorities? Perhaps, the uncertain genealogy of coins remained the biggest threat as foreign currencies remained in circulation, exchanging hands at dizzying speeds and at unaccountable volumes. Different public references for the circulating coins did not necessarily underscore their false origins but rather their impure and unknowable origins. "Bastard coins" and "mongrel money" would be frequently used to refer to these non-U.S. coins.[106] Despite circulating for decades before U.S. colonial occupation, these coins were designated as foreign to, and thus estranged from, America's genealogy. The expressions *bastard* and *mongrel* perhaps refer to the failure of a pure genealogy and hence the threat to future inheritance. As war continued, the future of American colonial authority was far from certain in the Philippines and experts faced several pressing concerns. Would the colonial monetary system be inherited by future American authorities in the archipelago? Or would so-called mongrel currencies continue to proliferate and corrupt any sort of American colonial inheritance?

Colonial currency reforms in the Philippines set a precedence for how American monetary authority would operate in other colonial spaces populated by other dark races. Conant's policy and the data collected from the Philippines, for instance, constituted a portfolio to be circulated throughout manifold places such as China, Mexico, Cuba, and Panama.[107] Through this process, experts such as Conant hoped to illustrate the racial capacity of white Americans to lead a racial capitalist and interimperial state world system. Emboldened by Conant's policies in the Philippine colony, the CIE and other economic experts would in turn sell their market knowledge to developing governments. Oftentimes U.S. firms and banks pressured these so-called developing governments—such as Haiti and Poland—into employing American economic experts, especially if these countries wished to appear as safe and secure economies for capital investment and accumulation. In turn, U.S. banks jockeyed for the opportunity to act as reserves for these new gold-based monetary systems, again following the colonial model in the Philippines.

The desire to transform "developing" silver markets into "gold countries" led to uneven results.[108] Much of the publicized success of currency reform had less to do with the soundness of economic knowledge and more to do with how the new monetary system benefitted from colonial contingencies. For instance, the Gold Reserve Fund remained at a surplus due to the continuous flows of U.S. military money to the islands.[109] Continuous militarized counter-decolonization campaigns thus kept the colonial state in the black. Despite the supposed modularity of Philippine currency reforms, what continued to remain occluded from U.S. imperial propaganda was the necessity of heavy policing within colonial borders and the suspicion of ongoing clandestine economic activities. Nervousness over economic activities on the ground also illustrate the ongoing antagonisms and unintended frontiers of escape that continued to plague the American colonial state long after the 1902 official declaration of the war's end. For at least the first decade and a half of colonial rule, militarized counter-decolonization would occupy the minds of U.S. officials.

Despite all this, some Americans in the Philippine colony believed state reports over what they witnessed on the ground. Looking back at this moment of transformation, Mary Fee described how they were "all relieved" by the news that Congress had adopted "Conant's system of currency."[110] As Fee remembers, there was some initial resistance to the reforms, but she contended that "on the whole the change went off quickly and without much friction." She noted in wonderment "how easily and quickly one circulating medium disappeared and another took its place." Yet, within Fee's narrative of almost instantaneous imperial transformation remained the cluster of memories that recalled "trouble about getting the poor people to recognize" the new currency form and the value it embodied. With a tone of disappointment, Fee recounted how "the Treasurer had a long line of delinquents before him each morning admonishing them that they could not play tricks with Uncle Sam's legal tender."[111] The observation, of "trouble about getting the poor people to recognize" the new coins, illustrates that there remained the haunting possibilities of unforeseen and unanticipated misrecognition of U.S. colonial currency in particular and American authority in general.[112]

Bad Money

3

On January 19, 1904, a Manila-based representative of the Hongkong and Shanghai Banking Corporation wrote to the civil colonial government, expressing concern over the potential introduction of a tax on non-American colonial currencies. The tax was intended to discourage the use of older currencies during the roll-out of the new U.S.-based coins. The letter, however, warned that the new currency would introduce too much of a "radical change" on a "financial system still based on a Spanish-Filipino-Mexican Currency." Not only was there not enough time for the banking, business, and retailing communities to adjust, but more significantly, the banker worried about how "the larger proportion of the population...widely spread and ignorant as it is, would be even aware of the proposed change, let alone prepare to act on it." The banker would go on to propose a delayed start date for the new currency, closer to the end of the calendar year. This year would allow for public announcements in "various dialects" that would ideally help ease the "friction and abuses" within urban areas like Manila. At the same time, however, even if the "ignorant natives" in Manila might be better prepared through market knowledge, the banker still expressed concern that those "in the provinces certainly would not be, where the natives would be hopelessly fleeced by Chino [sic] retailers."[1]

The new U.S. colonial currency was supposed to bring a sense of economic security to a territory that remained militarily contested and politically unsettled. News of a novel currency, however, seemed to bring about more nervousness than reassurance. There were too many possibilities that money could go bad, through hoarding, smuggling, or idleness, or by operating autonomously, turning against American authority. Despite the United States declaring the war settled in 1902, the long Philippine American War was far from over. For the next decade, movements for decolonization continued, within both the formal realm and the underground, through the political system and through guerilla conflicts, in the provincial frontiers and the urban centers. U.S. military and civil colonial authorities would respond to these antagonisms with counter-decolonization. Monetary authority was key to counter-decolonization and would operate at two registers. On one hand, monetary authority aided the military pacification and suppression of potential insecurities. On the other hand, monetary authority helped build ideological consent by providing security, safeguarding capital interests, and policing the habits of nonwhite colonial subjects.

This chapter examines the relationship between a new American-based colonial monetary system and strategies of counter-decolonization. First, it traces ongoing anxieties over the speed and spread of new colonial currency and the lingering presence of older currencies. The existence of older currencies enabled unsettling economic practices to persist. Ranging from wayward to unlawful, these economic practices were seen as potential threats to the normalization of American colonial sovereignty and racial orders. The policing of economic practices would take multiple forms. In one form, monetary authorities would attempt to elicit consent through collaboration. White Americans and Europeans in the banking and business communities who resisted using the new colonial currency were invited to collaborate with state decision-making. In another form, nonwhite colonial subjects, Natives and Chinese especially, were heavily policed and surveilled, suspected of undermining the new American monetary system. Additionally, this chapter tracks how counter-decolonization entailed building consent through the creation of infrastructure, particularly in territories on the periphery of urban centers of business.

In 1901 William McKinley, the famously proimperialist and procapitalist U.S. president, was assassinated in Buffalo, New York. Less than a year after inheriting the U.S. presidency, the imperial and military hawk, Theodore Roosevelt, declared the Philippine American War officially over. The July 1902 declaration was premature. For over a decade and a half, armed Filipino insurgencies would continue, necessitating the continued institutional presence of U.S. military in the archipelago. It would be the longest nonsettler direct U.S. war until the Iraq and Afghanistan Wars in the twenty-first century. Much to the chagrin of U.S. colonial officials, the shift to guerilla skirmishes throughout the archipelago would have disastrous effects on agricultural exports. The pretense of bringing capitalist development to, and securing capitalist accumulation in, the Philippine colony was constantly undermined by the disorder brought about by U.S. counter-decolonization violence. U.S. authorities believed that the survival of the civil colonial state meant the establishment of order and security, particularly in the Philippine hinterlands. Agrarian communities had, after all, been the main source of unruliness and restiveness for the Spanish colonial state before them. Even the Malolos Republic struggled to contain the revolutionary desires of peasants in the rural countryside.[2]

The pacification of peasants was therefore essential to colonial security. U.S. authorities understood, however, that military pacification would not be considered legitimate if it was not accompanied with so-called civil pacification, the establishment of a secure and orderly capitalist society. This meant that the economic life of colonial subjects had to be securitized, normalized, and domesticated. Monetary reforms—what American experts and authorities asserted was the stabilization of currency, exchange, and markets—was a key aspect of pacification. But without the establishment of normative institutions such as banks that peasants could access, the new currency would fail to circulate beyond urban and wealthy communities. Through banking services such as savings, credit, and loans, monetary reforms could be successfully distributed throughout the archipelago. In addition, banking would enable a sense of order and security for peasants who wanted to accumulate wealth (savings) or to have access to wealth (through credit and loans). It would simultaneously entangle peasants further within the economic world of the United States and force peasants to invest in the future order and security of the U.S. dollar, the basis of value for not only Philippine currency, but Philippine banking accounts. To U.S. colonial authorities, therefore, without banking, there could be no orderly or secure civil society.

At the same time, American economic experts rationalized the operations of capitalist empire through a racial paternalist logic. In this, the American expert exhibited both a racial affinity and rivalry with the Anglo–upper-class social reformers of the British Empire.[3] Eventually called Progressivism, this movement considered economic reform as part of the white man's burden. This conception obligated more advanced, civilized, and modern peoples, such as Anglo-Americans, to actively transform supposedly backward, savage, and primitive peoples. These invasive forms of social intervention were systemically nonconsensual, justified by the fact that racialized populations could not think or act properly if left to their own devices. Progressivist forms of intervention, which melded humanitarianism and scientific reason with public and foreign policy, reached a global scale, setting off a flurry of activities in the settler metropole and the extractive colonies.

Progressivism, as a movement, emerged from the material conditions of racial capitalist crisis throughout the last decades of the nineteenth century. U.S. racial capitalist accumulation was mainly generated by anti-Black slave plantations and by the expropriation of Indigenous lands through settlement and dispossession of Native peoples in the so-called frontiers of North America.[4] Despite the riches amassed by U.S. Empire, the end of the nineteenth century witnessed massive wealth inequalities amongst those considered part of U.S. civil society. Critics at the time would begin to call it the Gilded Age, a time in which a thin surface of gold concealed rampant corruption, greed, and exploitation. Progressivism was a reactionary movement to the Gilded Age that attempted to grapple with the material catastrophes and racial and colonial antagonisms of the late nineteenth century.[5] Despite its pessimism in contemporary material conditions, Progressives nevertheless held a kind of optimism in the reparative capacity of Western civilization and white supremacy.

A fantasy history of U.S. capitalism grounded this optimism toward the progress of capitalist modernity. In this fantasy history, Anglo-American wealth, prosperity, and security emerged out of the hard work and creativity of the self-sufficient white entrepreneur, the cultural investment in private property and individual personhood, and the legal protection and spread of the free market. This narrative was grounded in the disavowal of settler colonial land theft and Indigenous dispossession, the plundering of rival empires, the exploitation of imported labor from colonized and semi-colonized territories, and racial enslavement of Black peoples.[6] Instead of this history of crisis and violence, the traditional and dominant history of U.S. capitalism asserted a narrative of innovation, industry, and progress. Beginning with the Lockean notion of the settlement of idle lands and the establishment of private property and freedoms, the Jeffersonian ideal of yeomen farmers and self-sufficient liberty, all the way to the entrepreneurial spirit of industrial giants such as John Rockefeller and Andrew Carnegie: these narratives of economic development guided Progressive-era expertise.

Before arriving in the Philippine colony, many economic experts were shaped by Progressive views of race, capitalism, and empire. Many believed that human civilization followed a series of historic stages that began with the cultivation of agriculture and the protection of private property and the steady evolution and progress of U.S. society toward industrialization.[7] For experts, the Philippines was an ideal place to work out Progressive notions of racial paternalism and economic development. Moreover, in the colony, experts could experiment by creating new kinds of monetary and banking systems, from what they believed to be an economic tabula rasa. Through currency and banking experiments, experts would not only ideally prove their economic and racial theories, but also justify the necessity of monetary authority to the broader U.S. logic of counter-decolonization.

Policing and Punishing Bad Money

The main agent of monetary authority to institute counter-decolonization was the Division of Currency, headed by Edwin Kemmerer. The Division of Currency was not a permanent office, however. It was created as a two-year division implementing and administering the new currency brought about by the 1903 Philippine Gold Standard Act. In addition to instituting a new currency, the chief would be responsible for creating financial and banking institutions for the economic development of the Philippine colony.[8] The first two choices for the position were initially Charles Conant and Cornell University economist Jeremiah Jenks, leaders of the CIE. Although both would decline the offer, Jenks suggested his recently graduated doctoral student Kemmerer. This position would act as a significant stepping stone for Kemmerer's decades-long career. After his time in the Philippines, Kemmerer would regularly travel the world, employed as an economic advisor by multiple countries throughout Latin America and Europe. He would eventually become a professor at Princeton University, where he would retire. Throughout the 1920s and 1930s, Kemmerer's global profile would rise to the extent of being called the "Money Doctor" or "Money Wizard" by international presses.[9]

At the time of hiring, however, Kemmerer was still unknown and inexperienced, teaching as an entry-level instructor at Purdue University. He blamed his current professional anonymity on his seeming inability to command masculine authority in a world of experienced politicians and elder bureaucrats.[10] In several private correspondences to his mentor Jenks, Kemmerer expressed anxieties regarding his smaller physical build and his inability to make a lasting impression on men of political authority.[11] In the end, nepotism trumped presence, and Kemmerer was eventually hired for a two-year position as the Philippine colony's division chief on May 27, 1903.[12]

From the perspective of American experts and statesmen, currency reforms were intended to be a form of counter-decolonization. The establishment of a more secure and stable colonial currency would simultaneously aid in securitizing urban and commercial spaces of the archipelago and firmly legitimize American colonial sovereignty in the minds of merchants, bankers, and capitalists. However, despite the Secretary of Finance and Justice, Henry Ide, touting the massive success of monetary reforms in the beginning of 1904, the reality was that the security of the U.S. monetary system was far from settled.[13] There were still many ongoing frictions in public discourse, behind the scenes, and on the ground. Wayward practices, smuggling and hoarding, circulating illegal coins, and growing discontent and doubt continued to persist under the noses of authorities. Nevertheless, it was Kemmerer's job to make Ide's narrative of success a reality. Yet, there were multiple obstacles upon his arrival to the colony.

Two main monetary problems plagued Kemmerer during his tenure in the colony. The first involved a small circle of bankers and the second involved the broader population. More specifically, the first problem was the refusal of bankers to transition from older currencies to the new American colonial currency. Bankers in the main commercial areas of Manila, Iloilo, and Cebu were especially ambivalent about the speed of monetary reforms. Although they publicly welcomed the additional security and stability promised by the gold standard, they nevertheless believed changes were being imposed too quickly. Composed mostly of white Europeans, Filipino Mestizos, and some Americans, the banking community was mainly tied to London. Their interests, furthermore, was to keep exchange rates with British colonies—especially Singapore and Hong Kong—manageable and profitable. Moreover, although less stable, the bulk of the local currency cash balances of major banks was made up of Spanish-Filipino and Mexican currencies.[14] During this liminal moment of transition between currencies, the banking and business community took advantage of an unaware public. From the end of 1903 through the beginning of 1904, the general public continued to misapprehend the difference in values between the old and new currencies. Local wages and prices continued to be set according to Mexican dollar values. The older currencies also held less value than the new U.S. colonial currency. As a consequence, bankers, capitalists, and merchants continued to exploit the cheaper currency, both in terms of local payroll and purchases, and in terms of settling foreign balances.[15]

Several prominent American decision-makers were irritated by this practice, seeing it as a roadblock to establishing a colonial monetary system tied directly to the U.S. gold dollar. Yet, they were hamstrung by the fact that the use of Mexican currency was never made illegal. In response, so as to force bankers and business leaders to more rapidly accept the new colonial currency, several authorities began to publicly float the idea of imposing a 20 percent tax on Mexican currency at the end of January 1904. Bankers reacted strongly against the possible currency tax and complained that this was a radical attack on the financial community.[16] What was truly hindering the new colonial currency, as one banker argued, was not the banking community, but instead the ignorance of colonial society. Natives, according to this banker, did not have any market knowledge. They were therefore more liable to naively cling to the older and familiar Spanish-era currencies. Moreover, bankers believed the true culprit slowing down currency reforms for profit were the Chinese. According to rumors, the Chinese had "ransacked all the provinces" for Mexican currency in order to turn a profit in the international money markets.[17]

According to this logic, the true origins of the currency problems were rooted in the unscrupulous practices of the Chinese and the widespread ignorance of the Natives. Therefore, the colonial state should not punish bankers and business with a currency tax. Instead, authorities should first deal with the ignorance of the masses, and second, increase the policing of Chinese economic practices. If nothing changes, only then should the colonial state revisit imposing a currency tax. Moreover, if a currency tax were to be passed, bankers reasoned, the colonial state should intervene and guarantee a fixed rate of exchange, in order to curb any losses that banks may suffer.[18]

Kemmerer and Jenks agreed with many of the arguments made by bankers. This was not surprising. They both believed that the colonial state should do its best to not intervene in the capitalist market. In addition, they believed that the success of the new U.S. colonial currency was only possible with the full support of bankers and capitalists. Even Conant, a more hawkish policymaker, believed that the colonial state, in dealing with bankers and currency, should never "disregard vested rights and the freedom" of economic subjects.[19] Thus, Kemmerer and Jenks warned against creating friction with local bankers. Jenks, who was in China at the time, would lobby on behalf of Kemmerer and the Manila bankers, writing to the secretary of war and the Philippine governor general. Jenks would in turn parrot many of the policy suggestions made by bankers, especially arguing that colonial state officials were mistaken to threaten a currency tax. Although Jenks supported a theoretical tax, he believed the schedule suggested by colonial officials was far too aggressive. Instead, he argued to delay any action until October 1904 and to pursue the education of Natives on the new currency through the proliferation of public notices.[20] In this policy advice, Jenks asserted that the colonial state should stay out of the way of bankers, believing that the new currency would work its way into conventional use naturally through the logic of the capitalist market.[21]

On January 24, 1904, a private meeting between colonial officials and representatives from the main banks was held at Malacañang palace, the civil colonial government headquarters. Kemmerer would also attend this meeting. Frictions had intensified as "the Banks and the Chambers of Commerce...came out strongly in opposition" to the new tax, and the late-night meeting was organized to field suggestions from bankers on how best to transition from the Spanish-era currencies. The bankers eventually accepted a proposal by Kemmerer. The proposal promised to hold off on considering currency taxes until the month of October and instead focused on educating Natives through a colony-wide public relations campaign. According to Kemmerer, "People exchange their Philippine currency for Mexican because they either can't get its value at the stores, or can, only after considerable dickering. The plan I refer to is to provide cardboard notices, to the following effect, and induce the merchants, either by municipal ordinance or otherwise to post them in a conspicuous place in their stores."[22] These posters would indicate the going exchange rates for each currency, ideally illustrating the benefits and stability of using Philippine rather than Mexican currency. Kemmerer would later brag to Jenks about the success of this education policy. "It is now in the hands of the translators with instructions to rush as rapidly as possible, after being translated into a dozen or more dialects and languages it will be printed, and, then, if

October first has not by that time arrived, posted throughout the Provinces and published by '*bandilla*,' that is a sort of town cryer [*sic*]."[23]

By October 1904, Kemmerer would boast that the money markets had worked itself out, and bankers, on the whole, were now on board with promoting the new U.S. colonial currency over the Mexican currencies. Seen from a certain perspective, Kemmerer's strategy was correct. From May through August, commercial exchanges in Mexican currency had lost its profitability, prompting bankers to transition toward the U.S. colonial currency with less protest.[24] At the same time, the treatment of bankers on monetary reform illustrates the ways that the colonial state and economic experts viewed agents of capitalism. Refraining from the imposition of currency taxes and soliciting private meetings to decide colonial policy ultimately illuminates how the colonial state was ideologically and materially beholden to capitalist interests, specifically bankers. Upholding racial hierarchies, the colonial state considered white and European Mestizo bankers as sometimes rivals and sometimes collaborators who had to be convinced to maintain colonial economic security and support counter-decolonization efforts.

The practice of inviting bankers to cocreate colonial economic policy was vastly different from the treatment of Chinese and Natives. In the name of currency reform, colonial authorities would constantly carry out invasive profiling and audits. Racial paternalism justified this intensified policing in the eyes of authorities. Natives lacked market knowledge and because of this ignorance, the parasitic Chinese would prey on them. If these kinds of injustices accumulated, colonial authorities worried, it could possibly generate more political and economic insecurities, undermining counter-decolonization efforts.

With this in mind, and with the suggestion of bankers and capitalists, colonial authorities would switch focus from the Mexican dollar to copper currencies, the small denomination coins used by the masses. For authorities, how the colonized related to, and recognized, the use and security of colonial money was indicative of how the colonized felt about U.S. colonial sovereignty more generally. Kemmerer for instance boasted that the replacement of old Spanish-era currency with U.S. colonial currency was enthusiastically welcomed by the colonial public. "The crouds [*sic*] were so large that it took four policemen to control them, and there were a number of cases in which the people waited all day for two or three days to have a few pesos exchanged."[25] Despite Kemmerer's confidence, however, there remained suspicions of potential misuse or nonuse of colonial money, slowing down counter-decolonization efforts.

One such concern was the perception of rampant hoarding or smuggling of older currencies. Rather than target the more powerful and influential multicolonial banks, suspicions were cast immediately on Chinese moneychangers.[26] In Kemmerer's reports, the figure of the "Chinaman" would repeatedly become entangled with illicit matters. Chinese money exchangers for instance were believed to take advantage of the general public's confusion over the slow rollout of small denomination U.S. currency coins. "The enclosed complaint is against the custom of the Chinese of receiving ten centavos Philippine currency as the equivalent of eight dos cuarto pieces or ten centavos local currency, in other words of charging the same prices in Philippine currency that they formerly charged in local currency."[27] Even the most scandalous event in the financial community during the early years of U.S. colonialism, the bankruptcy of the American Bank, could be traced to suspicion over Chinese. Although the embezzler was not Chinese, he had used Chinese names to create numerous fake accounts. It was not until colonial authorities noticed the accumulation of Chinese-owned accounts that they became suspicious of foul play.[28]

Another example was the suspicion of Chinese smugglers. From 1905 until the middle of 1906, the price of silver once again violently changed, this time to a premium. As a result, an estimated half a million to one million pesos were smuggled out of the colony, through territories where there had yet to be a clear state monopolization of currency. Silver coins were then exported to Hong Kong, Amoy, and other Chinese coastal markets.[29] The Commission reacted by changing the silver bullion content of the coins, instituting a massive recoinage process that lasted two years between 1906 and 1908.[30] Moreover, there were reports of immense refusals from the frontier parts of the archipelago that were blamed mostly on Chinese merchant networks. After collaborating with Native businesses and foreign firms and companies, however, the colonial government was eventually able to discipline any public refusals. Considered resolved at the time, the recoinage process left unaccounted an estimated 2.7 million pesos worth of coins, most likely smuggled out and melted down to escape American transborder policing of various Asian ports.[31]

Because the colonial state introduced the new currency into circulation without any of the "subsidiary coins, minor coins, or silver certificates,"[32] the majority of the Philippine population still relied on the de facto currencies under Spanish colonialism. The vast majority of the colonized population, especially those in the border zones between civil and military governments, commonly used coins originating in Mexico, Latin America, and China or that were privately made by non-Christian Indigenous tribes. One particular nonsanctioned currency that irritated provincial officials were called "Igorotte coppers." These coins were named after an umbrella term for Indigenous peoples of the Cordillera mountain range of Northern Luzon. The Igorots were primarily considered non-Christian and savage, never quite domesticated by Spanish colonial authority. This is evident in the creation and circulation of the copper coin, which was conventionally traded alongside Spanish and Mexican coins. Some colonial officials claimed that these were "extremely rude counterfeit" coins. In many ways they were, for they were created by "private" and untraceable agents, and there was no sovereign bank or state to back up the value of the coins.[33] One had to merely place faith in the metallic content inherent in the coins themselves in order to give it value. Nevertheless, the coins circulated widely in the region by convention, and monetary authorities in Manila remained frustrated that even after the introduction of new copper denominations of the colonial peso, the Igorot copper endured in use.

The problem, according to several regional reports, was that despite it being half a year after the introduction of the new colonial coins, American regional authorities were still using Igorot copper.[34] In 1904, for instance, U.S. military government officials, in their haste for counter-decolonization, continued to disperse Igorot coins to pay for local and Native labor, food, and other supplies. Additionally, regional capitalists, the "business dons...of the Tao class," continued to use it for both business transactions and government obligations.[35] In a letter to Jenks, Kemmerer likened the use of Igorot coins to Mexican and Chinese copper coins that had been "smuggled into the country."[36] Due to the lack of Spanish colonial authority to properly regulate the currency, these coins, although illicit in origin, adopted the form and function of money.

Policing was not limited to non-Christian provinces. Monetary authority entailed practices of surveillance and profiling even in urban centers. Kemmerer, for instance, conducted surveillance at Divisoria market, one of the busiest commercial areas in Manila. As he recounted, Kemmerer "examined the cash boxes of some 24 small traders representing all classes, and found but seven cents local currency, five of which was a small Chinese five cent piece which had dropped into a crack in the box." Although he was relieved that there were fewer illegal coins in use at the market than he had expected, his experience illustrates the kinds of suspicions held by authorities of Natives and the pressing need to know what was truly hidden behind their practices of exchange and circulation.[37]

Authorities would also use suspicion over illegal money as pretext to stop and search market and street vendors at random. One colonial official stopped an "old woman selling native fruits" and searching "within her box of change" found illegal "local currency 'clackers.'" Instead of a mere warning, this official dragged the woman and her coppers with him to the municipal treasurer. He then forced her to not only exchange her coins for the new colonial currency in front of him, but he also forced her to make an "oath" and sign an "affidavit that she understood the currency laws, and would not hereafter transact any business in local currency without having...procured a license." Only after this public spectacle of punishment was she "released and instructed to return to her work."[38]

Authorities believed that the use of older coins was an affront to U.S. colonial sovereignty and American expertise. In correspondences, authorities would frequently refer to older coins as "bad money." One report from a provincial treasurer narrated an instance of a carpenter who had been informed that the currency he had been using was illegal. After some time the treasurer asked the carpenter if he had exchanged the coins for legal tender. The carpenter, with a smile, replied that "he had paid them to the market people who did not know they were bad money." This report proved to an expert like Kemmerer the deleterious effects of allowing "bad money" to circulate. It would allow those with knowledge of the coins' true value to prey on those of the "poorest, weakest, most ignorant people."[39] Through this seeming sense of justice, Kemmerer articulated a kind of racial paternalism. This racial paternalism was rooted in anxieties over the uninhibited continuation of certain nonnormative economic practices. These nonnormative practices could potentially sow insecurity in both colonial commerce and doubt about U.S. colonial authority. If Natives continued to use currencies beyond the control of the U.S. colonial state, this meant that a world could be carved out, autonomous from U.S. colonial control, rendering it useless. Eventually concern over the continued use of illegal coins and its skirting of U.S. authority pushed Governor General Luke Wright to outlaw copper coins, and the colonial state would purchase and take the coins out of circulation.[40]

Currency reforms were essential for direct and indirect forms of counter-decolonization. Directly, reforms aided the military with the logistics of counter-decolonization efforts, especially as it needed to move funds across the Pacific and throughout the archipelago to pay for labor, supplies, and infrastructural projects. Indirectly, reforms were necessary to establish ideological belief that the U.S. colonial occupation brought about commercial security. Nevertheless, ongoing practices of hoarding, smuggling, and the remnants of previous kinds of currencies also placed stress on monetary reforms. The fear was that the vast majority of the population would reject market knowledge and exclude American authorities. Under surveillance, Native and Chinese Filipinos would play along with American authority. Outside of the state's purview, however, Natives and Chinese would continue previous sorts of monetary practices and commercial exchange. This was not necessarily political resistance, but to American colonizers, it was ideologically unsettling. At the same time, some U.S. officials felt insulted by these wayward economic practices. They would in turn make a spectacle of enforcing monetary law. There was a fear that an affront to colonial law could spread and accumulate throughout the islands. As a consequence, in addition to purely punitive forms of counter-decolonization, authorities pursued counter-decolonization forms of attraction.[41] They sought ways for the "poorest, weakest, most ignorant people" in the archipelago to personally invest in a U.S.-based colonial economic system.

Racial Capacities for Saving and Sovereignty

A U.S. colonial banking system in the Philippines was a mode of both practical and ideological counter-decolonization. It would feed infrastructural needs, shore up an unstable property regime, and operate as a symbolic mode of deferring decolonization. Its creation was first instigated in January 1904, when the Division of Currency Chief Edwin Kemmerer overheard Howard Taft's desire for a Philippine agricultural and savings bank during a social gathering. Kemmerer was struck by this brief mention of colonial banks and believed it would be a career-advancing project before his two-year stint in the Philippines was completed.[42] Additionally, as warfare dragged on with threats to U.S. sovereignty emerging throughout the archipelago, Kemmerer felt an imperial and racial obligation to support the ongoing suppression of Philippine decolonization.

Over the next several months, Kemmerer would draft multiple designs for a postal savings bank and agricultural bank.[43] The U.S. monopolization of banking was considered necessary to deal with colonial insecurities, especially in the provinces. First, a centralized banking system, under U.S. colonial authority, would aid the work of military counter-decolonization. According to Kemmerer, for instance, those who led "a more or less nomadic life" such as American soldiers and the colonial policing force, the constabulary, would feel more secure by being able to deposit or withdraw their money wherever they were deployed throughout the archipelago.[44] Moreover, Kemmerer worried that agricultural land had turned idle as a result of war or abandonment. Idle land had to be developed, he warned, to provide a better sense of security for Natives and to weaken support for anticolonial guerila forces.[45]

While the agricultural bank would be delayed for years, Kemmerer's Postal Savings Bank (PSB) plan gained the most traction with colonial state decision-makers. After the termination of his position, Kemmerer visited multiple colonies throughout Asia, North Africa, and Europe before heading back to the U.S. settler metropole. Kemmerer would send back notes and revisions of his PSB design as a result of observing different banking and monetary systems established by rival capitalist empires.[46] As one American authority would later write, the PSB system was greatly influenced by banking established for "Oriental People somewhat similar in descent and environment to Filipino people" in a "primitive state of economic development."[47] In his revisions, Kemmerer asserted that the PSB would serve several crucial purposes for U.S. colonial authority in the islands, such as attracting private U.S. capital investment into the colonial banking system, breaking up the Native habit of hoarding, and securitizing and streamlining the movement of money throughout and without the archipelago. Transpacific order remittances through the post office, after all, had been heavily exploited by supposed foreigners, and the PSB system would help end "the evils of the practice."[48]

Yet, publicly for authorities, the most important purpose of the PSB was pedagogical. As Kemmerer revealed in his initial draft of the PSB bill in 1904, economic tutelage had always been the intention of a Philippine savings bank, which he believed would be vital in "educating the natives" of the values of "thrift and economy."[49] The PSB therefore was a colonial mechanism that would ideally transform the habits and practices of the Native at the quotidian level. To the colonial state, the Native was too idle and improvident, a threatening enemy to the political and economic security of the colonial state. Through learning to save, the Native would become an employable and responsible colonial subject, financially and ideologically invested in an American colonial future. There was even an increasingly popular belief from American authorities that the PSB experiment in the Philippines could be applied elsewhere within U.S. Empire, like the colony of Puerto Rico, or toward other nonwhite (and not quite white) peoples in the supposedly unsettled areas of the North American settler metropole.[50]

After Kemmerer's departure from the colony, the PSB project was taken up by Commissioner of Commerce and Police William Cameron Forbes. In May 1906, Forbes wrote in his journal that the PSB legislation, drawn up by

Kemmerer, was an "admirable document," which he "defended stoutly."[51] Forbes, in a later entry, wrote that the PSB would be "a great boon" in the American project of colonial education and uplift, teaching Natives how to properly manage their money. "Many of the people here save their money and bury it," Forbes mused to himself, "many would invest if there were anywhere to put it; hence they gamble. This new law puts an opportunity to invest within the reach of everybody. . . . It is going to be real good and incalculable in its advantages and results."[52] Forbes believed that the PSB would provide the Native with an opportunity to become a more efficient laborer and simultaneously take part in a capitalist world increasingly becoming dominated by financial institutions and relations. Freedom became essential in this type of colonial governance, for as Forbes argued: "If opportunity were given to laborers to invest their money, and education were given to them to demonstrate the wisdom of such investment, and by wise and cautious handling their confidence were gained, we should at one time provide the two great needs of the Islands namely labor and capital."[53] The PSB thus offered an alternative future for the Native, a world where labor could be converted into capital necessary to develop the Philippine Islands overall. As supposedly free subjects, however, Filipinos would have to paradoxically choose to follow the "opportunity" and "wisdom" offered by American economic tutelage, racial paternalism, and colonial subjugation.[54]

On May 24, 1906, the Postal Savings Bank Act was passed by colonial state lawmakers. On an accelerated timeline, the PSB system would be established and in operation a few months later. Bank leadership would be under the Chief of the Postal Savings Bank Division Ben F. Wright, a former bank examiner in the Philippines. Wright would carry on and expand much of Kemmerer's racial and colonial logic into the design and publicity materials of the PSB. The first bank branch in Manila would be opened in November 1906. By January of the following year, there were over sixty-two bank branches embedded in postal offices throughout the islands. The PSB system quickly gained popularity with Americans scattered throughout the archipelago due to its money order functions. In its first few months of operation, the PSB system was highly touted by the pro-American public in Manila.[55] Behind the scenes, however, Wright would often clash with the Director of Posts William Nolting, a long-time critic of Conant, Jenks, and Kemmerer. From Nolting's perspective, the PSB would bleed money, since Natives were too poor to make deposits. Wright, however, would counter that the Native's poverty was exactly the reason why the PSB was necessary. As a mechanism for colonial pedagogy, the PSB would "teach them [the

Natives] the necessity for industry and providence as a means of attaining a higher civilization."[56] Luckily for Wright, Nolting's superior, Forbes, was a firm believer in this paternalist mission.

At the same time, Wright would present savings as a crucial concrete and symbolic facet of counter-decolonization. Concretely, the PSB would serve two main counter-decolonization functions. First, it would extract personal wealth from individuals. As savings accounts, personal wealth would be converted to capital that would accumulate profits for the individual and the system itself through accruing interest. At the same time, the bank would collectively hoard these individual accounts and redistribute them as loans "at interest to farmers, merchants and manufacturers," thus creating more profit.[57] In addition, PSB loans would be made available to colonial state infrastructural projects and real estate development "in the cities of Manila, Iloilo, Cebu, and Zamboaga."[58] Those outside of urban areas were especially targeted by the PSB, for authorities believed that peasants usually stored their money "in the ground or about the house or placed in the hands of a friend for safe keeping."[59] Within these unsettling economic practices, money, to the chagrin of authorities, became hidden from state surveillance and held the potential to generate secret bonds and relations between people. Secret bonds, after all, could quickly turn into bonds of insurgency.

The PSB would ideally expand the territorial reach of the colonial state in terms of controlling the circulation of money throughout the settled parts of the archipelago. Previous savings banks under Spanish colonialism had been geographically limited to Manila and other urban areas.[60] Money, therefore, could only be deposited or withdrawn if one was in the city, not if one was in the provinces. Operating through post office branches, physical currency did not have to move from branch to branch. Proof of the deposit was a postage stamp, which stated an amount that could be withdrawn at any PSB location. The account holder would attach stamps of value (for example in units of five, ten, twenty centavos) onto a brightly colored and aesthetically eye-catching card. Money would thus move faster and more securely, through its conversion into stamps. At the same time, however, stamps could potentially destabilize money, by performing like currency, but at the same time, by being something else. As a consequence, additional security measures were created, which also doubled as a technology of surveillance and tracking. For instance, the section on the back of the card was designated for individual identification, not only by recording a name and address, but a square for a thumbprint and a space for a signature.

The PSB funds would also be used for personal loans. These loans would only be made available for those wishing to purchase or develop property. The procedure to secure a loan entailed a description of property, certificate of title and registration, and a statement of purpose of loan. The PSB, therefore, opened up the Native to further state surveillance and rendered the Native more invested in the regime of property. As a policy of attraction, savings as counter-decolonization was presented as work by and for Natives. As stated by Wright, "savings of these people may be put to work in the . . . improvement of the islands and their people."[61] The transformation of the unruly Native insurgent into a docile colonial subject was simultaneously the transformation of idle and unruly lands into valued property.

Ideologically, the Native would undergo transformation through the practice of depositing their wealth into the PSB. Whatever surplus they accumulated from their labor, the Native would give to a colonial state institution rather than for other purposes or creating other kinds of social ties, such as gifting, gambling, or informal credit. The Native would ideally depend on the colonial state to keep their personal wealth secure. If they wanted to profit from the interest, they had to invest in the colonial state's existence in the future. The PSB was also a paternalist project that intended to regulate Natives' habit of immediate pleasure in the present, replacing it with a new habit of deferring pleasure for the future. Wright, for instance, argued that Natives needed to learn the "proper discrimination in the valuation of the various commodities that enter in the daily life of the individual," or they would remain within "the lower scale of development."[62]

The Native, through savings, would be taught how to be a better decision-maker over the value of things, to learn when one should use their wealth to purchase things, and when one should refrain from purchasing. American authorities would guide Natives toward new normative wants and desires. It bound savings to the reproduction or lengthening of biological life. As Wright reasoned, savings led to "more sanitary lives, better food, and the development of a higher ideal of home life."[63] Most importantly, the PSB was supposed to accelerate the Native's investment into private property. The promise of a better and newer residence, home improvements, or sending your child to an American school to achieve a better life.[64] Indeed, it was the notion of accumulating capital through the reproduction of heteronormative life and private property that guided the PSB's pedagogical aims.

One large-scale example of this pedagogical function was the collaboration between the Bureau of Posts and the Bureau of Education. For this project, American authorities explicitly targeted the first generation to take shape under U.S. colonial rule, or what Wright called the "rising generation."[65] In this 1910 campaign, the Bureau of Education offered prizes and awards for those students who could deposit and save the most money.[66] The competition also entailed the writing of an essay on the importance of savings. The prize for the competition was a scholarship for technical education. At the same time, the prize was also dependent on whether one was gendered male or female. If the prize winner was a boy, he would receive a scholarship to a vocational school. If the prize winner was a girl, she would receive a scholarship to a normal (teacher's) school.[67] Savings was thus a form of learning to work more efficiently under heteronormative and gendered regimes of labor.

All these public campaigns were guided by the logic of counterdecolonization. For American authorities, if Natives could not save, they could not self-govern. In early 1907, experts such as Kemmerer and Wright went on an intense public campaign to link the relation between savings and self-government. Key to this was the concept that savings were fundamental for a civilized and modern society. Wright argued that "saving is one of the basic principles of our civilization" and that "without saving something for the morrow, no race of people would have risen out of their primitive conditions of savagery."[68] For Kemmerer, Natives could not yet properly grasp one of the most basic concepts of the modern age: abstract linear time. "Filipinos as a people have never developed the saving habit, and are deficient in foresight, the capacity to anticipate the future, and in self-control, the capacity to deny themselves the pleasures of the present for the more enduring ones for the future."[69] Unlike more modern and developed races, especially white Anglo-Americans, Filipinos were purely "creatures of the present."[70] As creatures of the present, rather than pursue "substantial advantages arising from an accumulated reserve," Filipinos submitted their wealth to the "momentary pleasures of the cockpits, the gambling table, of cheap jewelry, and of the holidays without number."[71] Through these pleasures of idleness, Natives wasted not only money and labor, but most egregiously, they wasted time.[72]

For Wright, this racial incapacity of the Native made him "an enemy to his country as well as to himself." The inability to make proper economic decisions left one vulnerable to exploitation, either through debt or dependency. For Wright, individual self-sufficiency led naturally to capital accumulation and autonomy. Natives' lack of savings led to insecurities in which more wealthy and powerful individuals and nations could easily exploit. "An intelligent, energetic, economical people will make a wise, powerful and prosperous nation, and just as truly will an ignorant, thriftless and improvident people make an unprogressive and unstable nation, subject to the vicissitudes of tyrannical rulers and destined sooner or later to become prey of some more powerful nation."[73]

The PSB was supposed to fix this racial incapacity of the Native. Despite the recognition by some American authorities that there were a few exceptional Native and Mestizo Filipino leaders able to comprehend modern knowledge, Kemmerer and Wright both believed this insufficient for immediate self-government. One article, for instance, would argue that it was "morality and not intellectuality" that was the "standard of self-government."[74] This lack of moral responsibility to save for the future could not be overcome by mere cleverness. Morality had to be taught to Natives. Just like saved-up capital, morality had to be maintained and accumulated over countless generations in order to bear fruit. In the interests of developing the Filipino capacity for future self-government, it was the paternalist responsibility of the American colonial state to cultivate such morality through the PSB. As Kemmerer boasted, "Few measures have been taken up by our government in the Philippine Islands of greater importance in the work of educating the Filipino for self-government than the recent creation by the Philippine Commission of a Philippine Postal Savings Bank."[75]

At the same time, however, Kemmerer and Wright's obsession of linking the Filipino incapacity for saving with the Filipino incapacity for self-government most likely had to do with the creation of the Philippine Assembly, the lower legislative house of the Philippine colonial government. The seats of the Philippine Assembly were to be occupied by representatives popularly elected by Filipinos in July 1907, therefore symbolically, if not politically, decreasing American authority.[76] Moreover, the impending election was a watershed moment for two reasons: first, it opened up to elected colonial subjects the ability to make law, and second, it opened up to colonial subjects, through a conditional suffrage, a horizon of democracy.

For some American authorities, the Philippine Assembly was seen as a crucial strategy in domesticating decolonization. By gifting conditional suffrage and partial representation, the colonial state hoped to resolve ongoing material antagonisms with the promise of political equality. Representative democracy would act as a substitute for revolution. As such, conditional decolonization would replace unconditional decolonization. Those such as Wright and Kemmerer, however, considered even the creation of the Philippine Assembly as a threat to the continuation of American presence in the Philippines. The stakes of which were bigger than merely Philippine colonialism, but U.S. transpacific empire more broadly. After all, Wright proudly claimed that the Philippine colony was "the permanent center of

American interest and influence in the Far East, the strategic point in the meeting of the oriental and occidental civilizations."[77]

The PSB was fundamental to this continued American presence. To prove that continued American presence was necessary, Kemmerer would gesture to recent data from the PSB system. By the end of 1906, and after only a few months of operation, the PSB had a total of 621 depositors. Of these depositors, Americans accounted for 82 percent, while the rest were assumed to be Filipinos. Kemmerer, in a newspaper in the settler metropole, would argue that these low numbers were due to Natives' "reputation of improvidence."[78] Wright would later unintentionally contradict Kemmerer, by arguing that the lack of Filipino savings accounts was most likely due to how Natives looked "with suspicion upon the motives of the government."[79]

On the whole, however, other public statements by Wright would support Kemmerer's logic that Filipinos remained incapable of self-government. Native leadership was the primary example of this racial incapacity for self-government. According to Kemmerer, several centuries of Spanish colonialism had taught Natives how to be politically crafty, resulting in a Native leadership that was completely corrupt and overly bureaucratic.[80] The few exceptional Filipinos in the bureaucracy were "appointed and not elected," and "a large proportion of them [we]re not of pure Filipino blood."[81] His assessment of the Filipino's inability to self-govern gained support from presses in the settler metropole and the Philippine colony. These articles would also reason that Natives remained too economically underdeveloped, living a "hand-to-mouth existence," and must be "educated in thrift" before they could be trusted with the power of suffrage.[82]

Public reaction to the counter-decolonization campaign led by Kemmerer and Wright was mixed. After delivering a speech at Cornell University critical of the Philippine self-government, Kemmerer was met with a "storm of protests" by Filipino students studying at Cornell.[83] Mostly from wealthier families, the "rising generation" of Filipinos studying in the U.S. settler metropole, also called *pensionados*, were offended by Kemmerer's broad brush that painted them all as part of some premodern race. A different type of opposition to Kemmerer appeared in the *Philadelphia Record*. Laced with irony, the *Record*'s article highlighted Kemmerer's argument for gradual progress under American rule. Specifically questioning the notion of benevolent empire, the *Record* asked: how can a people reduced to "great impoverishment" by war and faced with "hostile legislation of Congress upon their trade" hope to ever "make deposits of money?" The *Record* seemed to question the logic that Filipinos had to evolve under a system of political inequality and economic exploitation in order to realize true self-government. As the writer sarcastically stated, "Many of these natives who have no money to deposit in postal banks are actually so perverse as to earnestly desire a free government of their own."[84]

It is clear from his writings that news of the 1907 elections terrified Kemmerer. Although no longer residing in the Philippines, he could sense that the elections remained haunted by the spirits of the Philippine revolution and the ongoing desires for unconditional decolonization. Kemmerer described the election as "for the moment" fanning "the smouldering [sic] embers of the insurrection." With the proindependence political parties winning a convincing number of seats, Kemmerer described how some Filipinos "lost their heads, publicly paraded the *Katipunan*, the flag of the insurrection, and insulted the American flag." Trespassing over both economic and political boundaries, these and "other similar excesses" that poured out of Filipinos during the elections, according to Kemmerer, "aroused the better classes of Americans throughout the islands." In reaction, the Philippine Commission strengthened the sedition law and added an amendment that outlawed insurrection symbols, flags, and paraphernalia.[85]

The haunting threat of unconditional decolonization illuminates why authorities like Kemmerer and Wright would be so obsessed to connect the Native's racial incapacity to save to the Native's racial incapacity for self-government. In these brief moments in which people "lost their heads" over the promise of independence, revolutionary demands for unconditional decolonization would not come in some domesticated future but would arrive in the immediate present. Similar to the spendthrift and the excessive Native who stymied the accumulation of capital, the Native who demanded immediate independence in turn unsettled a future of American colonial authority. Consequently, this obsession in transforming the Native into a future-oriented saver and potential entrepreneur was inextricably bound to domesticating the ghosts of the revolution and warding off any possibility of unconditional decolonization

Counter-decolonization Logistics and Infrastructure

The Philippine American War persisted in the frontiers of the archipelago until at least 1913, remaining beyond the reach of military, capitalist, and infrastructural security. During this period, the Gold Standard Fund (GSF) was crucial in extending American colonial authority into heavily contested territories. As counter-decolonization in less "civilized" territories became more grueling and protracted, the GSF was vital for military logistics. Specifically, it would be a mechanism to more easily and rapidly move currency necessary to purchase supplies and labor for military occupation. The GSF also provided loans for different infrastructural projects in unsettled territories, embedding the ideological presence of American authority into the built environment. Counter-decolonization would operate through the funding of labor, new local markets, and structuring the physical space of Native life. The GSF would therefore directly and indirectly help shape a sense of security for individuals laboring and living under U.S. colonial occupation, potentially further entangling Native workers and peasants into an American-centric economy.

The GSF was crucial for militarized campaigns of counter-decolonization. In 1904, U.S. military expenditures on labor, resources, and infrastructural projects in the Philippine colony was estimated at $1 million a month.[86] At the same time, the institution of the new colonial currency benefitted from counter-decolonization military spending. As one of the major employers in the colony during the ongoing Philippine American War, all wages and debts had to be legally paid out in the new colonial currency.[87] The U.S. military spending would flood the archipelago market with new colonial money. However, because the money held in civil government treasury banks could not keep up with military spending, the GSF did most of the heavy lifting to keep cash flowing for military operations. The GSF was thus a vital lifeline for direct counter-decolonization military logistics. Additionally, military spending on counter-decolonization also helped generate more profits for Wall Street through the sale of drafts between Manila and New York banks.[88]

The relation between U.S. military needs and the GSF was not without frictions, however. Before he departed, Kemmerer warned that military dependence on the GSF could put too much strain on the new colonial currency system creating a situation of "currency redundancy."[89] To replenish the fund, more money had to be constantly sent from the settler metropole. If and when militarized counter-decolonization was completed, however, it would create a situation of overaccumulation. For Kemmerer, currency redundancy without military spending would create an excess of the money supply in the colony. Overaccumulation, according to Kemmerer, would lead to destabilization and insecurity, money would turn bad, and potentially undo counter-decolonization efforts. Currency redundancy never played out, but military spending in the archipelago, and more broadly in the region, would continue to depend on the colonial monetary system's currency funds. This dependence would require close scrutiny on the part of American authorities for the next several decades.

Other than benefitting military logistics, the GSF would do ideological work by helping form a narrative of colonial state success. To project to the public that the mission of monetary reform was successfully completed on schedule, the Division of Currency was dissolved in 1905. For years afterward, the colonial state would recurrently proclaim that the establishment of the U.S. colonial monetary system was a triumph. In September 1910, an article titled "Good Profit on Coinage" reprinted a statement from Conant on the "success of the experiment in the Philippines." Much like other colonial experiments, for instance in British India, the Philippine currency system proved the possibility of maintaining a racial and imperial hierarchy between metropole and colony while at the same time integrating economies. Moreover, despite the detrimental effects of the 1907 Payne-Aldrich Tariff Act, which established "free trade" between the extractive colonial economy of the Philippines and the U.S. settler colonial economy, the Philippine currency remained secured.[90] Conant boasted of the profits made from the GSF, mainly through "seigniorage on the coinage, the sale of drafts, and interest on deposits in American banks." In other words, the last decade of U.S. colonial currency in the Philippines had resulted in a self-financing monetary system and a mundane form of mass expropriation.[91] Through the maintenance of a massive currency system of about P51 million worth of circulating coins, U.S. colonial authorities had accumulated enough capital to fund the civil and military colonial governments, provide liquidity for U.S. private banks, and generate credit for future counter-decolonization projects.

Over the next several months, Conant would discuss with other authorities whether the profits were sustainable or were merely a temporary consequence of initial reforms. After all, the creation of multiple financial and banking mechanisms (drafts, securities, and loans) to ensure the replacement of Spanish-era currencies was intended to be temporary. Yet, Conant believed that these mechanisms should remain in place even though the monetary reforms were supposedly accomplished. Perhaps as a conservative policymaker, Conant believed that the work of colonial money in indirect counter-decolonization was far from finished. On one hand, U.S. colonial money, and by extension U.S. colonial authority, had to be further ingrained in the normative habits and practices of Native social life. On the other hand, Conant was a policymaker with global ambitions, and he believed that experiments in Philippine currency could result in a successful model that could be applied throughout the colonized and semicolonized world.[92]

One such experiment was developing the colonial currency from one based on metallic coins to one primarily based on paper. Although paper had been proven to be increasingly normative in many economies of the North Atlantic, the Philippines would be one of the largest nonwhite populations to achieve this goal. Paper currency, after all, proved a "prevailing confidence in the monetary system" and by extension confidence in American racial and colonial paternalism.[93] Bringing corporate logic to policy, Conant suggested that combining the GSF with the colonial state's treasury would enable more profit for the colonial state through various forms of securities.[94] However, others, like the head of the Bureau of Insular Affairs, Clarence Edwards, remained lukewarm on the idea of another monetary reform in the islands, believing there was little need to "earn additional income to the Philippine government."[95] Edwards would refuse to bring Conant's policy suggestions before the U.S. Congress.

As a result of this disagreement with Edwards, Conant would revive his gold-standard campaign at the turn of the century by appealing to public opinion. Along with other experts such as Jenks and Kemmerer, Conant would advocate for Philippine monetary reforms directly to Congress and the broader public. These reforms, they argued, would be in the interests of the further securitization of the monetary system as well as contribute to the colonial civil government's goal of fiscal self-sufficiency. This entailed several changes, including transferring the GSF to the colonial state treasury for "general fiscal purposes"; the creation of one unified Currency Reserve Fund to maintain parity between U.S. and Philippine currencies; the transfer of gold reserves to a Certificate Redemption Fund to increase securitization against fluctuation of coinage metal values; and the aforementioned increase of paper currency supply based on the gold-exchange standard. In sum, Conant wished to consolidate all of the discrete mechanisms, which were initially thought to be temporary strategies, into more permanent economic apparatuses of the Philippine colonial state.[96] By creating a more permanent structure for the colonial monetary system, it signaled the long-term intentions of Americans in the Philippines. Much to the chagrin of Edwards, Conant's policy changes began to gain support from top officials within the Philippine colonial state.

The support, however, had less to do with the notion of reform than with the highly coveted profits possible through the GSF. Since its establishment, the fund had provided loans to finance various colonial infrastructural projects. Interest on these loans had generated considerable profits, gaining the attention of ambitious officials. One ambitious official was William Cameron Forbes, who had grand plans of building a sophisticated railroad system to connect the non-Christian mountainous regions of Northern Luzon to the Christian regions of Southern Luzon. After serving as commissioner of Commerce and Police for several years, he officially became governor general in 1909. Forbes would oversee the passage of a Gold Standard Funds Act in December 1911 by the Philippine Legislature. The act made the interest received on loans available for "public works." The railroad would be one of these public works and would ideally aid the military settling of non-Christian frontiers and provide new pathways for capital to circulate and accumulate. Forbes would write to several authorities in the Bureau of Insular Affairs regarding his desire to build a railroad despite its unpopularity. "I take no shame in admitting that we are doing certain things which the Filipinos do not like," he would state in late December. Despite recognizing how unpopular a railroad was, Forbes asserted that if authorities were to wait for Natives to make correct decisions then there would be no use for American presence in the archipelago. To leave Natives "to their own judgment" would undermine the very logic of U.S. colonization after all. However, since the Native was "not in position to judge the value" of the railroad, Forbes declared that he had "no hesitancy judging for him."[97]

Despite Forbes's declaration of his superiority in decision-making, he nevertheless yielded portions of the fund to several pet projects of Filipino politicians. Forbes would approve the rerouting of several substantial loans to the Manila Hotel and other Manila municipal works, appeasing the Philippine business community and urban capitalists.[98] In the end, Forbes's railroad plan was never completed during his time in the Philippines due to routine economic and political frictions.[99] But his wheeling and dealing with Filipino members of the Philippine Assembly illustrates the broader reach and impact of the GSF. The fund's loans would provide seed money for infrastructural projects. In turn these projects would generate bonds and securities for local and foreign investors, further entangling U.S. finance capital with U.S. colonization efforts.

In addition to materially securitizing the islands through infrastructural projects, the fund also served ideological purposes. The profit generated from the fund and its capacity to provide loans was perceived as sound monetary management, instilling a sense of security from transpacific business and banking classes. Despite the frictions between the local capitalist classes and the colonial state in the initial years of colonization, Conant in 1914 stated that "the strong and consistent policy of the government... soon removed these doubts and assured confidence in the stability of the new system."[100] In addition to sound management was the colonial currency's profitability for the colony and the metropole. As stated by one U.S. congressperson to Philippine leader Manuel Quezon, "the Philippine Government," from 1903 to 1911, "received in the way of interest on its deposits in the United States the sum of $2,850,000, and has not lost one penny through insolvency of a depository or otherwise. Also the government has realized from sales of exchange in Manila against its funds on deposit in the United States the sum of $738,000 to June 30, 1911, a total profit on its deposits of $3,588,000."[101]

The profits of U.S. colonial currency not only enabled the Philippine colony to self-finance, but they also provided liquidity to U.S. banks in the settler metropole through deposits. According to this narrative, colonial currency economically benefited both the colonizer and colonized. It would, on one hand, further tighten the bonds between the overseas colony and the settler metropole with Philippine deposits, extracted from colonized subjects, held in U.S. banks. At the same time, colonial currency would reinforce the hierarchical relation between the Philippine colony and the U.S. settler metropole, with its very sense of economic security held mainly in Wall Street. Thus, through colonial currency, the Philippines was materially and ideologically bound to U.S. Empire and capital. To demand decolonization would be to demand the destruction of such a relationship and to lose present and future wealth. This was a risk that powerful Filipinos were not willing to take. This risk aversion by Filipino decision-makers, at least in monetary and banking matters, would be reproduced for decades to come.

By the mid-1910s both the PSB and the currency funds appeared as successful modes of capital accumulation and counter-decolonization. Authorities were pleased by how the surplus capital of the PSB system and currency funds could be mined for ongoing military and infrastructural projects. In addition, the PSB system aided in keeping up the morale of American civilians and soldiers. Through the PSB, Americans could deposit, withdraw, and remit money with less effort, making life as a colonial occupier relatively easier. Banking and currency, moreover, would aid in varied modes of securitizing areas where the peasant and working classes remained restive.

Authorities also saw the ideological benefit of a more stable currency and banking system, especially for counter-decolonization purposes. By collaborating with prominent bankers in the creation of monetary policy, the U.S. colonial state was able to shore up its authority as well as gain the confidence of the colonial banking and financial community. This collaboration between the colonial state and the banking community would continue over the next decade, creating more demand for financial and commercial institutions. Authorities believed that banking and business confidence in a state-backed colonial capitalist system would trickle down to Natives.

Yet, Native investment in the future of colonialism and capitalism did not occur as desired. Despite American authorities publicly stating that currency reforms and savings were a success, doubts would remain. Natives continued their wayward economic practices, threatening the economic security so coveted by authorities. Moreover, these ongoing practices and relations gestured not only to a kind of autonomy from colonial rule, but also to the possibility of a world without American authorities. For instance, the use of unofficial small denomination coins would remain an obsession of American authorities well into the late 1910s. Moreover, economic experts' anxieties about the Native capacity to defer desires of the present for stability and security in the future would also continue to haunt economic policies. American authorities and economic experts were especially terrified of the creeping Filipinization (the increase of Filipinos in the colonial state bureaucracy) of the colonial state, marked by the 1907 elections of the Philippine Assembly. As Filipinization continued over the next decades, colonial banking and currency would continue to be at the center of struggles between American authorities and an increasingly confident generation of Filipino lawmakers. Indeed, as the long Philippine American War would come to an end during the mid-1910s, both American and Filipino authorities would perceive the economic realm as one of the last frontiers in struggles over conditional decolonization.

An Orgy of Mismanagement

4

In 1921, retired U.S. Army Major General Leonard Wood and former Philippine Governor General William Cameron Forbes wrote and publicized an official report on the state of the American colonial Philippines. Commissioned by the incoming U.S. Republican administration, the report would dedicate a full section of its slim forty-six pages to the mismanagement of the PNB. The PNB's support of mass speculation during the wartime boom in prices, according to the report, led to "one of the most unfortunate and darkest pages in Philippine history."[1] Dripping with disdain, Wood and Forbes tersely narrated the tragic leadership of the PNB in two sentences: "A man presumed to be experienced in banking was brought from the United States and took the first presidency, which he had held a short time. An American inexperienced in banking was then put in charge, and upon his death a Filipino, also without banking experience became president."[2] For Wood and Forbes, the failure of the bank and its leadership was analogous to the failure of Filipino authorities and the previous American colonial regime, led by Democrats.

Wood would soon be appointed as the new governor general, and his primary goal was to roll back Filipino authority in the colony.

This chapter examines how and why, from the late 1910s and all throughout the 1920s, the PNB remained at the center of multiple struggles over decolonization and counter-decolonization. These struggles were highly public and oftentimes elevated to spectacle. At first, American authorities and Filipino authorities both desired the creation of an institution like the PNB. In the mid-1910s, the bank was conceived by American and Filipino lawmakers as a financial instrument of counter-decolonization, a way to simultaneously exploit and domesticate the restive provincial laboring population. Additionally, the bank was also expected to dispense agricultural credit, small denomination currency, and loans for infrastructure. The economic security brought about by the PNB would ideally be utilized to symbolically tout the accomplishment of *Filipinization*—the replacement of colonial state personnel with Filipino faces—under a Democratic imperial regime, and more broadly, the potential of conditional decolonization.

In the beginning of the 1920s, however, the dream of conditional decolonization had seemingly crumbled. The PNB was on the brink of insolvency and the Philippine colonial economy was in crisis. A new Republican imperial regime, under Governor General Wood, would colonially govern, aiming to repeal Filipinization and reestablish what the Republican regime nostalgically believed to be the halcyon days of the first decade of American colonial rule. The highly public feud between Wood and Filipino authorities would result in a spectacular storm of animosity, in which the bank would symbolically be the eye. This chapter tracks the various ways Filipino authorities would challenge this more spectacular form of counter-decolonization, by appropriating and reconfiguring American discourses of racial paternalism, imperial benevolence, and economic security.

The Great War, Conditional Decolonization, and Filipinization

The PNB was born in a world of speculation. Speculations on the future of Filipino nationalism, of the possibilities of finance capitalism, and of U.S. Empire's place in the world. These speculations would emerge during a time of massive changes. Shifting global economic conditions, transformations in the political milieu of U.S. Empire, and on-the-ground anxieties over capitalist security in the Philippine colony: these were some of the dramatic material changes that led to the PNB.

One of the key material changes was the increasing financial and banking power of the United States in the global capitalist system. This was intensified by the boom for war commodities and later, after Europe had been decimated by the Great War, agricultural commodities. A large portion of this financial explosion was due to imperial expansion in the Pacific, the Caribbean, and Latin America. Colonization and semicolonization entailed tying the monetary reserves of "developing" nations to U.S. banks. New York banks especially enjoyed the capital generated from foreign deposits and loans. Moreover, American financial advisors, armed with ideologies and narratives of U.S. capitalism would be deployed, creating new imperial markets for economic experts in the colonies.[3] Imperial expansion would thus place the United States as the leading lender of new capital to the world. Soon, only London, the longtime leader, was left to rival New York's financial global hegemony.[4]

Despite New York's newfound place as an imperial core in the global financial system, the United States nevertheless faltered behind other North Atlantic imperial accomplices and rivals in terms of managing and holding decision-making capacities over the flow of capital.[5] For instance, the United States remained one of the only major industrial powers without a central bank and whose currency did not serve as a major international currency.[6] To better deal with the insecurities inherent to capital accumulation and at the same time boost its global economic clout, the Federal Reserve System was established in 1913. Through the Federal Reserve, responsibility over possible bank and currency failures would shift from wealthy financiers and capitalists toward the masses, mainly by expropriating public funds as security. Subsequently the U.S. central banking system would attempt to entangle colonies and semicolonies closer to the U.S. economy and simultaneously create a model for how economic authorities could shape state decision-making.

The second material change was the shifting political climate in the U.S. settler metropole. The year 1913 marked the beginning of the Woodrow Wilson presidency. Wilson was a Democrat who planned to reverse many Republican policies in the Philippine colony. Racial paternalism shaped Wilson's desire to speed up independence. While the McKinley paternalist discourse of "little brown brother" invoked a kind of familial relation of benevolent adoption, Wilsonian paternalist discourse rejected this familial inheritance. The adoption of nine million brown bodies was not considered part of the natural relations of white America. The inheritance of Black and Indigenous bodies already exceeded Wilson's vision of American civil society. At the same time, Wilson could not grant immediate sovereignty to Filipinos, since that would admit that nonwhite peoples held the racial capacity for self-determination.[7] After all, for Wilson, self-determination was an inherent capacity of white nations under European empires, but not inherent to those of the darker nations. Furthermore, Wilson could never place the structures of imperialism and colonialism in peril. Even if there were unintended effects of his rhetoric of internationalism, as some have argued, Wilsonianism mainly strengthened the appeal of conditional decolonization over the threat of unconditional decolonization.[8]

Much to the chagrin of those serving under Republican regimes, many Filipino elites would welcome the Wilson regime. As one military commander stated in 1913, "the little people" (Filipinos) were visibly excited about the possibility of an "early passage" of independence.[9] Wilson's policy regarding the Philippines remained paternalist, but it found a loophole. By recognizing the current Filipino leadership, the "rising generation" under U.S. political, economic, and cultural tutelage, as more capable, then conditional decolonization could be more concretely pursued. Filipino lawmakers such as Manuel Quezon and Sergio Osmeña recognized this imperial strategy of conditional decolonization, and they adopted many of the market knowledge concepts to best negotiate and take advantage within these imperial conditions. Additionally, Filipino leadership was avowedly capitalist, considering capitalist security key to gaining international recognition as a self-sufficient society and capable of independence. Moreover, capitalist security would internally signal that all revolutionary desires had been domesticated. Unconditional decolonization, after all, would threaten the wealth and security that Filipino decision-makers in the colonial state had wrested from Americans over the last decade. Consequently, Filipino lawmakers were especially fundamentally invested in counter-decolonization. From their perspective, they could always offer their version of conditional decolonization as the more palatable alternative to revolution against an international order of racial capitalist empires.

The third material change concerned counter-decolonization operations in the colony. The Philippine American War, after all, continued well into the mid-1910s. As a consequence, insecurities over a restive peasantry incessantly weighed on the minds of colonial authorities. Monetary authorities saw the agricultural lands worked by peasants as fundamentally crucial to capitalist security and key to strategies of counter-decolonization. An agricultural bank was considered an apposite solution to secure land and the peasantry. On one hand, securitizing land and domesticating peasants would make the archipelago increasingly attractive to commercial and foreign investment.[10] On the other hand, land served as financial security for capital accumulation. It operated as collateral for bank bonds, for the production of rent profit, and as space for the infrastructural projects of heavy investments such as irrigation networks.[11]

With these material concerns in mind, an earlier plan of an agricultural bank was designed by former Division of Currency chief Edwin Kemmerer in 1904. Kemmerer's plan languished soon after his resignation. After several years of back and forth between American authorities and an increasingly more powerful group of Filipino lawmakers, an agricultural bank was finally instituted in 1908.[12] Initially, decisions over agricultural credit were under control of colonial state provincial treasurers. By the 1910s, however, provincial treasury positions fell increasingly under Filipino control. Provincial Filipino authorities would disproportionately favor wealthy landowners with bank credit, resulting in massive land consolidation and the increase of risky loans.[13] From 1912 through 1915, because of the intensified efforts of the colonial state to strengthen the land title system, applications for loans from the Agricultural Bank exponentially increased. At the same time, however, straining under the weight of all the accumulation of outstanding loans, as early as 1914, the Agricultural Bank's capital had been severely overstretched.

The intensified demand for credit during this time was most likely due to the Great War agribusiness boom. Beginning in 1914, Philippine exports of raw commodities such as copra, hemp, coconut oil, tobacco, and sugar exploded. By 1915 tensions intensified as angry farmers, who either owned smaller parcels of land or who did not have state-approved land titles, demanded equal access to government-backed agricultural credit.[14] Filipino capitalists, moreover, were frustrated by the capital limits imposed on the Agricultural Bank. Taking cues from Filipino capitalists, Filipino lawmakers would increase calls for a national bank, one that could expand capital accumulation in the islands. In agreement with Filipino lawmakers, American authorities believed that the colonial state's dominance over the economic boom was severely limited. Various multinational commercial banks, in particular British-owned institutions, greatly profited from booming export agricultural sales.[15] The creation of a national bank would help chip away at the United States' imperial rivals. Finally, some Filipino lawmakers, such as Osmeña, would argue that the establishment of a national bank would be a powerful symbol of Filipino nationalism.[16] In the end, authoritative Filipino politicians, such as Osmeña, would eventually win over lawmakers suspicious of foreign capital and subsequently work with American authorities to approve a national bank.

With support from Filipino lawmakers, Governor General Harrison and the Vice Governor General Henderson Martin made plans to create a government-owned "Insular Bank." BIA Chief Frank McIntyre, however, cautioned against increased intervention into the economic realm. He instead suggested withdrawing the colonial state entirely from the banking and credit business to allow American-owned commercial banks to take over in the Philippine colony.[17] The Philippine business bloc and Filipino politicians were split over the issue. Although both groups desired another state apparatus to do the heavy lifting of attracting capital to the colony, the potential authority that Americans would preserve nevertheless troubled both. In response, Manuel Quezon reached out to banking and financial expert Henry Parker Willis for advice.[18]

A renowned financial expert, Willis was instrumental in helping draft what eventually became the Federal Reserve Act of 1913.[19] He would go on to be appointed as the first secretary of the Federal Reserve Board and serve on several congressional committees dedicated to banking and currency. Willis would also hold several academic positions during his career, most notably at Washington and Lee University and Columbia University. Quezon's letter was not the first time Willis's career trajectory intersected with the Philippines. Working as an economic journalist in 1903, Willis was privately hired by American anti-imperialists to investigate and critique the political and economic conditions after the Philippine American War.[20] Because of his early anti-imperial work, he eventually became a sporadic contributor to Quezon's nationalist magazine, *The Filipino People*.

Despite, or perhaps because of, his past anti-imperialist stance, Willis was more than eager to lend his authoritative knowledge to the creation of a rapidly Filipinizing state bank. Putting aside Martin's bank proposal, Willis created his own version. He emphasized two elements that would, from his perspective, truly advance the economic life of the islands: investment into agriculture and eventually other natural resources; and commercial development through securities, deposits, and foreign credit markets.[21] In addition to these goals, Willis underscored the ways that a national bank would potentially solve several glaring problems within the monetary, banking, and fiscal systems in the colony and at the same time continue to aid the work of counter-decolonization.

For instance, the PNB was seen as a way to solve the scarcity problem of small-denomination coins. Access to small-denomination coins, in the eyes of authorities, was crucial to securitizing the worker and peasant classes of the colony. On one hand, an adequate supply of small-denomination coins meant that there would be less disturbance in the quotidian life of workers and peasants. On the other hand, daily interaction with American colonial money was ideologically necessary to reinforce American authority in general. For workers and peasants, small-denomination coins were their daily and repetitive reminder of American colonial sovereignty. Still, changes to Philippine colonial currency remained under the power of the U.S. executive branch. However, the PNB's autonomy from the colonial state enabled it to issue and circulate currency without waiting for the approval from Washington, DC. The solution, for American authorities, was to eventually commission the PNB to create smaller-denomination banknotes in lieu of coins made by the colonial state. The creation of PNB notes would also have an added practical bonus. In comparison to minting metal coins, the printing of paper banknotes would take less time. Additionally, the printing of smaller-denomination paper notes would cost much less than the P1, P2, and fifty centavo silver coins, which fluctuated according to the price of silver in international markets. Finally, by issuing currency, the PNB could reap great profits as the costs and reserves would be covered entirely by the Philippine colonial state.[22]

After being approved by the Insular (Philippine) Legislature on February 6, 1916, the PNB was quickly incorporated and opened for operation a mere four months later on July 24, 1916. The PNB consolidated many of the distinct state banking and credit institutions that had emerged throughout almost twenty years of American colonial occupation. The PNB's seeming rapid construction obscured its rather long embryonic life formed through years of battles among the contradictory interests of American colonial officials, economic experts, Filipino politicians, agricultural capitalists, and small landowning farmers. The result of these clashing interests was an institution composed of a complex tangle of functions such as agricultural development, investment and credit loaning, note and bond issuance, and caretaking of various public funds.[23]

One nagging question lingered throughout its construction, however. Who exactly had complete authority, and thus total responsibility, over PNB decisions? Would it be the PNB Board of Control or the PNB president? The board would be composed of the governor general, the president of the Senate, the speaker of the House, and other appointed members. The board, moreover, would have the most legal power, and if Filipinos held more seats on the board, then any form of American encroachment, even encroachment from the PNB president, could be theoretically challenged and blocked. Uncertainty over who held ultimate decision-making power would shape the life of the PNB moving forward.

At its founding, however, both Filipinos and Americans were full of enthusiasm about the PNB. With reassurances from multiple colonial state officials that he would have near complete authority over the PNB, Willis accepted the offer to be the first PNB bank president in 1916 [24] In later reports, Willis was often described as a shrewd conservative technocrat who desired to strengthen the influence of the U.S. dollar throughout Asia and the Pacific. [25] This notion of a stronger American global economic presence through the PNB was promoted publicly by Willis who claimed that the bank could fulfill the three main initial promises of colonization in the Philippines: a market for American manufacturers, the development of Filipino consumption capacities, and the "establishment of profitable and mutual trade relations." [26] Through the PNB, Willis was also eager to challenge British banks that had been profiting off the wartime export boom of Philippine commodities. [27] In addition, he promised to further tighten the bonds between the Philippine banking system and the U.S. banking system. Willis would eventually oversee the PNB's establishment as a foreign bank representative of the Federal Reserve and the creation of a New York branch of the PNB to deal with exchange and investments with the Atlantic financial market. [28] The PNB was thus envisioned as a critical step in further tightening the financial bonds between U.S. Empire's transpacific and transatlantic institutions.

Before his arrival, however, Willis was already suspicious of different tensions, allegiances, and collaborations on the ground, especially between those in the Harrison regime and agricultural capitalists in the colony. Almost immediately, Willis fell out of favor with other American and Filipino authorities in the Philippines. Willis blamed this alienation on the rapid Filipinization under Harrison. [29] Blocked from hiring American banking experts, Willis quickly found himself being outmaneuvered by the Filipino-dominated banking board. Without much political support, after less than a year, Willis resigned in February 1917, leaving the presidency to Samuel Ferguson. [30] Ferguson, a noneconomic expert, gained the position through his political proximity to Harrison and proved an inconsistent president due to chronic illness. Ferguson would not serve long, eventually passing away and being replaced by the staunch nationalist Venancio Concepción in March 1918. A former general in the Philippine American War, Concepción was openly rumored to have once saved Osmeña's life, thus ingratiating himself with the powerful Speaker of the Philippine House.[31] Concepción was described by American observers as an anti-intellectual, the complete opposite of Willis.[32] Many Filipinos, however, lauded Concepción's appointment as PNB president, seeing it as a significant step toward gaining more power over the economic realm. Filipino optimism would be short-lived, however, as crisis struck.

With the end of the Great War in 1919 a global recession would unfold. The recession would severely unsettle Philippine economic conditions. This would set off a disastrous chain reaction for the PNB. First, the speculative bubble for wartime agricultural commodities would immediately burst. Unfortunately, the PNB had helped inflate this bubble by loaning excessive amounts to sugar centrals and coconut oil factories. These speculative loans were made without a proper assessment of the true valuation of debtor assets, mostly properties and securities, put up as collateral. Consequently, the assets put up for loans were barely worth the amount owed, and the amount owed moreover was too great for even the most successful business to theoretically pay back within a reasonable time frame. The PNB had become nearly insolvent. By allowing its reserves to go well below what was required by banking law, the PNB's banknote circulation and public funds were also under threat. Moreover, the PNB had been secretly begging other banks, mostly foreign-owned banks located in Shanghai, not to redeem its banknotes and to delay calling in payment obligations.[33] Some experts warned that the PNB crisis could continue well into the middle of the following decade.[34]

As the PNB's financial value nose-dived, some Filipino authorities still recognized its political value. The PNB, after all, even in its weakened state, remained a powerful financial instrument that symbolically belonged to Filipino leadership. Yet the Filipino attempt to salvage the PNB would dovetail with the replacement of the pro-Filipinization Harrison regime by an avowedly anti-Filipinization Wood regime. For the next half decade, as a consequence of this new colonial regime, Filipino and American battles over the fate of the PNB would become rapidly antagonistic and unfold spectacularly in public.

The Spectacle of Counter-decolonization

Leonard Wood's regime as governor general was one of the most notorious in the history of the American colonial Philippines. Wood's notoriety, however, as a devoted and career imperialist, preceded his official tenure as

Philippine governor general. Achieving the rank of major general in the U.S. Army, serving as a military governor of Cuba, and appointed as Army chief of staff under President William Howard Taft, Wood had amassed a highly impressive résumé in imperial and counter-decolonization governance. In 1920, he was even considered a primary candidate to run on the Republican ticket for U.S. president. After his retirement from the U.S. Army in 1921 and the presidential election of Warren G. Harding, Wood was to serve as provost at the University of Pennsylvania. Before officially taking the university position, Wood, along with former Governor General Cameron Forbes, was sent to the Philippines on an investigative mission for the incoming Harding presidency. The counter-decolonization rhetoric of the *Wood-Forbes Report*, as it would be called, would receive a popular reception from Republicans and other proimperialists in the settler metropole. Wood was then tapped to be a temporary governor general overseeing the transition of colonial administrations. While in power, however, Wood decided to resign from the University of Pennsylvania and permanently remain as governor general.[35]

Throughout his tenure in the Philippines, Wood attempted to reverse any and all political authority gained by Filipino elites during the Harrison-Wilson era. Two main intertwining logics would shape his decision-making. The first was a nostalgic conception of the American colonial Philippines that preceded the Harrison regime, one in which American authority was respected by grateful Filipinos. The second was a notion that the state would refrain from intervening in capitalist matters.

The PNB was a prime target of Wood's counter-decolonization commitment. Through the PNB, Wood sought to publicly create a new narrative: the betrayal of American benevolence and the failure of Filipino authority. This narrative would justify his administration's burden and responsibility to revive American colonial sovereignty and white supremacy in the archipelago. A key tool to assembling this narrative was the 1921 *Wood-Forbes Report*, which was commissioned by U.S. President Harding and Secretary of War John Weeks. As an incoming Republican regime, both Harding and Weeks wanted to undermine Wilson and Harrison's assertion that the Philippines had been successfully moving toward self-government.[36] The prime evidence of the failures of Filipinization were the post–Great War economic crisis and the failure of the PNB. The *Wood-Forbes Report* would argue that Americans had overestimated the "ability of the [Filipino] people to absorb, digest, and make efficient practical use of what has taken other nations generations to absorb and apply, and in our critical impatience we forget the centuries of struggle through which our own race passed before it attained a well-balanced government."[37] According to the *Report*, altruism had blinded Americans to the true nature of Filipino racial capacities, endowing Natives with decision-making power for which they were ill-prepared. Under the Harrison regime, therefore, American authorities had moved far too fast in the Filipinization of colonial leadership.

Hoping to curry popular support for the incoming colonial regime, the War Department would leak the Wood-Forbes findings to newspapers, before the *Report* was officially complete. Weeks, after receiving a confidential cablegram from Wood on June 17, 1921, concerning the financial situation of the PNB and its entanglement with the treasury, decided to release the cable almost in its entirety to the press. The public response in the U.S. settler metropole especially, was rapid and politicized, intensifying already existing anti-Filipinization critiques. Many critics would claim that Filipinos squandered their increased autonomy and had driven the Philippine government itself to the brink of bankruptcy. Weeks most likely released this information to the public, in hopes of swaying Congress to double the Philippine government's legal debt to $30 million.[38] After eventually being approved, the BIA would use the increased loan from Congress to bail out the PNB. Through this increased loan, Weeks intended the PNB bailout to, on one hand, situate the War Department as saviors of the Philippine financial system and, on the other, illustrate that the incoming Harding regime was a more secure government in comparison to the previous Wilson regime.[39]

Despite the bailout, however, the public image of the PNB would deteriorate. Initially, this narrative of PNB crisis and failure would work in favor of the incoming Wood regime. Throughout 1921, the bank would be plagued by public speculations on who deserved the most blame for the chaos and crisis: corrupt and manipulative Filipinos or naïve and gullible American democrats. This attitude was guided by the Wood regime in the colony and the Republican regime in the settler metropole. Public scrutiny was especially intense since the PNB was responsible for a massive amount of public money, including currency reserves, fiscal funds, and government securities. The negative feelings toward the PNB would be amplified with the publication and circulation of the *Report*.

Several newspapers, long critical of Filipinization, blamed the Harrison regime for the "grave conditions" in the archipelago. According to one article, under Harrison's supervision, "American authority has been sadly impaired, fiscal affairs of the islands have been thrown into chaos, and things have gone backward instead of forward." Moreover, with the weakening of American authority "Japan would gradually reach out and impose her will on the islands."[40] Investigations were demanded into Francis Harrison, "the man upon whom rests the heaviest responsibility for the situation."[41] Throughout the most public struggles over the future of the PNB, Harrison would attempt to distance himself from any responsibility, claiming that he was physically "absent from the Philippines" while the speculative loans were distributed.[42] Harrison's alibi would only fuel public speculations of Filipino "demagogues" gone wild. Indeed, many saw the PNB crisis and economic mismanagement as "an index of what may be expected of Government control by . . . native politicians."[43]

For the Wood regime and many anti-Filipinization critics, the man who most embodied Filipino mismanagement and racial incapacity was PNB President Venancio Concepción.[44] Anti-Filipinization critics would rally against Concepción by demanding justice for the American and Filipino taxpayer, arguing that it was ultimately "the public who has to pay for these acts."[45] Public opinion of Concepción was greatly shaped by the *Wood-Forbes Report*. Yet, as nonexperts, Wood and Forbes relied instead on the market knowledge of American auditor Francis Coates. Coates was very vocal of his unfavorable impression of Concepción. This was not simply because of Concepción's anti-Americanism, but because, for Coates, Concepción represented all of the dangers and pitfalls of Filipinization.

Clearly politicized to cater to his Republican employers, Coates adopted paternalist language to racialize the incapacities of Filipinos to govern both the PNB and the colony in his audit. Submitted to the BIA on March 31, 1921, Coates's audit recounted the devolution of the bank under Filipino authority, beginning with Willis's departure in 1919. Coates described the PNB like a ship "drifting with an undisciplined crew, without rudder, compass or Captain." Coates asserted that experience under American colonial tutelage had been far too brief, leading to miseducation in economic matters. "As a race or nation," he stated of Filipinos, "they have only an elementary knowledge of financial affairs and they are seemingly lacking in the *inherited* keenness, resourcefulness, stability and ability that have come only through generations of training and environment to other nations, including Americans."[46] For the question of economic independence, Filipinos would have to devote "a generation or more to intensive study, and intensive practical experience, under the best trained and experienced banking talent available." But even then, Coates was skeptical that the capacity for independence "can be accomplished with the next generation."[47]

Coates's narrative of Filipinization failure was grounded in the racial incapacities of Filipinos to, first, properly manage capitalist time and, second, to properly apprehend market knowledge. To Coates, Filipinos possessed "no thought of individual responsibility beyond the present moment or the present consideration." This racial incapacity to work for the future proved "fatal to their operation and advancement in the fields of Finance." This inability to work for the future was especially embodied in Filipino PNB President Concepción, who quickly became lost to the "financial world of the white man."[48] Coates's critique of Concepción then extended more broadly into an indictment of the general inefficiency of colonial state authorities. Due to the inefficient administration of the government, Concepción, "a man who had had practically no banking training, knowledge or experience—who was known to be a politico" was promoted as PNB president. Concepción, it was argued, gained his position through political nepotism and systemic corruption. Continuing the supposed practice of nepotism, Concepción replaced American experts in favor of "Native Filipinos who were untrained and inexpert men, not familiar with banking and routine."[49]

Coates's evaluation of Concepción's financial ineptitude would serve as the basis for the *Wood-Forbes Report*'s assessment of, more broadly, the Filipino incapacity for sovereignty. Adding fuel to the fire was the notion of Concepción's nepotism and criminality. As evidence of nepotism, the public scrutinized the appointment of Concepción's son as PNB vice president as an indication of broader Filipino corruption.[50] Then came Concepción's arrest in June 1921, for illegally securing a loan for personal investment. Numerous presses would subsequently attempt to connect the bank's mismanagement to Filipino criminal acts.[51] Newspapers would even assert that the bank's corrupt culture would spread to other PNB branches, throughout the archipelago and abroad.[52]

Concepción would attempt to battle this public vilification by arguing that he had inherited a cluster of failures, chief of which was the American mismanagement of the currency reserves. On taking leadership, Concepción would claim that "the gold reserve was totally exhausted" and had been misused by the Insular Treasury and the bank's New York agency, two institutions under American authority. In addition, there was "something...a little queer," claimed Concepción. Not only was he being blamed for the failures of American authorities, but he and the bank were being "furiously attacked" by his own "brethren," other Filipino politicians and capitalists driven by "partisan passion." The scheming of Filipino collaborators, "seconding the work of destruction" was identified by Concepción as an even more inexcusable betrayal to the Philippine nation.[53]

For certain the articles make clear that Concepción attempted to shift blame and clear his name as public scrutiny intensified. At the same time, however, Concepción was correct that the Currency Reserve Fund (CRF) had been mismanaged before he had taken leadership of the bank. As private correspondences at the time illustrate, Concepción regularly reached out to Willis about the precarity of the CRF, with Willis regularly rebuffing Concepción from the New York branch.[54] Willis, in correspondences with the secretary of war and the BIA, would also regularly belittle Concepción as ignorant and without proper training, thus diminishing any impact of Concepción's concerns over the CRF when correspondences would reach the War Department.[55] Wood would carry on this practice of blaming Concepción for the mismanagement of the currency reserves. As historian Yoshiko Nagano cogently argues, American authorities would place the blame of the postwar financial crisis solely on the unsound and negligent Filipino mismanagement of the PNB, strategically obscuring the equally unsound and negligent white American mismanagement of Philippine currency.[56]

Problems with the CRF began when American authorities attempted to appropriate reserves for investment purposes during the wartime boom commodity. The two primary currency funds, the GSF and the Silver Certificate Fund, were necessary to maintain parity between the peso and the dollar and stabilize the price of silver currency to the world's gold prices.[57] Since the Conant-designed currency reforms of 1913, the GSF had been used to lend out money for different infrastructural projects. In addition to the GSF was the Silver Certificate Fund. Silver certificates remained crucial for ensuring that funds continued to flow to U.S. military operations in the Philippine colony, China, and other parts of Southeast Asia.[58] In 1917, these two funds would be combined and renamed the CRF. The CRF would be deposited in PNB branches throughout U.S. Empire as well as branches of the Federal Reserve Bank, further blurring the economic borders between the settler metropole and the overseas colony.

As the United States' involvement in the Great War increased, an alarming amount of the CRF was used, not to maintain parity as it had originally been intended, but rather to purchase Liberty Loan war bonds as well as speculative investments into war commodity production.[59] By 1919, due to the Great War boom, prices and credit inflated to such an extent that they threatened to drain the currency reserves.[60] The year 1920 saw the inflationary wartime bubble burst. This forced the Philippine peso to undergo rapid depreciation and exposed how a majority of speculative loans given out by state institutions were all on the brink of default.[61] The PNB, moreover, unable to call in its myriad loans and incapacitated by the amount of its currency notes still in circulation, suddenly faced a severe currency reserve shortage. In the eyes of the public, the colonial monetary system was on the brink of catastrophe. According to one article, "the bank is carrying virtually no reserves behind its $40,838,500 in deposits and $15,397,000 in circulating notes, which it is impossible for the bank to redeem in lawful money as required by law. . . . They [the PNB bank notes] therefore are a constant menace to the financial stability of the Government and private business."[62]

While the crisis spectacularly unfolded in public, the BIA had covertly sponsored several investigations of the fiscal and financial conditions of the colony. Since 1919, three separate investigations by different examining agents had been or were being conducted before the publication of the *Wood-Forbes Report*. The first was by Francis Coates Jr. in November 1919, the second by Haskins and Sells in May 1921, and the third by former PSB president and special bank examiner for the PNB, Ben F. Wright, who independently took it upon himself to investigate the PNB beginning in December 1920.[63] Despite possessing differing perspectives as to the causes and the subsequent solutions to the financial and monetary conditions of the colony, all three investigations identified exploitative loopholes in the currency reserve system. For all three, the roots of the crisis involved the mismanagement of the CRF not just the PNB. As already mentioned, the PNB was not a central bank, and thus the CRF was firmly the responsibility of the Philippine Department of Finance and Justice's Bureau of Treasury. Indeed, many economic experts hired by the colonial state were in fact very critical of the American-led Bureau of Treasury.[64] Although part of this criticism might have been aimed at the previous Harrison administration, this expert opinion nonetheless opened up to a broader critique of American authority in general. Wood would keep American expert criticisms of the CRF mismanagement under wraps, only leaking contextless data at moments that were politically advantageous.

Amid all this panic over the PNB and CRF crises, Wood would position his regime as the redeemer of the monetary system and the PNB. Pro-American newspapers would support this narrative. "Fortunately," as one newspaper claimed, "the notes circulate freely because the people know the Government is responsible for their redemption."[65] Under Wood, moreover, currency reforms were supposedly already under way. Wood claimed that a total of $23 million in bonds had been sold to ensure that "behind every

Treasury certificate there is a full face value in gold and silver." In addition, according to Wood, the GSF had become stable, "re-establishing the currency system" and securitizing the "international parity of the peso."[66]

The pro-American public in the colony seemed to have accepted the redemption narrative espoused by Wood. Subsequently he initiated several major reforms of the PNB. The first step for Wood was to replace Filipino leadership. With blessings from the War Department, Wood appointed E. R. Wilson as the new head of the bank in 1921. Before his arrival in the Philippines, Wilson worked as vice president of the Anglo-London-Paris Bank of San Francisco. Wilson would bring along with him a team of six "American experts," who he promised would "'aid Filipinos not replace them."[67] Upon his arrival Wilson would make the rounds to the business community, reassuring prominent Filipino capitalists that American experts were there to "assist them." At one Philippine Chamber of Commerce event, attended by over a hundred people, Wilson referred to the Coates Report's recommendations that banks were "purely technical" institutions and must be managed by experts.[68] Wilson had been vetted and coached by BIA Chief Frank McIntyre to attempt to soften the public image of Wood's counter-decolonization efforts in the PNB. For Wilson, the PNB could still be salvaged and instrumentalized to accumulate more capital for the benefit of U.S. Empire. Wood, however, would adopt a different perspective: the highly spectacular act of dismantling the PNB.

Wood believed the PNB was fundamentally flawed, for its commercial capacities structurally gave too much monetary authority to Filipinos. One article captured Wood's apprehension of the PNB: "The PNB was born in politics, has lived to the present time in politics, and promises to die in politics." For Wood, the politicization of the bank was synonymous with Filipinization. It was subsequently a threat to the notion of "the United States as sovereign power."[69] Thus, under this racial and colonial logic, the PNB had to be fundamentally stripped down, to revert back to what it had initially been proposed as: an agricultural bank under American authority. Wood immediately went public about his plans to turn the PNB into an institution that dealt strictly with small-scale agricultural credit. This plan, according to one newspaper, created a "veritable panic in Philippine commercial circles."[70]

Over the next three years of the Wood regime, intense unease would plague Filipino elites and capitalists. Political relations between Filipino lawmakers and the Wood regime would deteriorate, mainly along racial lines. In July 1923, the unbridled hostility would lead to the entirety of the

Filipino Council of State, the leading lawmakers of the colony, resigning in protest to what they saw as Wood's illegitimate authority. This event would later be named by historians as the Cabinet Crisis of 1923.[71] These struggles would be highly publicized. Wood even seemed to relish this public notoriety, especially as news of his anti-Filipinization efforts reached the settler metropole.

Wood would trigger these animosities by constantly feeding scandalous information to a rabid public. The most egregious "leak" to the public by Wood were the two-year-old audits by Wright and Haskins and Sells in September 1923. For months Wood had been infamously claiming that his voice was being "suppressed" by Filipino-controlled newspapers in the colony.[72] This leak would lead to Filipino authorities "condemning and protesting against Gov. Wood's actions."[73] In one collaborative press release in the *Far Eastern Review*, Wood asserted that the PNB had been "an orgy of mismanagement." He would go on to list all the different ways that the PNB wasted U.S. capital. This included losing the investment capital stock of P32 million, losing about 64% of its P47.5 million deposits in the bank, and most egregiously for Wood, having no reserves for P30.8 million worth of circulating banknotes.[74] Not only was this detrimental to the Philippine colony, but it also threatened the financial and currency system of the U.S. settler metropole.

Wood vowed, through severe measures, to clean up the mess made by the Harrison regime and unqualified Filipino authorities. With the full support of "the home government" Wood would ensure that the "insular government should be gotten out of business as rapidly as possible."[75] Wood's article in the *Far Eastern Review* was published alongside a vehemently anti-Filipinization essay titled "The Trend of Events in the Philippines: The High Cost of Altruism." The essay narrated the failure of the PNB as evidence of Filipino immaturity and racial incapacity for authority. "They [Filipinos] were like a child with a new toy," the article argued. "They laughed and cried over it [the PNB], hugged it and kissed it, fondled it, rocked it to sleep and then woke it up and jumped on it, banged it with a club, ripped it open and pulled the stuffing out of it."[76]

Despite appearing publicly united behind Wood, transpacific tensions brewed between American authorities. BIA Chief McIntyre, for instance, would take umbrage with the Coates audit, interpreting it as an attack on the BIA and the War Department.[77] McIntyre's dislike for Coates would eventually extend to another hired American expert, Benjamin Wright. This would in turn cause friction between McIntyre and Wood who frequently sought advice from the chief bank examiner and former Philippine PSB head. In Washington, there was much doubt of Wright's actual level of expertise. McIntyre, for instance, assessed Wright as an "incompetent" fraud who had "gotten altogether away from his appropriate functions" and had ingratiated himself with Wood and his American cabinet. Furthermore, despite not being "a financial expert in any sense of the word," according to McIntyre, Wright had managed to pass himself off as "something of an expert on currency and banking and general government finance" because of his "acquaintance with the early history of the establishment of the currency system in the Philippines." Wright had especially displeased McIntyre for he had begun a public feud with current PNB President Wilson, whom McIntyre fully supported.[78]

The animosity between Wright and Wilson swirled around the question of the PNB. Wright argued that Wilson had been keeping the bank alive in hopes of ingratiating himself with local Filipino politicians and businessmen. Wilson was making decisions that led to inefficiency and excess, according to Wright "throwing good money after bad."[79] Moreover, since the PNB was bound to fail, it would in turn prolong the crisis. But what bothered Wright the most was not that the bank was a failing business. Rather, Wright was infuriated that the PNB, and the parasitic companies that owed it money, despite being "legally and morally dead for at least two years," were being artificially kept alive by the Philippine colonial state. Through capital borrowed from the U.S. government, the Philippine colonial state had been forced to "inject into its [the PNB's] palsied body a semblance of life."[80] It was thus akin to a zombie, whose own toxic assets, which normally would have long been driven extinct according to the logic of market competition, was instead being kept alive by feeding off the fiscal funds of Philippine and American governments.

Wright concluded that to properly foster the economic development of Filipinos, the government bailout of private enterprises had to end. Wright repeatedly justified the shutdown of the PNB for three interrelated reasons. First, because the bank was almost completely owned by the colonial state, it appeared to play by different rules than commercial banks. Consequently, since the government could bail out the PNB's loans at any time, it scared away foreign capital investment from Philippine markets, killing competition. Second, although Wright believed that the Philippines should, like other nations, develop their own financial institution, they "must cease to lean upon a paternalistic Government," and achieve capitalist success though "their own initiative and ability." Finally, Filipinos had proven themselves incapable of playing the game of more advanced Western races, the game of finance capitalism. They had, instead, "lavishly used" government funds "in feverish speculation in the marketing of products rather than in their production."[81] In sum, Filipinos—because of their racial incapacity to comprehend the game of finance capitalism, their inability to calculate investment through knowledge of the market, and their juvenile expectation of a bailout-ready paternalistic state—ended up gambling away what they treated as an inexhaustible amount of government capital.

Wood was heavily enamored by Wright's assessment that Filipino racial incapacity led to the mismanagement of the PNB. The solution, as Wright saw it, was simple: government had to stay out of business. In the feud between Wright and Wilson, Wood unsurprisingly backed Wright. On April 7, 1923, after a "year and half feud," and much to the chagrin of McIntyre, Wilson was forced to retire his position as bank head. The highly publicized falling out was, according to some Filipino perspectives, due to Wood's obsession with "getting the Government out of business."[82] From Wood's viewpoint, Wilson had failed to "carry out the policy of the Board of Directors and Board of Control" and had thus failed to recognize his authority. Later in his confidential message to McIntyre, Wood expressed his hope that the replacement be a "capable American banker" with a view "to harmony and greater efficiency."[83] During the interim, however, career Filipino civil servant Rafael Corpus would serve as chairman of the PNB and theoretically have the most authority in day-to-day decisions. With this position, Corpus would work with other Filipino leaders to mount public challenges to the Wood regime.

Filipino Challenges and Appropriations

From 1921 to 1924, the Wood regime would come under attack from various prominent Filipino voices. Throughout the 1910s, there had been manifold political fracturing within Filipino leadership. The unintended outcome of Wood's vehement anti-Filipinization was a temporary ceasefire between different Filipino factions. With this short-term unity, Filipinos would attempt to subvert Wood's public narrative of the PNB and Filipino failure. Filipino politicians would take aim at both Wood and Wilson, through a mixture of nationalist and efficiency discourse. Much like Coates's and Wood-Forbes's assessments of the PNB management, which emphasized the waste of capital, career lawmakers such as Speaker of the House Sergio Osmeña criticized the use of public funds for the salaries of imported

American economic experts. In one highly public statement Osmeña listed the different pay rates of advisors, expressing shock by how "the country has had to pay 4 auditors at the rate of 50 dollars per day to some and other 100 dollars per day." Moreover, this exorbitant remuneration was for inefficient work. "To investigate a thing already investigated by Mr. Coates," reasoned Osmeña, was inefficiently redundant. Finally, Osmeña questioned the qualifications of men "who are anything but experts." He would go on to list their inadequate experience, naming one as "only a salesman," another as "merely an agent of the bank of Nicaragua," and finally, one as "but a clerk in the Anglo-London Bank of San Francisco, California." Osmeña thus highlighted that only through the logics of colonialism and white supremacy could inexperienced Americans suddenly be elevated to highly paid economic experts.[84]

In another example, one Filipino senator would argue that Filipinos had been wrongfully blamed for American waste. "Is there anyone who can affirm concretely that Filipinos are the ones who brought about the present condition of the National Bank?" he asked. According to the senator, Americans were "the ones who can withdraw the most money from the National Bank." Even if Filipino authorities were in leadership positions, the senator would go on to reason, it was ultimately the failure of American tutelage that was to blame. "Believing in reality that they could learn from these Americans," Filipinos had let "themselves be guided by them, and what was the result? The good faith of the directors of the National Bank was betrayed."[85] The senator had thus appropriated the paternalist language of the Wood regime. Rather than Filipinos betraying the trust of their father, the Americans, it was the Americans who had betrayed the trust of Filipinos, their adopted children.

Even leftist newspapers such as *Bagong Lipang Kalabaw* would put aside critiques of Filipino elites for the purpose of condemning American expertise. Written mainly in Tagalog, *Bagong Lipang Kalabaw* printed critiques of the PNB mismanagement and political infighting among Americans in the wake of the 1919 crisis.[86] *Bagong Lipang Kalabaw* dedicated several detailed editorials to the PNB and political cartoons, most likely to visually appeal to the less literate of the urban public. These articles did not dwell on the past criminal mismanagement of the PNB and instead focused on the unreasonable and, to their mind, wasteful employment of nonstate American experts.

In one editorial printed in November 1922, for instance, the writer argued that Wilson, and other technical advisors to the PNB, received "extraordinarily large salaries" in comparison to Filipino bank employees who were doing most of the work. Some of these salaries were thousands of dollars for weeks of work, equivalent to a typical annual salary of a Filipino civil servant.[87] Wright's salary was equally questioned. Referred to as a "puppet" of Wood, the bank examiner, according to the editorial, had received excessive compensation in addition to an already substantial salary as a college lecturer.[88] Another editorial featured a political cartoon of a snaking line of American experts carrying swollen sacks of money while a tiny tuxedoed figure labeled as the Philippine Legislature looked helplessly on.[89] The extraordinarily large salaries of American experts demonstrated the waste and nepotism on the part of the Wood regime. This critique was especially convincing, considering that American expert advisors did not create new capital but were receiving salaries for simply selling off existing toxic assets at immense losses.

The slow reform of the PNB subsequently kept it in the news well into the following year. On August 1923, *Bagong Lipang Kalabaw* printed a cartoon of Wood as the biblical Samson, blinded and haphazardly destroying the columns of an ancient Greek-inspired structure marked with "PNB."[90] The accompanying editorial stressed the wastefulness of the Wood regime by asserting that American leadership were "fools with public resources." Exhausted by the incessant threats by Wood of closing down the PNB, the writer focused on the assertion of "American imperialists" that Filipinos must first achieve "economic independence" before receiving political independence. The writer consequently pointed out the double bind faced by Filipinos, as they, on one hand, remained "fools to the guile of progress" and, on the other hand, were oriented toward a "higher career of civilization" to which they could never "graduate."[91] *Bagong Lipang Kalabaw*, in sum, saw the futility of struggling to advance on a civilizational and economic scale that could constantly and arbitrarily be adjusted by American imperialism.

In addition to battling through the press, Filipinos attempted to challenge the Wood regime by convincing the masses. Hoping to gain popular support in challenging American plans to "close the National Bank and sell out the centrals to private companies," Quezon and the Speaker of the House Manuel Roxas led a group of legislative delegates on a tour across the rural provinces in June 1923. During the tour, Filipino lawmakers made certain to assert that their nationalism did not come at the expense of capitalism in the archipelago. Roxas specifically asserted that they were not against "investment of American capital." Instead, they wanted to impart to the masses that American capital in the archipelago should only operate for the "national aspiration of the Filipinos."[92]

Even the most established Filipino politicians found inventive ways to critique the Wood regime without necessarily questioning the very racial and civilizational measurements constructed and reproduced by U.S. Empire. In the propagandistic 1924 text, *Governor-General Wood and the Filipino Cause*, Camilo Osias, President of the Philippine National University and long-time Philippine senator, adopted an intriguing rhetorical strategy. Rather than attempt to justify the errors made by Filipinos in the administration of the PNB, Osias instead concentrated on Wood's policy of keeping "Government out of business." While Wood argued that successful governance entailed keeping political agents out of the economic realm, Osias recast this decision to keep government out of business as not only unreasonable, but tragically naive. The senator highlighted Wood's policy as provincial by claiming it as "not an Anglo Saxon policy... European policy, and... not an Oriental policy."[93] Osias argued that keeping the Philippine government out of business would leave "the people of the Islands" to wage "an uneven and unequal, not to say, hopeless, economic fight."[94] Reversing the discourse of American imperial tutelage, Osias insisted that Wood's economic policy did not teach Filipinos how to economically stand on their own feet. Rather, the Wood regime had stripped the Philippines of its economic weaponry in an inimical capitalist world populated by rival and economically advanced nation-states. By denying the Philippines' capacity for economic self-defense, the United States was effectively reneging on its promise of racial and civilizational uplift. Invoking the imperial language of racial development through patrimony and filiation, Osias reasoned, "a father of vision, does not hesitate to incur obligations which he believes will benefit himself and his children."[95]

Despite engaging in a public and protracted battle, the Philippine Legislature eventually relinquished to many of the Wood reforms. On November 9, 1924, the PNB's operating capital was cut from $17.5 million to $5 million.[96] This was done, however, to save the PNB from being dismantled. Despite what seemed like a reduction of the PNB's power, some, like Wright, believed that the PNB reforms did not go far enough to punish Filipinos for their mismanagement. Wright believed that the reforms let Filipino authorities off the hook and declared the bank bill "worse than a disease." "Again," Wright reasoned, "the credit of a country is measured more largely by the stability of its currency than perhaps any other one thing. That our currency system will be greatly weakened by shifting to it

P30,000,000 of liabilities without corresponding assets is too obvious to need proof."[97] According to this narrative, Filipinos did not properly learn from the crisis and instead were bailed out by the American public and the U.S. government.

Filipinos would respond by arguing that Wright was politically motivated in his assessment, questioning his expertise and even his morality. In one statement, the officials and board of directors claimed that reports made by Wright were "written in a vindictive spirit and with a preconceived intent to prove, at all cost, that the officials of the bank were incompetent and negligent." They would also question his work ethic and yearly salary of P8,000, by arguing that Wright would frequently saddle most of his workload to "his assistants in the bank."[98] Ongoing internal frictions led to the public perception of the PNB as dysfunctional and systemically irreparable. One article in 1925 argued that the PNB "could not be fixed under" the "present system," and a "shake-up" was necessary.[99]

After several years of stagnation and public speculation on the PNB's future, Wood would pull a bank leadership coup. In January 1927, the governor general would appoint several Americans and pro-American Filipinos to the bank board, gaining a majority and thus authority over the PNB. Despite the walkout by then current PNB President Rafael Corpus, Wood had finally outmaneuvered Filipino authorities. Wood was able to gain a majority by repealing a bank law that allowed the "board of directors power to fill vacancies." With the repeal of the law, moreover, "the power of filling vacancies would revert to the stockholders, which means to the governor general."[100] This highly public coup would be challenged immediately by a newly united Nacionalista Party bloc led by Quezon and Roxas.

Filipinos would again argue that recent economic conditions "over which they had no control" were to blame for the PNB's failure, not Filipino leadership.[101] But the more popular Filipino challenge relied on the notion that the PNB remained an essential institution to the existence of the nation.[102] Filipino leaders were especially weary of another new round of imported American experts recruited by Wood to further dismantle the PNB.[103] One anonymous Filipino banker warned that "the preponderance of American directors in the PNB is almost certain to result in increased favorable attention to American clients at the expense of Filipino farmers." The bias of white American authorities for white "American businessmen" would in turn lead to Filipino capitalists withdrawing "their patronage of the bank."[104] The PNB, Filipino leaders feared, would lose its identity as a national institution and instead become recolonized by American capital.

On August 7, 1927, Wood would pass away from complications resulting from a brain tumor surgery. Nevertheless, Wright would carry on Wood's campaign of stripping Filipino authority over the PNB. Just a few months earlier, Wright expressed his optimism about counter-decolonization to friend and mentor, Edwin Kemmerer. "The day of a few thousand halfbreed [sic] politicians headed by Quezon, Osmeña, et al, actuated by the most greedy and selfish motives," he wrote, "is about over."[105] Even in July 1929, Filipinos feared the ongoing majority of American authorities in the PNB.[106] Despite what seemed like the tide turning against Filipinos, time had run out for Wood's Americanization of the PNB as new Governor General Henry Stimson would attempt to act, much to the chagrin of Wright, as "the great pacifier."[107]

In July 1929, Wright would resign, marking the end of any remnant of the Wood regime's PNB reforms. Feeling "double crossed" by Stimson's regime, Wright lamented the nine years he had spent attempting to fix the "awful mess" into which he had willfully walked. In a telling correspondence, Wright would briefly narrate his almost decade-long suffering at the hands of scheming Filipinos and spineless Americans to Kemmerer. Seeing himself as both victim and unrecognized savior, Wright wrote of how he valiantly attempted to bring the financial situation, the currency system, and PNB back in "proper order." Despite his self-proclaimed courageous effort, the "authority regained after a hard struggle," by Americans were "brought to naught by the...oriental ideals" of Filipino leaders.[108]

By the end of the 1920s the PNB's value as a highly charged symbol of both conditional decolonization and counter-decolonization had all but disappeared in the public. Although there were still concerns over the fate of the reforms, the PNB did not command the kind of spectacular attention that it once had under the Wood administration. Material conditions had certainly changed by the end of the decade. The sorts of speculation witnessed a decade earlier was less fashionable and transpacific trade continued to increase. Specifically, due to the harsher protective U.S. tariff policies for imported agricultural products, Philippine export commodities encountered far less international competition in the settler colony from the mid-1920s until the end of the decade. This so-called economic special relation between the Philippines and the United States was an unintended consequence of the three-decade-long "free market" agreement between the extractive colony and the settler colony. Just before the U.S. economic crash of 1929, both overall Philippine imports and exports levels enjoyed record success, exceeding the previous records set in the late 1910s.[109]

The seeming recovery in the global economy during the mid to late 1920s also led to a renarration of the PNB's history in the minds of Philippine statesmen, especially during U.S. Congressional debates over Philippine independence. Although Wood's rehabilitation was publicly memorialized as a failure, the PNB's survival into the 1930s unexpectedly became a source of great symbolic meaning for Filipinos agitating for sovereignty in Washington, DC. As one Philippine statesman argued: "When you consider that the current business depression has brought about the failure of more than 1,500 banks in the United States during the last two years, the fact that the national bank of the Philippine Islands has been able to maintain the soundness of its financial condition unimpaired speaks well for that institution."[110] Unlike a decade earlier, however, Filipinos during the early 1930s argued that the bank's survival was a result of Filipino—not American—stewardship. The bank's health, despite the Great Depression, gained new political resonance and produced a new narrative of the accomplishments of Filipino authorities. In this new narrative, with the security of capitalism ensured, Filipinos positioned themselves as capable students who, on one hand, had finally outgrown American tutelage, and on the other, were ready to graduate to conditional decolonization.

Under Common Wealth

5

In a radio address on November 14, 1939, Vice President Sergio Osmeña of the Philippine Commonwealth reflected on the last four years of semiautonomous Filipino government.

> The political phase of our struggle for freedom is ended; the capacity of our people to absorb democratic ideals and to manage the machinery of democracy has been proved; our right to be independent is recognized. It is in the economic field that a great deal of our work still lies ahead of us. In this task we cannot, we must not, fail. We must continue our efforts to build a solid economic structure for the nation so that when independence comes on July 4, 1946, the Philippine Republic will rest on a stable and enduring foundation.[1]

Osmeña was speaking at a moment of great global political and economic upheaval. He had addressed the supposed fears of American colonizers over the political disorder and tyranny that would ensue. Recalling the words of the *Wood-Forbes Report*, over a decade earlier, which claimed that Filipinos racially did not have the "ability of the people to absorb... what has taken other nations generations to absorb and apply,"[2] Osmeña proclaimed that the Filipino people had proved their capacity to "absorb democratic ideals and to manage the machinery of democracy." Despite this confidence in the Filipino's political capacity, Osmeña admitted that the Philippines' economic capacity remained wanting. Consequently, the securitization of the "economic structure" had to be urgently prioritized.[3]

This chapter examines the struggles over decolonization in the American colonial Philippines during the Great Depression. Through the suffering of the Depression, much of the world apprehended what it held in common, a planet structured by colonial and racial capitalism. Although felt unevenly and asymmetrically, capitalist crisis in the 1930s led to radical reimaginations of the political, economic, and social world. Some of these imaginations would follow the trajectory of economic nationalism, which demanded heavier policed borders between the foreign and domestic, metropole and colony, citizen and alien. Certain reactionary policies in the United States, such as protectionism and immigration bans, were framed as a solution to racial capitalist crisis. By economically protecting the nation from racialized commodities and bodies from the Philippine colony, the metropole would not only shore up its domestic market, but also securitize transpacific racial and imperial orders. The desire to more strictly segregate extractive colony from settler colony eventually led to what was unthinkable just a few decades earlier: an intense support from U.S. authorities and publics for Philippine independence.

Like American capitalists in the metropole, Filipino capitalists in the colony would conjure analogue economic nationalisms, explicitly tying it to desires for conditional decolonization. Some would propagandize nationalist protectionist policies and culture, while others would utilize racial paternalism to argue for capitalist security. Another path, novel at the time, was also carved out by a burgeoning self-conscious group of Filipino economic experts. Rife with tensions, expert logic valorized the universal laws of the capitalist market and the supposedly Indigenous knowledge of educated Filipinos. These economic experts would reaffirm monetary authority through the naturalization of gold, while simultaneously critiquing U.S. imperialism. Although these forms of economic nationalism followed different paths, they all nevertheless traveled the same direction. They all advocated for a form of conditional decolonization, where monetary authority remained in the hands of "Native" Filipinos.

In 1935, proponents of conditional decolonization would realize victory as the Philippines transitioned from a U.S. colonial possession to a more politically autonomous U.S. commonwealth. At the same time, the intensifying threat of unconditional decolonization continued to haunt monetary and state authorities. Akin to other parts of the colonial world, the Philippine radical tradition remained resilient throughout the 1920s. In the 1930s, however, anticolonial antagonisms became even more amplified by international racial capitalist crisis. Social experimentations and revolutionary imaginations would proliferate throughout the archipelago. In response to these unsettling threats to existing orders, Commonwealth authorities would adopt American forms of direct and indirect counter-decolonization strategies to ward off the possibility of unconditional decolonization.

The Depression, Economic Nationalisms, and Conditional Decolonization

The Great Depression was a crisis of global racial capitalism and interimperial monetary authority. Suspicion and paranoia between world decision-makers stressed interstate collaborations among imperial powers. Moreover, the Depression intensified already existing tensions among economic policymakers, state authorities, and various racialized publics across metropoles and colonies. As scholars have argued, the Great Depression was so vast, deep, and long, mainly due to the failure of monetary authorities to act quickly, decisively, and cooperatively to resolve the cascading effects of the financial defaults, panics, and crashes of the late 1920s and early 1930s. There were two interrelated reasons for this widespread impasse. The first was the diminishing global confidence in the gold-exchange standard to naturally fix massive gold imbalances between major economies, currency devaluations, and price declines.[4] The second was the lack of cooperation, if not outright suspicion, between monetary authorities.

The United States, the largest lender of new credit in the post–World War I world, exemplified the global climate of suspicion among monetary authorities well before the speculative Wall Street bubble burst in 1929. U.S. monetary authorities aggressively refused any imposition of a regulatory international body such as the League of Nations. Instead of cross-imperial cooperation, the Federal Reserve pursued a unilateral country-by-country approach, brokering credit with individual foreign countries through private banks and financial experts. This form of economic imperial rivalry was dubbed "dollar diplomacy."[5] Two years after the Wall Street crash, Austria and Germany's financial structure collapsed and the haphazard attempts to stop the rippling consequences had no lasting effect. Despite sporadic attempts by various combinations of international bodies, the path toward reestablishing the gold standard was quickly abandoned. In 1931 the British deserted the gold standard, forcibly taking all of its peripheral economies with it. Exacerbating the crisis, the incoming U.S. President, Franklin D. Roosevelt, refused in 1932 to honor the outgoing administration's extension of the war debt moratorium for most of Europe, plunging the world economy further into global crisis.[6]

Paranoia and suspicion were not limited to monetary authorities in the decade after the Great War. Many publics violently rejected interstate cooperation, opting to stoke the fires of economic nationalism and protectionism.[7] For most imperial societies, accumulated wealth from industrial production was severely threatened. Some nations witnessed almost a 140 percent reduction in production, a quarter of populations without work, routine financial and banking panics, and violently fluctuating prices for commodities. Rampant monetary contraction, moreover, led to unforgiving austerity policies. On one hand, these conditions bred an amplification of authoritarian state powers, seen most spectacularly in the majoritarian public affirmation of fascism, Nazism, and militarism. These reactionary movements promised economic security mainly through racist and imperial cultural imaginations and narratives of victimization. On the other hand, there were revolutionary imaginings of a world without capitalist crisis, primarily through the promise of a more just distribution of wealth and radically antiauthoritarian social life. Going beyond many Marxist, communist, or anarchist imaginations in Europe, however, antiauthoritarian imaginations in the "darker nations" additionally strove for the unconditional end of racial and colonial hierarchies.[8]

Protectionism would become the increasingly popular battle cry for proud economic nationalists, creating new alliances between tariff advocates and anti-immigrant organizations. U.S. protectionist policies were demanded by both corporations and populist publics to spectacularly exaggerate the borders between foreign and domestic, colony and metropole, migrant and citizen, white and nonwhite. In this way, U.S. publics were analogue to other empires that had openly developed fascist and militaristic forms of economic nationalism in the wake of the Great War.

Filipino bodies were racialized in new ways by the logic of economic nationalism. The Depression amplified long-brewing anti-Filipino aggression from white American settlers. Anti-Filipino migrant sentiment was especially acute along the U.S. Pacific coast states and the settler colony of Hawai'i, as evident in the institutional discrimination in housing, policing, and anti-miscegenation during the 1920s. Many of these institutional forms of racism were grounded in longer intertwining histories of anti-Asian, anti-Black, and anti-Indigenous structures. However, as a colonial subject, the Filipino race posed a conundrum for the existing U.S. immigration and legal systems that barred "Asiatic" aliens from naturalization. Filipinos were legally colonial subjects that were ambiguously both foreign and domestic to the settler metropole. As a consequence, they were recruited by Pacific coast agricultural capitalists hungry for low-wage and less-protected labor, a position formerly occupied by now excluded Asiatic migrant bodies. The 1920s witnessed a surge in Filipino migration to the North American continent, causing panic from settlers. As Rick Baldoz illustrates, a torrent of white supremacist anti-Filipino violence in the late 1920s and early 1930s would eventually culminate in calls for Filipino exclusion and Philippine independence to prevent colonial subjects from entering the settler metropole.[9]

In another register, the logic of economic nationalism racialized Filipino commodities in novel ways.[10] U.S. corporate blocs increased calls for trade protectionism. Many corporate lobbyists argued that U.S. colonies, such as the Philippines, held an unfair advantage in comparison to "domestic" businesses. Colonial conditions, which enabled fewer legal rights and protections to workers and the environment combined with lower living costs, enabled colonial producers of commodities such as fats and oils to undersell U.S. "domestic" commodities.[11] U.S. agribusiness cartels would go on to argue that Philippine companies were "foreign" despite being under U.S. imperial sovereignty and should be tariffed as such. Through the co-constitutive racialization of Philippine bodies and commodities, economic nationalism became a strategy to discursively and concretely deepen estrangement between extractive colony and settler metropole.[12]

Economic nationalism simultaneously intensified within Philippine colonial society, taking on more concentrated and institutional forms. Although its origins were not born from the Great Depression, the growing rhetorical popularity of Philippine economic nationalism was greatly augmented by capitalist crisis. In 1932, the total for Philippine imports and exports dropped to almost half of what it had been in 1929. Although trade would gradually begin to increase throughout the 1930s, it never reached pre-Depression levels until well after World War II.[13] In response to the contraction of the archipelago's largest export market, the United States, the Philippine colonial state during the early Depression years attempted to raise tariff rates on non-U.S. imports.

Discursively, therefore, the economy offered a site through which to critique colonial sovereignty and demand self-determination, but at the same time, never fundamentally challenge the logics of U.S. imperialism and racial capitalism. Through the optic of the capitalist market, two primary kinds of Philippine economic nationalism thrived during the late 1920s through the 1930s. The first kind was obsessed with protectionism, appropriating much of the logic of imperial economics. The second valorized expertise. Protectionists were mainly capitalists who developed nationalist notions of business, commerce, and trade. Economic experts were grounded in a libertarian understanding of the national economy, primarily basing their logic on abstract conceptions of the securitization of capitalism on both local and global registers. While protectionists relied mainly on the logic of profits, experts relied on the logic of the market as a whole. Despite tensions between logics, these two kinds of Philippine economic nationalism ultimately fed off one another.

Protectionism entailed convincing the consuming public to give cultural and legal preference to "Native" Filipino commodities and gained traction in 1934 with the founding of the National Economic Protectionism Association (NEPA). Despite NEPA's public stance of keeping government out of business, its origins emerged from the colonial state itself, beginning as a fact-finding group under Governor General Frank Murphy.[14] In its mission, NEPA framed its right to protectionism as a right to self-determination.[15] Self-defined as "semi-governmental," NEPA's primary members would include wealthy financiers, such as Salvador Araneta, and career politicians, such as Vice President Osmeña.[16] Of all the different organizations of Commonwealth-era economic nationalism, NEPA was publicly the most patriotic and reactionary. However, this had more to do with its officially quasi-state status rather than any deep ideological exceptionalism.

During the Commonwealth era, NEPA would pave the way for President Quezon to launch more explicitly state-backed protectionist entities: the National Economic Council and the National Development Company.[17] Due to Japan's colonial occupation of the Philippines in 1941, it is difficult to tell whether protectionism would have benefited the broad population of the Philippines as NEPA promised. However, it is clear that the National Economic Council and National Development Company were successful in accumulating capital for the already wealthy, siphoning public funds into private and elite hands. Thus, the protectionist logic of economic nationalism, which was spearheaded by Filipino capitalists touting "Native" trade and "Native" economic security, in many ways worked for Filipino capitalists, who asymmetrically benefited from the economic security it provided.[18]

In addition to the intensification of economic nationalism, the Great Depression restaged debates over Philippine decolonization in new ways. This is especially clear in the U.S. Congressional hearings for the 1932 Hawes-Cutting bill. Like the 1930 deliberations over the anti-Filipino Welch bill (which demanded the banning and repatriation of Filipino migrants in the United States), the Congressional hearings were saturated by debates over the economic consequences of U.S. Empire. The primary question of the hearings was centered around "economic security," or the securitization of capitalism after Philippine national sovereignty. During the hearings, clashing narratives of capitalist security and insecurity would come to light. On one side, those in favor of maintaining colonialism narrated a history of Philippine economic insecurity. On the other side, those in favor of decolonization narrated a history of Filipino responsibility and security, with the monetary and banking systems held up as evidence of capable decision-making.

For advocates against decolonization, Philippine independence would lead to insecurity and catastrophe. The loudest voice of this perspective during the hearings was the Hoover administration, represented by Secretary of War Patrick J. Hurley. The secretary's language was especially paternalist, positioning Filipinos as a race that had yet to reach maturity— socially, politically, and especially economically. Granting independence would go against the natural order of a more advanced nation (the United States) supervising and guiding the less advanced nation (the Philippines) along the path of political and economic modernity.[19] The Philippines, after all, was radically dependent on U.S. trade, not only for economic vitality, but also for political and social stability. Because U.S. trade accounted for almost double all other combined foreign trade, it would be economic suicide if the Philippines lost its colonial privilege of tariff-free trade.[20]

Hurley explicitly connected what he saw as the racial incapacity of Filipinos to ensure capitalist security in the archipelago and the racial incapacity of Filipinos for self-government. Like numerous American imperial officials before him, Hurley kept the criteria for sovereignty conveniently vague, arguing: "All the measures necessary for the attainment of economic independence c[ould] not be determined in advance."[21] What was especially clear in the secretary's mind was a terrifying future of antiauthoritarian disorder if the United States left the Islands to Filipino self-government. "Until the Filipino people have made greater progress toward economic independence," he warned, "political independence would merely invite chaos and revolution."[22] Unconditional decolonization would therefore lead to "financial crisis," "widespread bank failures," and the "loss of public and private deposits." These economic disruptions would set off a chain reaction in terms of social and political crisis: "widespread unemployment and discontent; public disorders which the weakened government would be helpless to repress; revolution; chaos; and absorption by some stronger power." These catastrophes would not only have dire local consequences, but they would severely hamstring any interventions by the ill-prepared and incapable Filipino-run government. These catastrophes in the former colony would have broader geopolitical consequences for it would ultimately, according to Hurley, "weaken the power and prestige of the United States."[23]

The nebulous and ever-oscillating criteria for independence was strongly condemned by the Philippine Commission for Independence, the special committee formed by Filipino statesmen advocating for conditional decolonization in Washington, DC. In making their case, the commission referred to a series of tariff acts imposed by the United States on the Philippines. These warnings would prove true after two decades of free trade with the United States that would create "artificial conditions" for the Philippine economy.[24] After over three decades of "free trade" with the United States, Philippine industry specialized in only a handful of commodities desired by American markets. Defined mainly by monocrops and undermechanized production, the Philippines was completely unprepared to globally compete with industrialized and diversified economies, especially during the Depression. To avoid this dreaded scenario, the commission proposed a "readjustment" period of five years in which to diversify the nation's economy. Readjustment would also entail stabilizing local "economic conditions" and setting "economic development on solid and lasting foundations" and simultaneously maintaining tariff-free access to the U.S. market.[25]

Readjustment was a prime example of conditional decolonization, a way of buying time for Filipino capitalists while simultaneously maintaining economic security in the archipelago. To assuage American doubts that Filipinos held the capacity to "readjust" the economy within five years, the commission held up as evidence the securitization of the colonial monetary and banking systems throughout the 1920s. Indeed, the stability of Philippine currency, government debt, and government-backed credit was a particular source of pride for Filipino statesmen. This performance of stability was especially significant during the insecure times of the Great Depression, a period that saw many other currencies—both imperial and colonial—become wildly unstable. As commission member Manuel Roxas proudly proclaimed, the Depression had "not had any effect on the currency of the Philippine Islands" while the "currencies of other countries have faltered or actually depreciated."[26]

Roxas would push the language of racial capitalist paternalism into an affirmation of Philippine independence. The Filipino statesman asserted that "the task America had set out to accomplish in the Philippines is completed." "We do not contend that the Filipinos have reached the highest peak of progress and culture and economic advancement attainable," Roxas continued, "but we believe we have reached the limit of progress, advancement, and education in democracy that we can achieve under American guardianship."[27] With these words, Roxas predicted how postcolonial national sovereignty did not contradict a world order structured by racial capitalism and imperial states. Instead, the Philippines would be the "broadcasting station for America's ennobling principles," teaching "the subject peoples of the world that the road to freedom is through self-training, self-education, self-mastery, and discipline" and not "armed or violent revolution." For Roxas, therefore, Philippine decolonization—based on racial paternalism and capitalist security—would serve as an aspirational narrative that could be held up for "India, Indochina, Korea, Java, and all of those other countries inhabited by dependent peoples."[28] Conditional decolonization in the Philippines, therefore, would necessitate the continued existence of U.S. imperial and racial capitalist power, not only in the Philippines, but for the entire colonial world.

In 1932, the U.S. Congress would pass the Hare-Hawes-Cutting Act. The act promised to recognize the Philippines as a sovereign nation-state after a period of ten years.[29] Although both outgoing U.S. President Herbert Hoover and the Philippine Senate eventually rejected the Hare-Hawes-Cutting Act, the political momentum proved far too strong. The act was revived with some provisional changes in the Tydings-McDuffie Act of 1934, which concretized a ten-year timeline for Philippine independence. The act would also establish the Philippines as a U.S. commonwealth rather than a U.S. possession. Commonwealth status meant the complete Filipinization of the legislative and executive branches of the colonial state. The Philippine political realm would soon belong completely to Filipino leaders. However, Filipino sovereignty, which is to say Filipino decision-making, would be limited to the colonial territory. So-called foreign relations policies, in particular authority over military and economic security, would remain under U.S. sovereignty. Of these two, capitalist security would be the greatest public obsession of Filipino economic experts during the Commonwealth era.

Monetary authority would play a highly significant role in illustrating the political fitness of Filipino decision-makers as it was ready to transition to commonwealth status. In August 1935, Filipino bureaucrats would boast of how the Philippine currency remained "strong and sound." As evidence, the acting Insular treasurer reported that the cash reserves had a surplus that exceeded the 25 percent legal limit by almost P17 million. Proving the Philippine Commonwealth's continued tie to the United States was the substantial amount of the reserves deposited in U.S. Federal Reserve banks as well as private repositories, such as Chase National Bank. Cash reserves were additionally in the combination of over P4.6 million and $1.6 million, illustrating how much of the Philippine monetary system remained entangled with the U.S. dollar.[30]

In the minds of Philippine statesmen, economic security would only be recognized by American authorities if the Philippine monetary system remained bound to the U.S. dollar. Loyalty to U.S. Empire would be the official position of the Commonwealth government, with Commonwealth President Manuel Quezon in 1934 declaring that "there is no foundation for the belief that a change in the Philippine currency is being contemplated."[31] Despite this promise, however, other Filipinos would not be so publicly loyal to U.S. Empire. A new kind of critique would emerge in the years around the Commonwealth's founding. This critique claimed that economic security could only be achieved through increased autonomy from U.S. rule and more fidelity to the natural laws of the global capitalist system.

Filipino Expertise, Fantasies of Gold,
and the Wish for Monetary Authority

Throughout the 1930s, majoritarian arguments for conditional decolonization were buttressed by Filipino economic expertise. Filipino experts desired authority over an autonomous monetary system in the Philippines, challenging U.S. Empire without fundamentally undermining its racial and colonial logic. Instead, Filipino experts deployed normative notions of racial hierarchies to question the utility of American racial paternalism and the artificiality of U.S. imperial policy. At the same time, unlike previous generations of

American authorities, Filipino experts declared themselves possessors of both "Native" and "universal" market knowledge that remained beyond the comprehension of Americans and other foreigners. Arguing against "aping the ways of other governments," Filipino experts instead proposed to pursue economic planning grounded in a "scientific attitude about the approach to any problem."[32]

Interrogating U.S. imperial sovereignty through market knowledge rather than through political rights or nationalist protectionism was a radical departure from previous anti-imperialist critiques. In this, Filipino experts of the 1930s adopted much of the rhetorical logic deployed by American experts in the 1910s and 1920s. For over three decades American experts grounded these economic critiques in the basis of racial capacities of colonial subjects to perform intellectual and manual labor. Filipino experts inherited this kind of American expertise, not necessarily through formal education, but rather through the day-to-day grind of administering state policies through bureaucratic offices. Many became experts through the experience of working within a constantly changing colonial state, under American bureaucrats, auditors, and advisors, formally educated in economics, business, or accounting.[33] Subsequently, the majority of these experts professionally cut their teeth in the 1920s, during the brutal public debates over the PNB crisis. The language of efficiency and utility, therefore, saturated many of their economic critiques during the lead-up to, and initial years of, the Commonwealth period.

One of the primary terrains of anti-American criticism was the monetary system. An eventual governor of the future Central Bank of the Philippines, Andres V. Castillo, declared in 1936 that the "currency problem" was "the most delicate and complicated of our economic problems." As one of the first possessors of a doctorate in economics in the Philippine government, Castillo believed himself privy to what had been "a sealed mystery to the great mass." As "the currency systems of the world have been undergoing radical changes even those that have been most stable, our currency system," had "suffered in common with the rest."[34] Loyalty toward the U.S. dollar had failed to protect the Philippines from the effects of worldwide capitalist crisis, a universal affliction that every nation on the planet felt "in common." Whether the devaluation profit would be inevitably credited to the Philippines, Castillo argued that the Commonwealth should nevertheless pursue an independent monetary system.[35]

Another primary concern for experts was what they considered U.S. Empire's unpaid debt to the Philippines. Beginning in 1933, the United

States decided to manipulate the gold value of the dollar. Pressured by an American bloc of agribusiness owners, industrialists, bankers, and other corporate interests desperate to get prices back to pre–Great Depression levels, newly elected U.S. President Franklin Delano Roosevelt signed Executive Order 6102 dedicated to slowing down the Depression's monetary crisis. The executive order had three main consequences for the U.S. economy. First, it outlawed the possession or trade of gold as money by citizens and subjects anywhere in the world. Second, it required all gold to be deposited in the Federal Reserve. Third, it embargoed the exportation of gold. In tandem with the executive order, Roosevelt declared a Banking Holiday, which shut down the banking system throughout the empire for several days. According to Filipino authorities, this would lead to a massive loss of profits for the Philippine economy, which had not been as deeply affected by the Depression as the settler metropole.[36] The following year, as a reinforcement of the executive order, Congress enacted the 1934 Gold Reserve Act, which required all personal gold and gold certificates to be deposited into the U.S. Treasury and set an artificial dollar price on gold, thus devaluing the dollar's worth in gold.[37] Consequently, $2 billion of the profits from the devaluation of the dollar were put into the establishment of a federal fund to stabilize exchange against foreign currencies.[38]

Once the U.S. dollar left gold, so too did the Philippine peso. As a result, no longer was the Philippines on a gold-exchange standard with the United States, but rather it was on a formal dollar-exchange system.[39] The peso was now bound by law to back its currency, not by the value of an idealized metal, but strictly by the U.S. economy.[40] At first, devaluation was thought to be beneficial to the Philippines. In April 1934, the joint Philippine-American government headed by Murphy, Quezon, and Osmeña announced that the government, due to its U.S. gold deposits, was set to make approximately P47 million in net profit. Some in the Philippine business community championed this profit as a triumph second only to the passing of the Tydings-McDuffie Act. Some others, additionally, had opinions on what to do with the unexpected windfall. Many opportunists suggested buying U.S. bonds to safeguard against future national debt, while others recommended injecting the money into local circulation in order to augment the growth of national businesses. Acting Secretary of Finance Vicente Singson Encarnacion, taking a different and more long-term approach, announced from Washington, DC, that he was drafting a plan to use the money to establish an autonomous central bank and currency system.[41]

None of these options were ever realized, however, since the United States refused to pay this debt during the life of the Commonwealth government. Philippine economic experts would subsequently fixate on the debt. Later termed the "devaluation profit" by Filipinos, the debt was frequently fought over during the political debates leading to the Tydings-McDuffie Act. It would remain deferred throughout the Commonwealth's life.[42] Indeed, not until the end of Japanese occupation in 1945 would the U.S. Congress add the amount owed into the reparation fund for the reconstruction of the newly independent Philippine Republic.[43] Obsessed with the devaluation profit, experts demanded repayment through a logic that was simultaneously anti-imperial and reactionary.

After the U.S. dollar abandoned gold, Filipino experts would claim that forcing the Philippine currency to leave gold would have several devastating consequences. First, the gold content of the dollar value was changed to such an extent that major discrepancies with the gold content of the peso value caused mass confusion, particularly in trade and currency conversion with countries other than the United States. Second, according to Filipino experts, the deflation of the dollar—the proposed solution to raising American prices back to pre-Depression levels—caused undue hardship in the Philippines, whose local prices and purchasing power remained at the same Depression-era levels. Third, despite being nominally on a gold-exchange standard, the Philippine monetary system was nevertheless bound to the whims of the dollar's value, again restricting trade possibilities with other countries and limiting the growth of new capital.[44]

In November 1936, Auditor General Hernandez dredged up seemingly long-buried memories of this imperial debt. Written just over a year after the establishment of the Philippine Commonwealth, Hernandez's article provides a glimpse of the Philippine state's difficulties governing under conditions of political decolonization. To illustrate the Philippines' lack of authority, Hernandez recalled the unilateral decision made by the U.S. federal government in 1933 to go against the gold standard and artificially reinflate the value of the dollar back to levels before the Great Depression. Unlike the United States who "profited by the devaluation of the dollar," the Philippine Treasury saw no profits and only losses. Despite the fact that both Americans and Filipinos recognized this debt, according to Hernandez, the odds of repayment were "very problematical," reminding the Philippine public that "an independent currency system" was one "of the major questions that require immediate attention and proper solution by the Commonwealth Government."[45]

Rather than dwell on the question of monetary repayment of the debt, however, Hernandez shifted attention to an alternative form of settlement: namely substituting monetary liberty for monetary debt. Hernandez was troubled by the automatic dependency of the peso to the dollar; a dependency that he believed was determined not by the natural laws of the capitalist market but by political constraints. "Owing to the difference in the economic and financial conditions of the United States and the Philippine Islands," he reasoned, "I see no valid reason for tying up the Peso to the Dollar." Underscoring difference, Hernandez asserted that the "purposes and problems of Philippine currency" were not only "not identical with those of the United States dollar," but in reality, "may be inimical." In its stead he proposed an independent Philippine currency that would be "more economical" and "better adapted to our present economic condition."[46]

In addition to imperial debt, arguments for national economic liberty and a Philippine monetary authority were additionally situated within the language of war and self-defense. As early as 1933, for instance, the head of the Economics Department at National University, Jose Celeste, asserted that in "economic warfare, currency has been used as one of the effective weapons." Entrenched in the Great Depression, Celeste argued that an economic war was being waged between nationalists and internationalists. On one side were those whose motives were "mainly their desires for national economic advantage rather than an interest in world recovery." On the other side were those "who stress above all else the importance of a stable medium of international exchange."[47] Because the peso and the Philippine economy were subject to currency manipulations made in Washington, DC, Celeste's critique of a unilateral nationalist monetary policy was aimed directly at the United States.

Challenging the supposed uneconomical relationship between the peso and the dollar, Celeste grounded his call for an autonomous monetary system in the essentialized difference between the Philippines and the United States. "The main objective, therefore, of an independent system" and "absolute control in currency," reasoned Celeste, was "to enable the country to manage it in accordance with its conception of its own needs." Without complete authority over an autonomous monetary system, Celeste continued, "the Philippines will always be forced to follow whatever policy they have in the United States and, considering that the conditions in these two countries are different, it cannot be expected that a reform of the currency in the United States which is calculated to improve its conditions, will also bring the same result here." For Celeste, the solution was clear. "It is better and safer for the Islands to have an independent currency system."[48]

Arguments for an autonomous monetary system were deeply tied to a nostalgic wish to return to the gold standard. In 1933, Celeste asserted that "the Gold Exchange Standard, our present system, would still be the best for an independent Philippines."[49] A few years later, Hernandez proposed rejecting the "Philippine-American exchange standard" in order to adopt "an independent gold standard."[50] This logic was based on the notion that a gold-exchange standard, unfettered to any particular imperial nation, would enable more autonomy from U.S. Empire. For Celeste, true national independence meant the removal of "the defects which are not inherent to the system but are forced upon it by virtue of our political relation with the United States."[51] By removing the unnatural defects that were artificially attached to the Philippine monetary system by American colonial authorities, the peso could be deployed to promote new trade partnerships with other nations and speed up economic recovery. Despite the fact that the monetary system had already operated as a dollar-exchange system since the 1920s, Celeste nevertheless desired to remove what he believed to be the artificial political constraints of the American imperial state from one supposedly more natural: the gold-exchange standard.[52]

Another goal of experts was to achieve monetary authority. This entailed the establishment of a central bank. A central bank was seen as necessary in properly mediating between the national economy and the global capitalist system primarily through controlling a country's currency and credit supply. Through a central bank, a postcolonial Philippine government could ideally redistribute currency funds from U.S. reserves into other countries' central banks, advancing trade and easing payments with those countries. For instance, former Secretary of Finance Vicente Singson Encarnacion in 1934 declared that "however good the monetary system that we have may be, if we do not have a Central Bank to safeguard its stability and integrity in the market, we shall always be confronted with economic stagnation if not absolute economic failure."[53]

Encarnacion emphasized the necessary co-constitution of a centralized Philippine monetary authority and a completely sovereign Philippine government. Because political independence from empire was still contingent upon the achievement of proper representative democracy, Encarnacion argued that the central bank should be "intimately linked with the government of the nation." In addition, he supported the belief that a democratically elected government should be empowered to appoint the central bank's governor and vice governor, as well as maintain "rigid and constant supervision of its reserves and its operations." Still, in regard to a monetary authority, Encarnacion distrusted the state and the political realm in general. "It is," he warned, "very dangerous for the government to have absolute control of the monetary system." Liberty from both the American imperial state and the Philippine state would guarantee that decisions concerning the national economy would be kept "far from the control and easy manipulation of politics."[54]

The establishment of a Philippine central bank, free from politically motivated constraints, would thus have the capacity to wield the monetary system for the continued growth of the nation's wealth. In response to colonial doubts that the Philippines remained too "undeveloped" to soundly wield authority over money, Encarnacion pointed to several resolutions passed in international financial and economic conferences in 1920 and 1934. Rather than rely on measurements of Philippine racial capacities made by American authorities, Encarnacion looked to an international congregation of finance and economic experts. In these conferences, international experts asserted that there was "no better medium for the development of credit in a gradual and healthy way in any country than through the establishment of a Central Bank."[55] Encarnacion thus deployed the language of an international body of experts to argue for an autonomous monetary system and central bank. Moreover, these foreign experts were not only concerned with their respective economies, but also with the stabilization of the entire world monetary order and the global capitalist system. Encarnacion's support for the establishment of a central bank, therefore, was not merely a nationalist performance. Instead, he believed that a Philippine central bank would not only benefit the national economy, but also through cooperation with other monetary authorities around the world, a Philippine central bank would help securitize the ever-expanding growth of the global capitalist system as a whole.

Expert demands would additionally dovetail with a new American fetish for gold mining in the Philippines. In the first years of the Depression, Americans paid close attention to the Philippine gold mining industry and how to continue to profit from it, even after the increased autonomy of the islands. The governor general insisted in using the newly mined gold for the Philippine reserves held in U.S. banks.[56] Subsequently American authorities became deeply invested in policing the exportation of recently mined gold. According to Roosevelt's executive order, gold mined in the Philippines could only leave the colony to be deposited with the U.S.

Mint.[57] On the quotidian level, Americans made sure gold exportation would remain beyond the control of Filipino officials, stating: "the intervention of a Philippine Officer is not contemplated nor would it appear to be necessary in connection with the deposit of gold."[58] Smuggling would also occupy the minds of American authorities. Those who were conventionally racialized as foreign and alien, particularly the Chinese, were frequently under surveillance.[59]

The Filipino public would also speculate on gold, especially in the years leading up to the founding of the Commonwealth. A critical mass of gold mining companies would be rapidly established. Many amateur investors would also pour their savings into gold, a seemingly natural commodity that investors would flock to during times of capitalist crisis. This would create a financial bubble in anything related to gold, especially as more of the mineral was discovered in the so-called uncivilized frontiers of the archipelago.[60] As one article publicized, many would lose what little income they received in the daily fluctuations of gold stocks.[61]

Filipino experts, at the same time, similarly speculated on the gold resources of the Philippines, fantasizing about how the nation's gold would provide the foundation on which a new and independent Philippine monetary system could flourish. The notion that the land of the nation would naturally contain wealth that would provide for a postindependence state during a time of crisis was a seductive one. The return to the supposed naturalness of gold and the gold standard, a universal standard of value, was thus paradoxically analogous to the supposed naturalness of Native control of national wealth. This return to Native control, however, did not threaten capitalist security, but instead it placed capitalism on even more secure grounds.

The public and expert turn to the earth itself was perhaps a wish for a stable source of wealth within a political and economic world whose grounds remained unsettled. Castillo saw gold as key to achieving an independent monetary system despite the ongoing effects of the Depression.

> We are a gold producing country, our yearly production amounts to about P40,000,000, and we could buy this gold and use them as reserves. The establishment of a Central Bank is part of the reform to be carried out and shall have the monopoly of note issue; it shall also be the keeper of the gold reserves for the currency. The Central Bank shall issue its notes to pay for the necessary amount of gold reserves.[62]

For Castillo, the desire to base an independent Philippine monetary system on gold mined from the nation was simultaneously a desire to latch onto something that was seemingly more natural to achieve a greater sense of security and autonomy.

Castillo's wish for an independent monetary system and monetary authority was a desire for greater security in a gravely insecure world. Worldwide recovery from the Depression still remained a faint horizon, while the Commonwealth's economic future under the political constraints of decolonization remained precarious. By mining into the depths of the nation, with the intent to expropriate wealth from every prehistoric cavity held within the nation's imagined and policed territory, Castillo hoped to create a new standard, a new order from which to base an autonomous economy. In Castillo's mind, true liberty from U.S. Empire entailed not only the extraction of the nation's long dormant wealth but also to convert the nation's wealth into money. This money would not, however, simply circulate within the nation, but it would be offered up to the world market, to circulate through the governance of a Philippine central bank.

Various plans for a central bank and an autonomous monetary system based on gold would continue well into the Commonwealth era. One Filipino lawmaker, Benito Solivan, for instance, introduced a bill in 1937 to create an independent national currency based on a classical gold standard. Solivan's plan was based mainly on the devaluation profit of P47 million owed by the United States. The U.S. Congress, however, refused to pay this debt without hard evidence that the 1933–1934 devaluation policies harmed the Philippine economy rather than aided recovery. Since the United States continued to refuse to acknowledge its debt to the Philippines, Solivan looked instead to gold. Solivan reasoned that the mid-1930s boom in Philippine gold mining would provide the reserves necessary to back the new currency.[63] In the end, Solivan's plan would fail to gain traction with other, less speculative, Filipino lawmakers. Indeed, all these Commonwealth plans to change the monetary system to the gold or gold exchange standard eventually failed. Despite this, the desire to return to a gold-based system nevertheless illustrates the uncertain confidence Filipino experts had in the U.S. dollar and, more broadly, the U.S. imperial economy during the 1930s.

Not all Filipino experts would argue for an independent currency based on a nostalgic notion of gold. For instance in 1937, Miguel Cuaderno, the future (and first) governor of the Central Bank of the Philippines, argued that the Philippines, over the last thirty years, had "stood the test of time better than the experience of many of the principal countries, not excepting the United States." This economic security was dependent on stable exchange rates and relative prices, all of which were enabled by the U.S. dollar. For Cuaderno, cutting ties with the U.S. dollar would mean disaster for Philippine trade, creating even more insecurities for an international capitalist system increasingly unstable due to militaristic aggression, protectionism, and credit scarcity. Cuaderno even addressed the fantasy of going back to gold, either through the gold mined from the Philippines or purchasing gold with the U.S. dollars held in reserve by the Commonwealth government. For both options, the high price of gold bullion would end up creating a more insecure base for the Philippine monetary system. As a consequence, Cuaderno asserted that conditional decolonization, one that economically relied on the United States, was far more secure. This was especially true in a time when "the principal countries of the world" were "still grappling with huge problems of currency stabilization," and "the future of our trade and financial relationship with the United States" remained unknown. As a consequence, it would be "untimely and illogical to discard a monetary system which has served the country comparatively well." In the end, to ensure the economic security of conditional decolonization meant the simple continuation of the colonial monetary status quo.[64]

The Threat of Unconditional Decolonization

Although the Depression was unevenly felt throughout the archipelago, and was often dependent on regional markets, local economies, and ecological vicissitudes, it nevertheless commonly shaped the everyday experiences of workers and peasants.[65] The shrinking of export markets in the United States and the ensuing hoarding panic by capitalists and financiers in the Philippine colony had drastically contracted the circulation of money in the early 1930s. For those in the nonindustrialized colonies, global capitalist crisis made structural poverty even more acute. The colony's money supply decreased from 124 million pesos in 1929 to 88 million pesos in 1932, and it would not be until 1937 that the money supply would return to pre-Depression levels.[66] After a tour of the agricultural provinces of central Luzon, the governor general at the time, Theodore Roosevelt Jr., asserted that although he saw no money being exchanged, he also saw no one starving.[67] Roosevelt most likely disavowed or misrecognized the deteriorating situation in the rural provinces of central and northern Luzon. For although people might not have been visibly starving, they had most likely accrued devastating debt in order to survive.[68]

Money shortage led to manifold intraregion traders, retailers, money-lenders, and landowners losing access to bank loans or credit, which in turn led to a drastic scarcity of loans to tenant farmers or landless workers.[69] For the first three decades of colonial rule, American authorities constantly attempted to institutionalize rural and agrarian credit. This concern over rural credit did not change during the Great Depression. For instance, American experts, such as "money doctor" Edwin Kemmerer, would again be employed by the colonial state to give advice on agricultural banking and rural credit.[70] Imported American expertise would do little for impoverished peasants already reeling from the effects of the global economic crisis. Moneylenders or landowners, moreover, in the face of economic uncertainty panicked and either violently recalled loans or charged even more exorbitant interest rates. Unregulated and informal credit practices, frequently publicly denounced as usury, proliferated.[71] This is especially apparent in the antiusury campaigns and propaganda that saturated the public at the time.[72]

At the same time, even if tenant farmers and landless workers found alternate ways to navigate the market without access to cash, taxes and other municipal government fees forced many to enter into asymmetrical and exploitative credit agreements with predatory lenders. As the Philippine Bank commissioner stated in 1933, the "common taos" remained in the "clutches of the loan sharks." Subsequently, the bank commissioner suggested using the PNB to lower interests, so that private banks may follow suit.[73] It would take several years, however, for the Philippine Commonwealth to actualize any bank to deal with the problem of predatory debt for peasants in the provinces. By the time the Agricultural and Industrial Bank was created in 1940, the Philippines was on the cusp of being occupied by Japanese forces.[74]

Those in the rice-growing regions in central Luzon in the early 1930s were especially hard hit by these material conditions. Desires to mechanize the mode of production and lower wages by capitalist landowners, the tightening or shutting down of customary interest-free food credit by traders and landowners, the swollen amount of refugee populations from other regions due to rampant dispossession during the 1920s, and the increased exportation of rice to other export-oriented regions: all of these contingencies led to an increasing number of tenant farmers and agricultural workers finding themselves caught in a seemingly hopeless economic cycle of debt and dispossession.[75] Subsequently, Commonwealth authorities declared a rice crisis during the mid-1930s, exacerbating already existing problems of poverty and debt.

According to President Quezon, Filipinos like "most other Orientals" were existentially dependent on rice. During the period of American colonial rule, Filipinos had become artificially reliant on imported rice that had reached over P25 million a year in imports. Despite seemingly being able to grow enough rice locally, the combination of price manipulations by speculative rice merchants, and mistimed floods and typhoons, had led to "a growing discontent on the part of the rice growers, especially the tenants or kasamas, who are earning less than is required for the bare necessities of life."[76] Consequently, the provinces surrounding Manila rapidly became, at least according to the Philippine press, a frontier populated by violent riots, spontaneous uprisings, and lawless bandits.[77] These provinces surrounding the north of Manila, like Nueva Ecija, Pangasinan, and Bulacan, became the primary hotbeds for organized labor and militant activism.[78]

Despite these economic pressures, farmers and peasants experimented with new modes of collective survival. Although they remained trapped within the circuits of capital, they nevertheless developed creative ways to share what little resources they held in common. Some, for instance, practiced a "share-the-poverty" practice, in which tenant farmers paid landless workers a percentage of the harvest before splitting the harvest with the landlord. Others used the *pulot* (to retrieve from the ground) custom, which allowed first access to those in most economic need to collect discarded grain thought to be worthless to the market and thus commonly accessible.[79] Others would develop a makeshift cooperative credit system, in which machines would be collectively owned and available for cheap rent to each member.[80] All these instances illuminate peasant survival strategies that were not complete refusal or flight, but rather were an attempt to bend the technologies of modernity away from the logic of private property toward a more ethical form of life in common.

Peasant social experiments and forms of life created fertile ground for novel articulations of labor and radical organizing. Many of the worker organizations or labor unions that had existed in the 1920s, such as the Kalipunang Pambansa ng mga Magsasaka sa Pilipinas (National Association of Peasants in the Philippines), saw a significant increase in membership.[81] One labor organizer recalled that although many might not have officially paid the membership dues, depending on the region, most likely 10 to 40 percent of agricultural workers identified as part of the Kalipunang Pambansa ng mga Magsasaka sa Pilipinas.[82] In addition to well-known unions such as the Kalipunang Pambansa ng mga Magsasaka sa Pilipinas, there were countless others, with varying membership numbers and diverse compositions, but nevertheless expressing similar critiques and making analogous demands.[83] Mounting organized militancy in the hinterlands was anxiously scrutinized by the urban public, as illustrated by the proliferation of Manila newsprint stories concerning tenant strikes, petitions, and protests.[84] Many of these new radical organizations tapped into these makeshift solidarities, economic networks, and commonly held experiences of exploitation under racial and colonial capitalism. Those in power—American officials, Filipino elite, and wealthy landowners— became increasingly unsettled by these collective survival techniques, especially as organized movements became more militantly anticolonial, antiracist, and anticapitalist. In the first half of the 1930s, the two most heavily policed militant organizations were the Partido Komunista ng Pilipinas (PKP; The Communist Party of the Philippines) and the Sakdalista movement.

The PKP was forged through deeply anticommunist colonial conditions. Since the 1917 Russian Revolution, the threat of an anti-colonial communist movement in the Philippines consistently gnawed at the minds of both American and Filipino authorities. Colonial presses during the late 1920s and 1930s would make a spectacle of the "red scare," nervously portraying it as a foreign threat to conditional decolonization.[85] Frequently, Filipino communism—which was simultaneously anticolonial, anticapitalist, and nationalist—would be lumped together with imperial, reactionary, and racist forms of nationalisms, fascism, and Nazism.[86]

Despite the public caricature of communism presented by colonial presses, authorities nevertheless remained genuinely nervous about communist notions of decolonization and anticapitalism. A primary example of this anticapitalist form of decolonization can be found in an earlier work of Crisanto Evangelista, a long-time labor organizer and a key founder of the PKP. In the short 1928 book *Nasyonalismo Proteksiyonismo vs. Internasyonalismo Radikal*, Evangelista emphasized what he saw as two possible political economic futures for the Philippines: nationalist protectionism or radical internationalism.[87] On one hand, there was the future proposed by Filipino protectionists, which would lead to racial chauvinism and an unproductive trade policy of isolationism. Chauvinism and isolationism would destroy international demand for Philippine commodities, leading to the rapid decline in commodity prices and wages and eventually mass unemployment. Filipino workers, desperate for work and wages, would flee the Philippines in even greater numbers to other territories that were under the "grasp of imperialism." These imperialized territories included Hawai'i, and even

Mindanao, which Evangelista argued was under the informal colonialism of "Foreign Investment."[88]

In opposition to nationalist protectionism, Evangelista proposed radical internationalism. Liberation had to be conceived as a radical overturning of the entire world, not simply the achievement of national sovereignty. "The independence of the Filipino people is dependent on the problem and the fate of the other colonies and semi-colonies," declared Evangelista.[89] This analysis was generalizing and systemic, focusing on the struggles of the colonized against the structures of an imperial world system. Rather than the "narrow, conservative, and reactionary nationalism" of Filipino statesmen and protectionists, the struggle for true Philippine decolonization necessitated a connection to the broader struggle of international anticolonialisms. As he proclaimed, "If we are freed, it would change the shape of colonialism in the world." Philippine decolonization, as Evangelista envisioned, could operate as "an outbreak of fire that would burn and smolder inside the people of Taiwan and Korea to fight against Japan; the Indonesian against the Netherlands; in Indo-China against France and Portugal; the Indians, the Malaysians and other English colonies against England."[90]

Despite Evangelista's belief that a proletariat revolution was imminent in the Philippines, immediately after its founding in 1930, the PKP was violently policed by anticommunist state authorities and public paranoia. In 1931, hundreds gathered in Manila to pay their respects to the suspicious death of charismatic communist leader Antonio Ora. Public anxieties arose over the explosive display of red flags leading up to Ora's funeral.[91] In response, state authorities outlawed any type of communist-related assembly or exhibitionism.[92] Violent clashes between protesting mourners and colonial police resulted in the jailing of hundreds.[93] After these clashes, the PKP was forced underground with a few members remaining in the public and organizing nominally as socialist parties or labor unions.[94]

After the establishment of the Philippine Commonwealth, the PKP was allowed to operate legally. State recognition, however, led to massive purges of the most revolutionary within the party. In the late 1930s, the PKP and the socialist party would officially merge.[95] The aboveground operations would almost immediately end as Japan colonized the Philippines in 1941. Communists were instantaneously outlawed by Japanese authorities, and soon Evangelista would be captured and executed, violently marking the end of organized communism's first wave in the Philippines. Although relatively short-lived, there was great anxiety on the part of Philippine and American authorities that the PKP could potentially ally with the Sakdalista movement, the largest radical threat to Filipino authorities for most of the 1930s.[96]

The Sakdal movement emerged in 1930 against white supremacist events in the Philippine colony and the settler metropole. The combination of anti-Filipino American vigilante violence in Watsonville, California, and a white American teacher's chronic abuse of high school students in Manila triggered a cascade of mass protest movements.[97] These expressions of public dissent against white supremacy and U.S. colonialism inspired Benigno Ramos, a disgruntled former Quezon supporter and colonial state official. Ramos would attempt to domesticate these insurgent energies through the establishment of a newspaper called *Sakdal* (accusation in Tagalog). The Sakdal movement, however, immediately unfolded in directions unintended and unforeseen by Ramos. Through the circulation of the *Sakdal* newspaper, a network of committed organizers and activists spanning Manila's agricultural hinterlands rapidly developed over the next two years. From this network emerged the Partido Sakdalista (Sakdal Party) on October 23, 1933, which captured a few congressional and provincial government seats. Although some of the rhetoric of certain organizers, leaders, and activists were peppered with millenarian language and a strange adulation of Japanese imperial power, Sakdalistas demanded urgent and concrete social, political, and economic justice. Many of their demands, moreover, were in direct response to the uneven and unjust distribution of economic wealth in the colony, a condition amplified by the Depression.[98]

Increased wages for agricultural and urban workers, the abolition of taxes, land redistribution and common ownership of property: these and other demands were clear calls for revolutionary change to the economic status quo of Philippine capitalist society. The demands of Sakdalistas, in addition, were inherently global. They understood that low wages, land dispossession, and ever-increasing debt were inextricably bound to the geopolitical relations among the Philippine colonial state, U.S. Empire, and the global capitalist system.[99] The growing political and organizing power of increasingly militant rural workers alarmed local and colonial state authorities. In response to constant harassment and arrests by police and believing the shift to commonwealth status as opportune political conditions, the more militant wings of the Sakdalistas organized an uprising on May 2, 1935. Lasting for a brief two days, poorly trained, equipped with rusted weapons, and awaiting popular support that never came, Sakdalistas were massacred in confrontations with constabulary forces. Dozens were killed and wounded, while hundreds were arrested and jailed.[100]

Although only lasting less than forty-eight hours, the insurgency sent shockwaves throughout the entire Philippines. The Sakdalista uprising especially unsettled American and Filipino authorities who were obsessed with administering the orderly political transition of the Philippines from Insular Possession to Commonwealth. A fact-finding committee, consisting of U.S. military officers, were deployed by the acting governor general to analyze the root cause of the uprising. The committee argued that economic insecurity was the primary reason for the insurgency. For the poor, life was "harder than before the depression."[101] Many were additionally "harassed with debts" and "had a family income of only a few pesos a month." The report then claimed that despite some of the Filipino national leaders having "sympathy with the bottom man" it was the "personnel in the machine between the leaders and the bottom strata, cloaked with power as provincial and municipal officials, and others of standing and means outside of the government service" who treated "the poor with scant attention."[102]

Unsurprisingly, American authorities placed sole blame on Filipino capitalists and politicians, not on the conditions created by U.S. colonialism. According to the report, those involved in the uprisings were ultimately misguided by their own people and subsequently suffered as a result. All in all, the report acted as an alibi for conditional decolonization, defending the continued semi-colonialism of the Commonwealth government and especially the continuation of American-style capitalism in the archipelago. Continuing the logic of racial paternalism, American authorities dismissed Sakdalista demands for unconditional decolonization, propagating instead a simple narrative of class discontent against the Filipino wealthy.

The Commonwealth government, run by the Quezon regime, would incorporate this narrative of class discontent into its public promise of social justice. For Quezon, social justice was synonymous with economic security and order. "The promotion of social justice," for Quezon, was "to insure the wellbeing and economic security of all the people.[103] To maintain order and security, Quezon would use state strategies of repression inherited from American colonial authorities. Through what was publicly called the "mailed fist" approach, the Commonwealth state would deploy local police, constabulary, and fascist militias to violently repress Sakdalistas, communists, socialists, and other various labor organizations.[104]

At the same time, the Quezon regime promoted what it called "progressive conservatism," a vow to resolve economic antagonisms without disturbing already existing racial and colonial hierarchies.[105] Similar to "New Deal" strategies in the U.S. settler metropole, Quezon would deploy "policies of attraction."[106] Through money, these policies intended to lure peasants and workers from revolutionary movements. Like the American colonial state, the Commonwealth eyed the CRF to bankroll different promises of land reform, increased minimum wages, state-backed credit, and infrastructural projects, such as irrigation and roads.[107] In 1938, for instance, the Agricultural and Industrial Bank was established with P150 million to supposedly benefit smaller landowners.[108]

Despite its highly publicized promises, the Commonwealth campaign of "Social Justice" failed to create any sense of economic security for the vast majority of Filipinos and only increased repression in the name of order. Average wages just before the 1941 Japanese occupation ranged between twenty-five and forty-five cents a day. Under the Commonwealth, wealth inequality remained severe. Poorer families averaged $62.50 a year, most of which was paid in kind. The top 1 percent of income earners, however, averaged $500 a year and accounted for over one-third of the total national income.[109] Moreover, even though this data indicates a monetary increase over the life of the Commonwealth, this increase did not correspond to the rising cost of commodities during the period. Thus, the immediate years before World War II witnessed a drastic disconnect between the rate of price inflation and real wages.[110] Radical leaders, for instance, reported that 1.5 million were unemployed by the end of the decade, a stark contrast from the official reports of the Commonwealth.[111] The combination of wage stagnation and rising unemployment, therefore, illustrates the failures of Quezon's "Social Justice" campaigns to adequately address the intensifying forms of economic injustice in the archipelago.

Militant organizers, activists, and union members doubted the Commonwealth state's rural credit strategy. They believed rural credit reforms would simply reinforce land title regimes that benefited large landowners and punished landless peasants.[112] Many former Sakdalistas would end up joining the socialist-led "United Front" radical movement from 1939 to 1941.[113] Some in the last years of the 1930s, however, would end up joining pro-Quezon paramilitary reactionary organizations such as the Kawal ng Kapayapaan (Soldiers of Peace), which publicly paraded as a conservative labor union.[114] Landowners would also pursue extra-state forms of antiradicalism, by bankrolling so-called labor organizations to actively clash with leftist groups. Many of these frictions and conflicts would occur in the rice- and sugar-growing provinces of Luzon, such as Tarlac, Bulacan, and Pampanga.[115]

Even as Japan steadily increased its colonial presence throughout East Asia in 1941, Quezon remained focused on programs of counter-decolonization. In a February address to the National Assembly, the Commonwealth president relayed the state's commitment to "social justice," chief of which was establishing "order to reduce evils." Order would come about mainly through the disbursement of credit and loans to fund infrastructural projects, real estate, and the resettlement of the unemployed into "non-Christian" lands. Several extra-state institutions, similar to the PNB and the Agricultural and Industrial Bank would also be established, such as the People's Homesite Corporation and the National Land Settlement Administration.[116]

The goal of these policies and institutions was to domesticate the surplus of unemployed and landless peasants and workers through financialized debt. For example, the PNB would disburse P1 million in loans to tenants and small farmers; the National Land Resettlement Administration would spend P1.5 million to acquire land to rent out to a hundred thousand new settlers; the People's Homesite Corporation would spend P2 million to build model home communities for low-income laborers to rent; and the Agricultural and Industrial Bank would have an initial capital of P25 million made available strictly as loans to agricultural and industrial capitalists. The Quezon regime, therefore, took advantage of the ongoing capitalist crisis caused by the Depression and the intensifying war in Europe to fund a panoply of pet projects and state corporations.[117] In the end, rather than social justice, all these publicly funded projects were counter-decolonization strategies, benefitting both the security of the Commonwealth state and the already wealthy.

The passage of the 1934 Tydings-McDuffie Act changed the colonial status of the Philippines from a possession to a commonwealth and set an official temporal limit of ten years of U.S. imperial sovereignty in the archipelago. The subsequent establishment of the Commonwealth government in 1935 was a moment of possibility for many, a liminal condition in which radical transformations of existing economic structures and relations were imaginable. Although these imaginations ranged wildly from fascist, to liberal, to nationalist, and even to revolutionary, they nevertheless expressed anxieties over the limitations of Filipino sovereignty within a planet structured by racism, capitalism, and empire. Reactionary logics such as protectionism, paternalism, and expertise proposed different ways of carving out Philippine autonomy without challenging the normative structures of the world. Concepts such as racial difference, the capitalist market, and gold became naturalized objects utilized for "Native" Filipino monetary authority. Although varied, all these forms of reactionary logics affirmed the notion of "naturalness" of Filipino authorities versus the artificiality of U.S. imperial sovereignty.

These reactionary logics, nevertheless, coalesced to repress the possibilities of unconditional decolonization. The Depression, after all, also created conditions in which social experiments and antagonisms against and beyond racial and colonial capitalism could be felt, enacted, and imagined. These collective movements were sources of insecurity and appeared to monetary authorities merely as disorder, threatening the very foundations of the Commonwealth state. Through counter-decolonization tactics, the Commonwealth state would perform its fantasy of sovereignty on the local level and on Native bodies and practices. Although harshly repressed by state and extra-state forces, the revolutionary energies of unconditional decolonization would live on beyond the Commonwealth. These revolutionary desires would continue to haunt the Japanese colonial occupation during World War II and even after the Philippines' nominal independence in 1946.

Conclusion: Decolonization

Except in a few instances, every independent country in the world today has a central bank. Our country is now free and independent and in the exercise of its right of economic self-determination, it is its earnest desire to lay the foundation of our currency and banking system on a sound basis, and to administer it so that the system will promote a rising level of production, employment and real income.

Miguel Cuaderno, *Guideposts to Economic Stability and Progress*

The Filipino moves about in an American-made world.... The value of his peso depends entirely on the value of the American dollar. The very home he lives in (if he lives in the city) is virtually American-made: the corrugated iron roof, the nails in the walls, the electric light bulbs, the electric wiring and switches, the kitchen utensils, the plates and spoons, his toothbrush, the bed clothes, the ring with which he weds his wife. And finally, of American make, are the guns, the tanks, the planes, the artillery, the vehicles, and even the uniforms of the troops that have been used to shoot down the Filipino people who would like to see a Filipino-made future for their children.

Luis Taruc, *Born of the People*

These epigraphs were written in the immediate years after the Philippines' supposed national independence. The first quote is from Miguel Cuaderno's speech titled "The Philippine Currency and Banking System" and the second quote is from Luis Taruc's autobiography. Cuaderno, on one hand, was a proto-technocrat, one of the so-called founding fathers of the Philippines and the first president of the Central Bank of the Philippines (Bangko Sentral ng Pilipinas). Taruc, on the other hand, was a communist guerilla, one of the leaders of the Hukbahalap (later called the Huks). The Huks were an anticolonial militant organization that took up arms to fight against Japanese imperialism during World War II. They would continue their armed insurgency by resisting the repression of both U.S. imperialism and the newly independent Philippine state. For the Huks, the Philippine government merely reproduced colonial conditions in which the poor remained unfree and the wealthy remained in power. On one hand, Cuaderno believed the key to Philippine decolonization was capitalism. On the other hand, Taruc believed the key to Philippine decolonization was communism.

Normatively considered a time of transition, historians mark the immediate years after World War II as the era of decolonization, the moment when the Philippines turned from colony to independent nation-state. Once nominally free, the postcolonial nation set out to erect a panoply of state institutions to prove its sovereignty to other capitalist nation-states. As Cuaderno declared in his speech, the establishment of the Central Bank signaled to the international community that the Philippines would be a chief collaborator in ensuring the economic security of domestic and international capitalism. The Central Bank, according to Cuaderno, would set out to increase "production, employment, and real income" and simultaneously illustrate the Philippine "right of economic self-determination."[1] For Taruc, however, as long as capitalism and imperialism existed, "self-determination" could never truly be achieved. Writing in 1949, he saw the "postcolonial" relationship between the Philippines, the United States, and global capitalism after World War II as simply a continuation of the colonialism of the last four centuries. Despite possessing state sovereignty, Taruc argued that the Philippines remained economically unsovereign, beholden to the U.S. imperial economy and global capitalism more broadly.

I shed light on these two quotes and these two figures to illustrate two incommensurable conceptions of decolonization. On one side was conditional decolonization and on the other side was unconditional decolonization. Proponents of conditional decolonization, such as Cuaderno, coveted the sovereign power of the state. They declared that the formerly colonized nation would wield monetary authority better than their former colonizers had. They were willing to maintain colonial systems and institutions as long as the colonizers relinquished monetary authority and sovereign power to a Filipino-led state. Under conditional decolonization, therefore, all the norms of racial and colonial capitalism were relatively guaranteed to be reproduced and passed down to "postcolonial" descendants. Moreover, conditional decolonization meant the rebranding of the imperial-state order as a nation-state system hierarchized according to race and driven by the logic of global capitalism. Under conditional decolonization, the world remained recognizable. On one side remained the wealthy and powerful peoples, rich from centuries of colonial and racial capitalism. On the other side remained the impoverished and vulnerable peoples, poor from centuries of colonial and racial capitalism.

Through the Central Bank, Cuaderno promised to wield monetary authority—an assemblage of policies, institutions, and knowledge—to ensure that decolonization profited both the colonized and the colonizer. The formerly colonized Philippines would benefit from the rules set up through racial capitalism and imperialism. Through the proper and sound management of capitalist money, the Central Bank would ideally lift the Philippines out of the category of poorer nations and into the wealthy. At the same time, the Central Bank would help securitize global capital flows that moved throughout, and capital that accumulated within, the Philippines. The prime benefactor of this securitization was the United States, as it was, by the end of World War II, the undisputed capitalist hegemon on the planet. At the same time, since the United States had gained the most from colonial and racial capitalism, it had the most to lose. This is why conditional decolonization, the transfer of state sovereignty from colonizer to colonized, was preferable to the alternative, unconditional decolonization.

As I observed through researching and writing this book, conditional decolonization could only exist in and through the threat of unconditional decolonization. While proponents of conditional decolonization desired ownership of their own piece of the recognizable world, those who desired unconditional decolonization sought to destroy the recognizable world. But what kind of world did they recognize? For them the world was racial, colonial, and capitalist. To Taruc, the postcolonial felt similar to the colonial. As he declared, the Filipino was "forced to move around in an American made world." The Filipino remained dependent on an environment saturated by U.S. commodities and money. This material unfreedom structured every moment of "postcolonial" life, the quotidian and the exceptional.

Capitalist money, moreover, had two opposing meanings to Cuaderno and Taruc. For Cuaderno, capitalist money was a pathway to exercising the sovereign right of economic self-determination. For Taruc, even if Philippine currency became Filipinized, capitalist money ultimately remained beholden to imperial forces. As Taruc argued "the value of his peso depends entirely on the value of the American dollar." And it was capitalist money, extracted from Filipino resources, labor, and consumption, that led to the proliferation of more American-made weapons. Proponents of conditional decolonization, in the name of Philippine state sovereignty, then collaborated with U.S. Empire, deploying militarized violence against Filipinos who desired unconditional decolonization. Taruc thus succinctly captured how and why conditional decolonization—which is the securitization of the recognizable world of racial capitalism and racial empires—was radically dependent on the fear of unconditional decolonization.

Throughout this book I explored the role of monetary authority as a crucial component in strategies of counter-decolonization. For over four decades in the American colonial Philippines, monetary authority utilized the colonial monetary and banking system to, on one hand, sustain counter-decolonization logistics and infrastructure and, on the other hand, police the economic activities of colonial society. To legitimize monetary authority, economic experts produced and deployed market knowledge. Crucial to market knowledge was its ability to naturalize and fortify colonial relations of power. Market knowledge naturalized racial hierarchies, the laws of the capitalist market, and the dependency of colonial sovereignty on monetary authority. Finally, I charted how monetary authority served as a terrain for political recognition, a terrain on which struggles between conditional and unconditional decolonization would also unfold.

Observing the late nineteenth century, I explored the ways desires for decolonization ultimately took two routes in the Philippine colony: conditional decolonization and unconditional decolonization. The former left intact imperial and racial capitalist structures in exchange for political sovereignty and the potential recognition of the nation. The latter demanded an absolutely different world, one in which colonial and racial capitalist structures were radically exorcised from social life. I traced how currency, taxation, banking, and labor systems were primary sites for demands for decolonization in the Philippines. Some demands were mere reforms, asking that increased authority over capitalist institutions and structures be possessed by Native hands. This would prove the racial capacity of Native Filipinos for sovereign power. Other demands, however, were a direct challenge to colonial and capitalist authority. The 1896 Revolution and a cacophony of labor strikes during the Philippine American War illustrated how political revolutions did not necessarily mean social revolution and that they were perhaps radically heterogeneous to one another. I was especially drawn to how Philippine nationalists desired authority over capital and labor, wishing to wield this power to gain political recognition. It is the tension between these two desires that led to the domestication of unconditional decolonization and the future collaboration between Philippine nationalist authorities and American colonial authorities.

I then demonstrated how American monetary authority was essential to the establishment of U.S. counter-decolonization in the archipelago. Focusing on colonial currency policies during the long Philippine American War, I uncovered how political security went hand in hand with military occupation and the enforcement of a seemingly more secure universal standard of measurement, the gold standard. Forcefully tying the Philippines to the gold standard not only sent a message to the interimperial community that the U.S. Empire was following the global and interimperial norms of the capitalist system. In addition, tying the Philippines to the gold standard pushed forward the notion that Americans were creating a more secure world through its currency, the U.S. dollar. At the same time, the colonization of Philippine currency could only be rationalized as part of a larger ideological and material assemblage of white supremacy: namely the notion that these universal standards of capitalism, invented by Anglo-Americans, represented the progress of human civilization. In this way, the global securitization of capitalism, through the gold standard, would not only benefit those with accumulated wealth. In addition, the gold standard would help uplift nonwhite savage races in the Philippines.

The desire for decolonization did not die down after the official end of the Philippine American War in 1902. For the first decade and a half of the twentieth century especially, U.S. colonial occupation in the Philippines was in a permanent state of insecurity and colonial authorities remained troubled by wayward colonial subjects. American plans for postwar reconstruction were constantly plagued by, on one hand, ongoing revolutionary insurgencies throughout the islands, and on the other hand, non-Christian Native resistance in the so-called frontiers of the archipelago. For authorities, the securitization of capital and labor went hand in hand with the militarized eradication of these ongoing political disturbances. Economic security, through multipronged modes of policing, could eliminate Native desires for decolonization. Colonial authorities consequently became obsessed with producing the Native as a proper and normative American colonial subject, a subject that could control one's immediate desires for the production and reproduction of a normative capitalist and imperialist future. Economic habits of the Filipino were attributed as racial habits and vice versa. Specifically, individual incapacity to accumulate personal wealth or manage debt meant that Filipinos as a race did not possess the collective capacity to accumulate or manage large-scale capital. According to this logic, unconditional decolonization had to be delayed.

During the 1910s, U.S. and Philippine racial capitalist conditions would be transformed by the Great War economic boom and subsequent crisis. To try and cash in on the global boom in wartime commodities, the colonial state created the PNB, a more centralized government apparatus that would manage investments in colonial agribusiness. The Filipinization of economic institutions was an experiment in conditional decolonization. At first, Filipinization seemed to be a success, with many of those already wealthy profiting off the wartime boom and those already powerful gaining more political control. But this success proved short-lived, as the PNB underwent crisis after the post–World War I recession.

The PNB then became a highly charged site of Filipino racial and economic incapacities. Imperial authorities argued that the failure of the PNB demonstrated that decolonization had to remain conditional, a slow process overseen by white American experts and guided by racial paternalism. American authorities during the 1920s adopted spectacular forms of counter-decolonization, propagating narratives of both white victimhood and imperial redemption. In the eyes of American authorities, the norms of the global imperial state system and the racial capitalist economic system had to be upheld, even if Philippine lawmakers gained more political authority. As authority over the economic realm remained heavily policed by American authorities, it increasingly became an object of desire, and crucial to Filipino nationalists' conception of conditional decolonization.

During the Great Depression, anxieties over Filipino bodies and commodities flooding the "domestic" United States accelerated public calls for decolonization in the U.S. settler metropole. Moreover, the Depression also led to reassessments of nineteenth-century normative concepts such as free trade or the gold standard. These concepts were suddenly contested and debated by not only imperial authorities but also those colonized. In the

Philippines, concerns over the racial and economic capacities of Filipinos would determine these contestations in surprising ways. Racial nativism and economic nationalism, for instance, led to unforeseen claims to monetary authority in the Philippines. According to this logic, Americans, as non-Indigenous foreigners to the archipelago, no longer held the capacity to legitimately control the Philippine economy. At the same time, the Great Depression also unleashed myriad desires for unconditional decolonization. I traced the various ways workers and peasants attempted to imagine futures without the racial capitalist world system that they had been forced to inherit. Although these movements for unconditional decolonization would be violently repressed by the Commonwealth state, their revolutionary energies would continue to haunt both Filipino and American authorities well into the 1940s.

In 1941 the Philippines would again be occupied by a different colonial force, the Japanese Empire. Drawn into World War II by both its former colonizers and its current colonizers, myriad Filipinos desired a different kind of decolonization, one that sought to radically overturn not only colonial life, but racialized and capitalist forms of life as well. Yet, the end of the war would not be kind to those who dreamt of a radical overturning of the world. Instead, "universal" concepts such as free trade and the gold standard would be reinvented, this time under new interstate assemblages such as the Bretton Woods system and the General Agreement on Tariffs and Trade. The security of these assemblages would be guaranteed by U.S. Empire, the newly undisputed global hegemon of the capitalist world-system.

After the end of World War II, which kicked off the so-called age of decolonization, the Philippine nation-state would at last achieve nominal state sovereignty. Filipino nationalist authorities would squash any kind of dreams of unconditional decolonization, espousing anticommunism in the name of democracy while proclaiming itself a beacon to other nations striving for conditional decolonization. Filipino national authorities would quickly ally themselves to the "First World." Philippine monetary authorities would immediately commit to the Bretton Woods system and General Agreement on Tariffs and Trade, while rhetorically grumbling about the imperialism of the U.S. dollar. And Manila, for instance, would be the founding site of the 1954 Southeast Asia Treaty Organization. State sovereignty would trump all other Filipino desires, leaving them strangely a part of the Third World, but also antagonistic to many of the revolutionary movements and radical reimaginings of decolonization ongoing elsewhere.

The legacy of conditional decolonization has continued to shape the contemporary Philippines. It is a kind of national chauvinism that does not see Filipinos akin to other racialized and colonized peoples. Nor does it conceive Filipinos as part of what Prashad calls "the darker nations" or "the poorer nations," at least in a shared affective sense.[2] Instead, many of those in power in the Philippines and in the diaspora have continued to cling to aspirations of capitalist security and the violent fantasy of state sovereignty. With this in mind, this book's interrogation of conditional decolonization has sought to illustrate that what differentiates the postcolonial Philippines from the colonial Philippines is perhaps more a difference in degree rather than a difference in kind. Despite this gloomy analysis, this book nevertheless sheds light on the residues and possibilities of unconditional decolonization that continues to haunt the now, an unfulfilled promise that animates contemporary intersectional movements for collective liberation, transformative justice, and self-determination in the Philippines and elsewhere.

Notes

INTRODUCTION

1 Vijay Prashad, *The Darker Nations: A People's History of the Third World* (New York: The New Press, 2007).

2 Notorious white supremacist Lothrop Stoddard feared that the twentieth century could possibly end white political and economic control over the world. Lothrop Stoddard, *The Rising Tide of Color: Against White World Supremacy* (New York: Charles Scribner's Sons, 1920). W. E. B. Du Bois, *The Souls of Black Folk* (1903; repr., New Haven, CT: Yale University Press, 2015), v.

3 *Independence for the Philippine Islands: Hearings before the Committee on Territories and Insular Affairs* (Washington, DC: U.S. Government Printing Office, 1932), 46.

4 *Independence for the Philippine Islands*, 47.

5 *Independence for the Philippine Islands*, 48.

6 For more on U.S. imperial formation within settler colonial capitalism see the following: Jodi A. Byrd, Alyosha Goldstein, Jodi Melamed, and Chandan Reddy, "Predatory Value: Economies of Dispossession and Disturbed Relationalities," *Social Text* 135, no. 36.2 (2018): 1–18; Glen Coulthard, *Red Skin, White Masks: Rejecting the Colonial Politics of Recognition* (Minneapolis: University of Minnesota Press, 2014); Iyko Day, *Alien Capital: Asian Racialization and the Logic of Settler Colonial Capitalism* (Durham, NC: Duke University Press, 2016); Nick Estes, *Our History Is the Future: Standing Rock versus the Dakota Access Pipeline, and the Long Tradition of Indigenous Resistance* (Brooklyn, NY: Verso, 2019); Manu Karuka, *Empire's Tracks: Indigenous Nations, Chinese Workers, and the Transcontinental Railroad* (Berkeley: University of California Press, 2019).

7 Karuka develops this concept of countersovereignty through the thinking of radical Indigenous feminist thinkers. Karuka, *Empire's Tracks*, xii.

8 For more on U.S. imperial formation in relation to global capitalism see Giovanni Arrighi, "Hegemony Unraveling 1," *New Left Review* 32 (2005): 23–80; Sam Gindin and Leo Panitch, *The Making of Global Capitalism: The Political Economy of American Empire* (London: Verso, 2013); and David Harvey, *The New Imperialism* (Oxford: Oxford University Press, 2003). For more on the relation between imperialism and money capital more generally, see V. I. Lenin, *Imperialism, the Highest Stage of Capitalism* (1916; repr., Moscow: Foreign Languages Publishing House, 1961), and Rudolf Hilferding, *Finance Capital: A Study of the Latest Phase of Capitalist Development* (1910; repr., London: Routledge and Kegan Paul, 1981). For more on the notion of the United States as being profoundly shaped by economic imperialism, see the so-called Wisconsin school analysis of diplomatic history, particularly made famous by scholars such as Fred Harvey Harrington, William Appleman Williams, Walter LaFeber, and Carl Parrini. Thomas J. McCormick and Walter LaFeber, eds., *Behind the Throne: Servants of Power to Imperial Presidents, 1898–1968* (Madison: University of Wisconsin Press, 1993); Carl Parrini, *Heir to Empire: United States Economic Diplomacy, 1916–1923* (Pittsburgh: University of Pittsburgh Press, 1969); Emily Rosenberg, *Financial Missionaries to the World: the Politics and Culture of Dollar Diplomacy, 1900–1930* (Durham, NC: Duke University Press, 2004); William Appleman Williams, *The Tragedy of American Diplomacy* (New York: W. W. Norton, 1972). See also Joseph A. Fry's detailed assessment of the impact of the Wisconsin school in "From Open Door to World Systems: Economic Interpretations of Late Nineteenth Century American Foreign Relations," *Pacific Historical Review* 65, no. 2 (1996): 277–303.

9 On the racial capitalist transformations of U.S. continental empire in the first half of the nineteenth century see Walter Johnson, *The Broken Heart of America: St. Louis and the Violent History of the United States* (New York: Basic Books, 2020). On the hemispheric imperial framework of the mid-nineteenth century provided by the Monroe Doctrine, see Jay Sexton, *The Monroe Doctrine: Empire and Nation in Nineteenth-Century America* (New York: Hill and Wang, 2011).

10 Allan E. S. Lumba, "Empire, Expansion, and Its Consequences," in *A Companion to the Gilded Age and Progressive Era*, ed. Christopher Nichols and Nancy Unger (Oxford: Wiley-Blackwell, 2017): 399–409.

11 Neferti X. M. Tadiar, *Fantasy-Production: Sexual Economies and Other Philippine Consequences for the New World Order* (Quezon City, Philippines: Ateneo de Manila University Press, 2004), 8.

12 For a better understanding of the dialectic relation between academic expertise and state policymaking see Peter Hudson, *Bankers and Empire: How Wall Street Colonized the Caribbean* (Chicago: University of Chicago Press, 2017); Timothy Mitchell, *Rule of Experts: Egypt, Techno-Politics, Modernity* (Berkeley: University of California Press, 2002); Dorothy Ross, *The Origins of American Social Science* (Cambridge: Cambridge University Press, 1991); Parrini, *Heir to Empire*; Rosenberg, *Financial Missionaries to the World*; Cyrus Veeser, *A World Safe for Capitalism:*

Dollar Diplomacy and America's Rise to Global Power (New York: Columbia University Press, 2002).

13 Onofre D. Corpuz, *An Economic History of the Philippines* (Quezon City: University of the Philippines Press, 1997); Frank Golay, *Face of Empire: United States–Philippines Relations, 1898–1946* (Quezon City, Philippines: Ateneo de Manila University Press; Madison: University of Wisconsin Press, 1998); Yoshiko Nagano, *The Philippine National Bank: The American Colonial State and Finance, 1898–1941* (Quezon City, Philippines: Ateneo de Manila University Press; Singapore: National University Press, 2015); Paul Hutchcroft, *Booty Capitalism: The Politics of Banking in the Philippines* (Ithaca, NY: Cornell University Press, 1998); and Peter W. Stanley, *A Nation in the Making: The Philippines and the United States, 1899–1921* (Cambridge. MA: Harvard University Press, 1974).

14 Cedric Robinson, *Black Marxism: The Making of the Black Radical Tradition* (Chapel Hill: University of North Carolina Press, 2000), 2. For more on racial capitalism see W. E. B. Du Bois, *Black Reconstruction in America* (1935; repr., New York: The Free Press, 1998); Frantz Fanon, *The Wretched of the Earth* (New York: Grove Press, 2004); C. L. R. James, *The Black Jacobins: Toussaint L'Ouverture and the San Domingo Revolution* (New York: Vintage Books, 1989); Walter Rodney, *How Europe Underdeveloped Africa* (London: Verso, 2018); Eric Williams, *Capitalism and Slavery* (Chapel Hill: University of North Carolina Press, 1994). For more on the South African intellectual tradition of thinking about racial capitalism that predates Cedric Robinson's conceptualization see Peter Hudson, "Racial Capitalism and the Black Proletariat," *Boston Review: Forum 1* (Winter 2017): 59–66. Finally, there has been an intensified return to the provocations of Robinson's *Black Marxism* in academia. For example see Ruth Gilmore, *Golden Gulag: Prisons, Surplus, Crisis, and Opposition in Globalizing California* (Berkeley: University of California Press, 2007); Peter Hudson, *Bankers and Empire: How Wall Street Colonized the Caribbean* (Chicago: University of Chicago Press, 2017); Destin Jenkins and Justin Leroy, eds., *Histories of Racial Capitalism* (New York: Columbia University Press, 2021); Walter Johnson, *River of Dark Dreams: Slavery and Empire in the Cotton Kingdom* (Cambridge, MA: Harvard University Press, 2013); Lisa Lowe, *The Intimacies of Four Continents* (Durham, NC: Duke University Press, 2015); Jodi Melamed, *Represent and Destroy: Rationalizing Violence in the New Racial Capitalism* (Minneapolis: University of Minnesota Press, 2011). In addition, the following articles are especially useful in thinking through racial capitalism: Walter Johnson, "To Remake the World: Slavery, Racial Capitalism, and Justice," *Boston Review,* Forum 1 (2017), https://bostonreview.net/forum/walter-johnson-to-remake-the-world; Manu Karuka (also Manu Vimalassery), "The Wealth of the Natives: Toward a Critique of Settler Colonial Political Economy," *Settler Colonial Studies* 3, nos. 3–4 (2013): 295–310.

15 Warwick Anderson, *Colonial Pathologies: American Tropical Medicine, Race, and Hygiene in the Philippines* (Durham, NC: Duke University Press, 2006), 2.

16 The full quote reveals much on Fanon's thinking about racial and colonial capitalism: "In the colonies the economic infrastructure is also a superstructure. The cause is effect: You are rich because you are white, you are white because you are

rich. This is why a Marxist analysis should always be slightly stretched when it comes to addressing the colonial issue." Fanon, *The Wretched of the Earth*, 5.

17 Although these academics tend to ignore reading race beyond a superstructural epiphenomenon, there is nevertheless a vast literature of macroeconomic history, in particular world-systems theory, which identifies the exploitation of colonial economies with the violence against racialized labor. See especially Andre Gunder Frank, *ReOrient: Global Economy in the Asian Age* (Berkeley: University of California Press, 1998); Janet Abu-Lughod, *Before European Hegemony: The World System A.D. 1250–1350* (Oxford: Oxford University Press, 1989); Timothy Mitchell, "The Stage of Modernity," in *Questions of Modernity*, ed. Timothy Mitchell (Minneapolis: University of Minnesota Press, 2000); and Immanuel Wallerstein, *The Capitalist World-Economy* (New York: Maison des Sciences de l'Homme; Cambridge: Cambridge University Press, 1979). For more regional applications of the world-systems approach and its relation to race see Lucie Cheng and Edna Bonacich, *Labor Immigration under Capitalism: Asian Workers in the United States before World War II* (Berkeley: University of California Press, 1984); John H. Elliott, *Empires of the Atlantic World: Britain and Spain in America 1492–1830* (New Haven, CT: Yale University Press, 2006); Sidney W. Mintz, *Sweetness and Power: The Place of Sugar in Modern History* (New York: Penguin Books, 1986); and John Thornton, *Africa and Africans in the Making of the Atlantic World, 1400–1800* (Cambridge: Cambridge University Press, 1998).

18 Vicente L. Rafael, *White Love and Other Events in Filipino History* (Durham, NC: Duke University Press, 2000).

19 Tadiar, *Fantasy-Production*, 14.

20 For more on intersectional theory and its emergence from a radical Black feminist and women of color feminist tradition see Cathy Cohen, "Punks, Bulldaggers, and Welfare Queens: The Radical Potential of Queer Politics?" GLQ 3 (1997): 437–465; Patricia Hill Collins, *Black Feminist Thought: Knowledge, Consciousness, and the Politics of Empowerment* (New York: Routledge, 1991); The Combahee River Collective, *The Combahee River Collective Statement: Black Feminist Organizing in the Seventies and Eighties* (Albany, NY: Kitchen Table: Women of Color Press, 1986); Kimberle Crenshaw, "Demarginalizing the Intersection of Race and Sex: A Black Feminist Critique of Antidiscrimination Doctrine, Feminist Theory and Antiracist Politics," *The University of Chicago Legal Forum Volume: Feminism in the Law: Theory, Practice and Criticism* 8 (1989): 139–167; and "Mapping the Margins: Intersectionality, Identity Politics, and Violence against Women of Color," *Stanford Law Review* 6 (1991): 1241–1299; Audre Lorde, *Sister Outsider: Essays and Speeches* (Trumansburg, NY: Crossing Press, 1984).

21 Here I build off Philippine scholarship that looks especially at the historical intersections of gendered, racial, religious, and sexual power, especially Rick Baldoz, *The Third Asiatic Invasion: Migration and Empire in Filipino America, 1898–1946* (New York: New York University Press, 2011); Genevieve Clutario, "The Appearance of Filipina Nationalism: Body, Nation, Empire" (PhD diss., University of Illinois at Urbana-Champaign, 2014); Deirdre de la Cruz, *Mother*

Figured: Marian Apparitions and the Making of a Filipino Universal (Chicago: University of Chicago Press, 2015); Caroline Hau, *Necessary Fictions: Philippine Literature and the Nation, 1946–1980* (Quezon City, Philippines: Ateneo de Manila University Press, 2000); Victor Mendoza, *Metroimperial Intimacies: Fantasy, Racial-Sexual Governance, and the Philippines in U.S. Imperialism, 1899–1913* (Durham, NC: Duke University Press, 2015); Rafael, *White Love and Other Events in Filipino History*; Neferti X. M. Tadiar, *Fantasy Production*, and *Things Fall Away: Philippine Historical Experience and the Makings of Globalization* (Durham, NC: Duke University Press, 2009).

22 Paul A. Kramer, *The Blood of Government: Race, Empire, the United States, and the Philippines* (Chapel Hill: The University of North Carolina Press, 2006), 18.

23 This academic field is vast. The ones most resonant for this book's thesis has been Anderson, *Colonial Pathologies*, Kramer, *The Blood of Government*; and Alfred McCoy, *Policing America's Empire: The United States, the Philippines, and the Rise of the Surveillance State* (Madison: University of Wisconsin Press, 2009). In addition, there have been several anthologies that contain several useful essays on American colonial state formation and the creation of imperial institutions in the Philippines. Julian Go and Ann Foster, eds., *The American Colonial State in the Philippines: Global Perspectives* (Durham, NC: Duke University Press, 2003), and Alfred McCoy and Francisco Scarano eds., *Colonial Crucible: Empire in the Making of the Modern American State* (Madison: University of Wisconsin Press, 2009). Finally, for a good overview of scholarly works on the Philippines through a U.S. imperial framework see Paul A. Kramer, "How Not to Write the History of U.S. Empire," *Diplomatic History* 42, no. 4 (2018): 911–931.

24 *Filipinization* refers to the process of Filipino lawmakers and civil servants replacing American personnel in the colonial state. From 1902 to 1946, during different periods, the American colonial state underwent Filipinization at varying speeds.

25 My thinking on the radical difference between conditional and unconditional decolonization is especially indebted to Indigenous studies, particularly in the North American settler colony. Although the literature by Indigenous scholars is vast, some recommended works are Joanne Barker, *Critically Sovereign: Indigenous Gender, Sexuality, and Feminist Studies* (Durham, NC: Duke University Press, 2017); Ned Blackhawk, *Violence over the Land: Indians and Empires in the Early American West* (Cambridge, MA: Harvard University Press, 2006); Jodi Byrd, *The Transit of Empire: Indigenous Critiques of Colonialism* (Minneapolis: University of Minnesota Press, 2011); Audra Simpson, "Sovereignty, Sympathy, and Indigeneity," in *Ethnographies of U.S. Empire*, eds. John Collins and Carole McGranahan (Durham, NC: Duke University Press, 2018), 72–89; Haunani-Kay Trask, *From a Native Daughter: Colonialism and Sovereignty in Hawai'i* (Honolulu: University of Hawai'i Press, 1999). For more general theorization on settler colonialism see Patrick Wolfe, *Settler Colonialism and the Transformation of Anthropology* (London: Cassell, 1999), and "Land, Labor, and Difference: Elementary Structures of Race," *American Historical Review* 106, no. 3 (2001): 866–905.

55555555555

Parts of this chapter were initially published in Allan E. S. Lumba, "Philippine Colonial Money and the Futures of Spanish Empire," in *The Cultural History of Money and Credit: A Global Perspective*, ed. Thomas Luckett, Chia Yin Hsu, and Erika Vause (Lanham, MD: Lexington Books, 2016), 97–111.

1 Francisco Aguilar y Biosca, *Legislación Sobre Moneda* (1893) reprinted in *Barrilla: The Central Bank Money Museum Quarterly* 6, no. 2 (1979): 60.

2 Biosca, *Legislación Sobre Moneda*, 62.

3 The contemporary words *Philippine* (*Las Filipinas*) and *Filipino* are referents only made possible through the historical process of Spanish colonization. One of the primary sources for understanding the crucial link between national identity and naming is Vicente Rafael, *The Promise of the Foreign: Nationalism and the Technics of Translation in the Spanish Philippines* (Durham, NC: Duke University Press, 2005).

4 Angelita Ganzon de Legarda, *Piloncitos to Pesos: A Brief History of Coinage in the Philippines* (Manila: Bancom Development, 1976), 8.

5 Patricio N. Abinales and Donna J. Amoroso, *State and Society in the Philippines* (New York: Roman and Littlefield, 2005), 42–45.

6 Andre Gunder Frank, *ReOrient: Global Economy in the Asian Age* (Berkeley: University of California Press, 1998), and Cedric Robinson, *Black Marxism: The Making of the Black Radical Tradition* (Chapel Hill: The University of North Carolina Press, 2000).

7 For more on the post-Galleon Era colonial economy see Benito Legarda, *After the Galleons: Foreign Trade, Economic Change and Entrepreneurship in the Nineteenth Century Philippines* (Quezon City, Philippines: Ateneo de Manila University Press; Madison: University of Wisconsin Press, 1999).

8 Quioquiap [pseud.], "El Giro con Filipinas," *La Politica de España en Filipinas* 4, no. 89 (1894): 177.

9 "Press Abstract No. 11," March 29, 1902, box 107, folder 56, Records of the Bureau of Insular Affairs, Record Group 350, National Archives and Records Administration.

10 Legarda, *Piloncitos to Pesos*, 32.

11 Legarda, *Piloncitos to Pesos*, 28–31.

12 Legarda, *Piloncitos to Pesos*, 44.

13 For more on the intricacies of the global shift to the gold standard and the consequences on Philippine monetary legislation see Edwin Kemmerer, *Modern Currency Reforms: A History and Discussion of Recent Currency Reforms in India, Puerto Rico, Philippine Islands, Straits Settlements and Mexico* (New York: Macmillan Company, 1916); George F. Luthringer, *The Gold-Exchange Standards in the Philippines* (Princeton, NJ: Princeton University Press, 1934); Francisco Godinez, *Regularizar la Situación Monetaria en las Islas Filipinas* (Madrid: Imprenta de Luis Aguado, 1894); F. Aguilar y Biosca, *Legislación Sobre Moneda*; and Commission On International Exchange, *Gold Standard in International Trade: Report on the Introduction of the Gold-Exchange Standard into China, the Philippine Islands, Panama,*

and Other Silver-Using Countries and on the Stability of Exchange (Washington, DC: Government Printing, 1904).

14 Maria Serena Diokno, "The Political Aspect of the Monetary Crisis in the 1880s," Kasarinlan 14, no. 1 (1998): 23.

15 Legarda, Piloncitos to Pesos, 28–35.

16 "Ben F. Wright to F. A. Branagan," July 22, 1904, box 198, folder 6, Edwin W. Kemmerer Papers (MC146), Public Policy Papers, Department of Special Collections, Princeton University Library.

17 Josep Fradera, "The Historical Origins of the Philippine Economy: A Survey of Recent Research of the Spanish Colonial Era," Australian Economic History Review 44, no. 3 (2004): 313.

18 Fradera, "Historical Origins of the Philippine Economy," 314.

19 Fradera, "Historical Origins of the Philippine Economy," 314–315.

20 In the Spanish Catholic tradition, secular signified a kind of priest that did not belong to an established monastic order.

21 Jose Rizal, El Filibusterismo, trans. Ma. Soledad Lacson-Locsin (1891; repr., Makati: The Bookmark, 2004); and chapter 2 of Rafael, Promise of the Foreign. For more on the possible revolutionary tradition in the Philippines see Benedict Anderson, Under Three Flags: Anarchism and the Anti-Colonial Imagination (New York: Verso, 2005).

22 Diokno, "Political Aspect of the Monetary Crisis in the 1880s," 24.

23 Jose Feced, "El Cambio de Moneda en Filipinas," La Politica 4, no. 96 (1894): 272–273, and Diokno, "Political Aspect of the Monetary Crisis in the 1880s," 25.

24 A. A. O. [pseud.], "La Cuestion Monetaria," La Politica de España en Filipinas 7, no. 170 (1897): 443. Criollos, in the Spanish Philippines, usually referred to the legal, political, and racial category of a Spaniard born in the Philippine colony. In relation, Mestizo referred to those categorized of "mixed-race" origins. Although originally meaning a "mix" between Chinese and Native subjects, by the end of the nineteenth century the lines of categorization had blurred to potentially include anyone of supposedly "Spaniard" descent.

25 "El Duro Peninsular en Filipinas," originally in El Nuevo Mundo, May 15, 1894, reprinted in La Solidaridad, vol. 6, trans. Guadalupe Forés-Ganzon and Luis Mañeru (Manila: Fundacion Santiago, 1996), 215.

26 Q. [pseud.], "El Cambio," La Politica de España en Filipinas 4, no. 99: (November 20, 1894): 315, and A. A. O., "La Cuestion Monetaria," 458.

27 Q., "La Cuestion Monetaria," La Politica de España en Filipinas 4, no. 101 (December 18, 1894): 330.

28 Quioquiap, "El Peso Mejicano," La Politica de España en Filipinas 4, no. 87 (1894): 162.

29 Quioquiap, "El Giro con Filipinas," 177–178, and "El Peso Mejicano," 293–294.

30 For more on the historical relationship between the capitalist market, the figure of the Chinese in the Philippines, and Philippine nationalism see Richard Chu, The Chinese and Chinese Mestizos of Manila: Family, Identity, and Culture 1860s to 1930s (Leiden: E. J. Brill, 2010); Caroline Hau, The Chinese Question: Ethnicity, Nation, and Region in and beyond the Philippines (Singapore: National University of

Singapore Press, 2014); Edgar Wickberg, *The Chinese in Philippine Life 1850–1898* (Quezon City, Philippines: Ateneo De Manila, University Press, 2000); Andrew R. Wilson, *Ambition and Identity: Chinese Merchant Elites in Colonial Manila, 1880–1916* (Honolulu: University of Hawai'i Press, 2004).

31 See chapters 2 and 3 of Wickberg, *Chinese in Philippine Life 1850–1898*.

32 Abinales and Amoroso, *State and Society in the Philippines*, 76–78.

33 Wickberg, *Chinese in Philippine Life*, 73.

34 John Murray, "Chinese-Filipino Wage Differentials in Early-Twentieth-Century Manila," *Journal of Economic History* 62, no. 3 (2002): 775.

35 Caroline Hau, "'The Chinese Question': A Marxist Interpretation," in *Marxism in the Philippines: Continuing Engagements*, ed. Teresa Tadem (Manila: Anvil Publishing and University of the Philippines Third World Studies Center, 2010), 163.

36 Q., "El Peso Mejicano," 162; Feced, "El Cambio de Moneda en Filipinas," 272; and Willem Wolters, "How Were Labourers Paid in the Philippine Islands during the 19th Century?" in *Wages and Currency: Global Comparisons from Antiquity to the Twentieth Century*, ed. Jan Lucassen (Bern, Switzerland: Peter Lang AG, 2007), 153.

37 Hau, "The Chinese Question," 165.

38 Rizal, *El Filibusterismo*, 169, 175.

39 J. F. [pseud.], "La Cuestion de Plata: El Contrabando, los cambios," *La Politica de España en Filipinas* 3, no. 64 (1893): 176.

40 M. H. del Pilar Gatmaitan (Marcelo del Pilar), "Soluciones Monetarias," January 31, 1895; reprinted in *La Solidaridad*, vol. 7, trans. Guadalupe Forés-Ganzon and Luis Mañeru (Manila: Fundacion Santiago, 1996), 39.

41 "El Duro Peninsular en Filipinas," 212–215.

42 "El Duro Peninsular en Filipinas," 257.

43 Francisco Godinez, "Papel Moneda en Filipinas" (originally in *El Nuevo Mundo*, July 15, 1894) in *La Solidaridad*, vol. 6, 307.

44 Godinez, "Papel Moneda en Filipinas," 307.

45 Godinez, "Papel Moneda en Filipinas," 309.

46 For more on the colonial rendering of the Indigenous as "savage" see Frank Wilderson III, *Red, White and Black: Cinema and the Structure of U.S. Antagonisms* (Durham, NC: Duke University Press, 2010). On the role of colonial hierarchy based on the difference between Christians and non-Christians in the Spanish Philippines see Vicente Rafael, *Contracting Colonialism: Translation and Christian Conversion in Tagalog Society under Early Spanish Rule* (Durham, NC: Duke University Press, 1992).

47 Godinez, "Papel Moneda en Filipinas," 307.

48 Godinez, "Papel Moneda en Filipinas," 307.

49 Godinez, "Papel Moneda en Filipinas," 309.

50 For more on the significance of Mestizo identity in the Spanish Philippines see Vicente Rafael, *White Love and Other Events in Filipino History* (Durham, NC: Duke University Press, 2000): 6–7.

51 Godinez, "Papel Moneda en Filipinas," 309.

52 Godinez, "Papel Moneda en Filipinas," 309.

53 Godinez, "Papel Moneda en Filipinas," 307.

54 Del Pilar, "Soluciones Monetarias," 39.

55 Del Pilar, "Soluciones Monetarias," 41.

56 Del Pilar, "Soluciones Monetarias," 41.

57 The nation as a figure of the organic in opposition to the artificial state is explored by Pheng Cheah, *Spectral Nationality: Passages of Freedom from Kant to Postcolonial Literatures of Liberation* (New York: Columbia University Press, 2003).

58 Del Pilar, "*Soluciones Monetarias*," 41.

59 Del Pilar, "*Soluciones Monetarias*," 45.

60 The official full name in Tagalog is *Kataas-taasan, Kagalang-galangang Katipunan ng mga Anak ng Bayan* and may be translated as the Highest and Most Honorable Society of the Children of the Homeland.

61 Milagros Guerrero, "Luzon at War: Contradictions in Philippine Society, 1898–1902" (PhD diss., University of Michigan, 1977), 114.

62 See especially the first chapter of Reynaldo Ileto, *Pasyon and Revolution: Popular Movements in the Philippines, 1840–1910* (Quezon City, Philippines: Ateneo de Manila University Press, 1998).

63 Still, as Rafael points out, the revolution did not eliminate the idea of sovereignty altogether. In its stead, the revolution displaced imperial legacies unto other forms such as the notion of "popular sovereignty." Vicente L. Rafael, "Welcoming What Comes: Sovereignty and Revolution in the Colonial Philippines," *Comparative Studies in Society and History* 52, no. 1 (2010): 165.

64 Although this topic is covered in chapter 2, for more on the U.S. timeline leading up to the Spanish American War see Walter LaFeber, *The New Empire: An Interpretation of American Expansion, 1860–1898* (Ithaca, NY: Cornell University Press, 1963); Emily Rosenberg, *Spreading the American Dream: American Economic and Cultural Expansion, 1890–1945* (New York: Hill and Wang, 1982); William Appleman Williams, *The Tragedy of American Diplomacy* (New York: W. W. Norton and Company, 1972).

65 Guerrero, *Luzon at War*, 113.

66 "Emilio Aguinaldo to Provinces," November 24, 1898, *Philippine Insurgent Records: 1896–1901* (hereafter PIR), reel 18, folder 212.

67 "Secretary of War to Secretary of Interior," February 10, 1899, PIR, reel 25, folder 360.

68 "Act Providing for a Domestic Loan," November 30, 1898, PIR, reel 16, folder 184.

69 "Act Providing for a Domestic Loan."

70 "Act Providing for a Domestic Loan."

71 "Act Providing for a Domestic Loan."

72 "Act Providing for a Foreign Loan," July 13, 1899, PIR, reel 22, folder 287.

73 Emilio Aguinaldo and Mariano Trias, "Decree of November 26, 1898," in *The Laws of the First Philippine Republic*, ed. Sulpicio Guevara (Manila: National Historical Commission, 1972), article 3, 72.

74 P. A. Paterno, "Decree of June 30, 1899," *The Laws of the First Philippine Republic*, 168.

75 *The Malolos Constitution*, article 68, section 6. *Official Gazette of the Republic of the Philippines*, https://www.officialgazette.gov.ph/constitutions/the-1899-malolos-constitution/.

76 Legarda, *Piloncitos to Pesos*, 49.

77 "Monetary System of the Philippine Republic" in *The Tribune Magazine*, February 8, 1931, reprinted in Neil Shafer, *A Guide Book of Philippine Paper Money* (Racine, WI: Whitman, 1964), 14.

78 Gregorio Sancianco y Goson, *The Progress of the Philippines: Economic, Administrative and Political Studies*, trans. Encarnacion Alzona (1881; repr., Manila: National Historical Institute, 1975), 81.

79 "Instruction for the Collection of War Tax Known as Certificate of Citizenship," March 1899, PIR, reel 23, folder 303.

80 "Instruction for the Collection of War Tax."

81 "P. Garcia to Military Headquarters," September 11, 1898, PIR, reel 70, folder 1138.

82 "Decree from Emilio Aguinaldo and Mariano Trias," October 3, 1898, PIR, reel 18, folder 213.

83 "Official Form that Recognizes the Collector," December 1898, PIR, reel 18, folder 213.

84 "Instruction for the Collection of War Tax."

85 "Instruction for the Collection of War Tax."

86 "J. Quesada to Luis A. Callanda," April 27, 1899, PIR, reel 16, folder 184.

87 "Response of Arcadio Rosario (Secretary of Department of Treasury)," March 4, 1899, PIR, reel 17, folder 199.

88 "J. Quesada to Citizen del Rosario," January 7, 1899, PIR, reel 22, folder 287.

89 Guerrero, *Luzon at War*, 119.

90 Guerrero, *Luzon at War*, 120.

91 "Proclamation of the President of the Filipino Government," September 23, 1898, PIR, reel 60, folder 989.

92 "Proclamation of the President of the Filipino Government."

93 Guerrero, *Luzon at War*, 117, and Ileto, *Pasyon and Revolution*, 152–153.

94 "Proclamation of the President of the Filipino Government."

95 "Proclamation of the President of the Filipino Government."

96 "Ambrosio Flores to the Inhabitants of the Province of Manila," September 23, 1898, PIR, reel 23, folder 301.

97 "Ambrosio Flores to the Inhabitants of the Province of Manila."

98 "Ambrosio Flores to the Inhabitants of the Province of Manila."

99 "Ambrosio Flores to the Inhabitants of the Province of Manila."

100 Frantz Fanon, *The Wretched of the Earth* (New York: Grove Press, 2004), 1.

2. MONGREL CURRENCIES

Parts of this chapter were initially published in Allan E. S. Lumba, "Imperial Standards: Colonial Currencies, Racial Capacities, and Economic Knowledge during the Philippine American War," *Diplomatic History* 39, no. 4 (September 2015): 603–628.

1   Mary H. Fee, *A Woman's Impressions of the Philippines* (Chicago: A. C. McClurg, 1910), 100.

2   Fee, *A Woman's Impressions of the Philippines*, 160.

3   Fee, *A Woman's Impressions of the Philippines*, 161.

4   Fee, *A Woman's Impressions of the Philippines*, 162.

5   Omar H. Ali, *In the Lion's Mouth: Black Populism in the New South, 1886–1900* (Oxford: University of Mississippi Press, 2010), 113–115.

6   The emergence of the Democratic Party and organized formal political counter Reconstruction from the white planter class is analyzed in W. E. B. Du Bois, *Black Reconstruction in America* (1935; repr., New York: The Free Press, 1998), 373.

7   Gretchen Ritter, *Goldbugs and Greenbacks: The Antimonopoly Tradition and the Politics of Finance in America* (Cambridge: Cambridge University Press, 1999), and Barry Eichengreen, *Golden Fetters: The Gold Standard and the Great Depression, 1919–1939* (New York: Oxford University Press, 1992). The theorized connection between the "Money Question" and "open door" imperial expansionist shaped what would be considered the "Wisconsin school" analysis of diplomatic history, particularly made famous by scholars such as Fred Harvey Harrington, William Appleman Williams, Walter LaFeber, and Carl Parrini. See especially Joseph A. Fry's detailed assessment of the impact of the Wisconsin school in "From Open Door to World Systems: Economic Interpretations of Late Nineteenth Century American Foreign Relations," *Pacific Historical Review* 65, no. 2 (1996): 277–303.

8   There is a vast literature on the "Money Question" in U.S. history. Some helpful texts include Carl Parrini and Martin Sklar, "New Thinking about the Market, 1896–1904: Some American Economists on Investment and the Theory of Surplus Capital," *Journal of Economic History* 43, no. 3 (1983): 559–578; Walter Benn Michaels, *The Gold Standard and the Logic of Naturalism: American Literature at the Turn of the Century* (Berkeley: University of California Press, 1987); and Jeffrey Sklansky, *Sovereign of the Market: The Money Question in Early America* (Chicago: University of Chicago Press, 2017). In addition, the "naturalness" of the market and its relation to economic liberalist thinking is intensely interrogated in the second chapter of Michel Foucault, *The Birth of Biopolitics: Lectures at the College de France 1978–1979* (New York: Palgrave Macmillan, 2008).

9   The quote is from Arthur Twining Hadley's presidential address in Murray N. Rothbard, *A History of Money and Banking in the United States: The Colonial Era to World War II* (Auburn, AL: Ludwig von Mises Institute, 2002), 216. Although Rothbard's overall libertarian antigovernment analysis is suspect, the quote itself speaks to the emerging kinds of allegiances between the state and expertise.

10 For more on the CIE see the first chapter of Emily Rosenberg, *Financial Missionaries to the World: The Politics and Culture of Dollar Diplomacy, 1900–1930* (Durham, NC: Duke University Press, 2004).

11 For more on international relations and bankers in the colonial world, see Rosenberg's *Financial Missionaries to the World* and Peter Hudson, *Bankers and Empire: How Wall Street Colonized the Caribbean* (Chicago: University of Chicago Press, 2017). See also Sam Gindin and Leo Panitch, *The Making of Global Capitalism: The Political Economy of American Empire* (London: Verso, 2013).

12 Charles A. Conant, *A Special Report on Coinage and Banking in the Philippine Islands* (Washington, DC: U.S. Government Printing Office, 1901), 15.

13 For a more in-depth account of Charles Conant's social and professional connections to both the banking community and the McKinley administration see Carl Parrini's detailed chapter "Charles A. Conant, Economic Crises and Foreign Policy, 1896–1903," in *Behind the Throne: Servants of Power to Imperial Presidents, 1898–1968*, ed. Thomas J. McCormick and Walter LaFeber (Madison: The University of Wisconsin Press, 1993), 35. And for more writings in which Conant attempts to analyze capitalist crisis and theorize a solution of both fiscal and monetary policy see "Can New Openings Be Found for Capital," *Atlantic Monthly* 84 (1899): 600–608; "Recent Economic Tendencies," *Atlantic Monthly* 85 (1900): 736–748; and "Crises and Their Management," *Yale Review* 9 (1901): 374–398.

14 Charles A. Conant, "The Economic Basis of 'Imperialism,'" *North American Review* 167, no. 502 (1898): 326.

15 Although it was not blatantly stated, Conant most likely meant Anglo-American as synonymous with white. By saying Anglo-American, he is not only differentiating white Americans from other kinds of citizens of the United States, such as African Americans who were excluded politically, economically, and culturally from U.S. society, but also from other gradients of Euro-Americans who were placed below Anglo-Americans in terms of not being fully white. For more on the category of whiteness as one rife with tensions and uncertainties see Matthew Frye Jacobsen, *Whiteness of a Different Color: European Immigrants and the Alchemy of Race* (Cambridge, MA: Harvard University Press, 1998), and David Roediger, *The Wages of Whiteness: Race and the Making of the American Working Class* (London: Verso, 1991).

16 Conant, "Economic Basis of 'Imperialism,'" 326.

17 Charles A. Conant, "Currency Problems in the Orient—Discussion," *American Economic Association* 4, no. 1 (1903): 281.

18 Conant, "Economic Basis of 'Imperialism,'" 337.

19 Conant, "Economic Basis of 'Imperialism,'" 338.

20 Conant, "Economic Basis of 'Imperialism,'" 340.

21 Conant's emphasis on protecting capitalist competition—no matter what nation-state was in charge over the territory—problematizes the Open Door thesis (and others like it). The Open Door thesis strictly considers the market as an instrument of American imperial sovereignty. According to Conant's theoretical gymnastics, however, the growth of American capital simultaneously indicated the growth of global capital in general. Conant, "Can New Openings Be Found for Capital?," 608. For more on the invention of the free market by British imperial thinkers, see chapter 1 of Karl Polanyi, *The Great Transformation: The Political and Economic Origins of Our Time* (Boston: Beacon Press, 2001).

22 Conant, "Economic Basis of 'Imperialism,'" 338.

23 Clarence R. Edwards, *Memorandum for Secretary of War on Currency and Exchange in the Philippines* (Washington, DC: U.S. Government Printing Office, 1900), 62.

24 Although the history of the Philippine American War is extremely complex, the rival claims to sovereignty by both the United States and the Philippine Republic

(Malolos Republic) led to almost a decade and a half of brutal warfare. This protracted war would entail intense skirmish strategies on the part of Filipino guerillas, who were subsequently labeled by Americans as insurrectionists (or *insurectos* in Spanish).

25   Edwin Walter Kemmerer, *Modern Currency Reforms: A History and Discussion of Recent Currency Reforms in India, Puerto Rico, Philippine Islands, Straits Settlements and Mexico* (New York: Macmillan Company, 1916), 263.

26   "Surgeon General to the Secretary of War," May 5, 1899, box 106, folder 808, Records of the Bureau of Insular Affairs, Record Group 350, National Archives and Records Administration (hereafter BIA RG350, NARA).

27   Edwards, *Currency and Exchange in the Philippines*, 7.

28   "Manila Currency Problems," *Manila Times*, June 8, 1899, box 106, folder 808, BIA RG350, NARA.

29   "Dept. of Treasury, Secretary of War Endorsement," June 14, 1899, box 106, folder 808, BIA RG350, NARA. "L. J. Gage, to Root," June 27, 1899, box 106, folder 808, BIA RG350, NARA.

30   "Secretary of War to Secretary of Treasury," June 8, 1899, box 106, folder 808, BIA RG350, NARA.

31   "Secretary of War to Secretary of Treasury."

32   "Canadian Bank of Commerce," August 20, 1900, box 106, folder 808, BIA RG350, NARA.

33   Edwards, *Currency and Exchange in the Philippines*, 52.

34   Cuartos were referred to as "cualta" in Tagalog. Edwards, *Currency and Exchange in the Philippines*, 53.

35   Willem Wolters, "How Were Labourers Paid in the Philippine Islands during the 19th Century?" in *Wages and Currency: Global Comparisons from Antiquity to the Twentieth Century*, ed. Jan Lucassen (Bern, Switzerland: Peter Lang AG, 2007), 151–153.

36   Edwards, *Currency and Exchange in the Philippines*, 53.

37   Kemmerer, *Modern Currency Reforms*, 269. For the broader history of the Boxer Rebellion see, for example, Robert Bickers and R. G. Tiedemann eds., *The Boxers, China, and the World* (Lanham, MD: Rowman and Littlefield, 2007); Paul A. Cohen, *History in Three Keys: The Boxers as Event, Experience, and Myth* (New York, NY: Columbia University Press, 1997); Joseph Esherick, *The Origins of the Boxer Uprising* (Berkeley: University of California Press, 1987); and David Silbey, *The Boxer Rebellion and the Great Game in China* (New York: Hill and Wang, 2012).

38   "MacArthur to War Department," August 3, 1900, box 106, folder 808, BIA RG350, NARA.

39   "Canadian Bank of Commerce."

40   *Reports of the Taft Philippine Commission* (Washington, DC: U.S. Government Printing Office, 1901), 85.

41   See Francisco Godinez, *Regularizar la Situación Monetaria en las Islas Filipinas* (Madrid: Imprenta de Luis Aguado, 1894), 4; and Francisco Aguilar y Biosca, *Legislación Sobre Moneda* (1893) reprinted in *Barrilla: The Central Bank Money Museum Quarterly* 6, no. 2 (1979): 62–63.

42   *Reports of the Taft Philippine Commission*, 86.

43   "MacArthur to Secretary of War," August 9, 1900, box 106, folder 808, BIA RG350, NARA.

44   Edwards, *Currency and Exchange in the Philippines*, 46–47.

45   Edwards, *Currency and Exchange in the Philippines*, 46–47. Also see the first chapter, concerning the inherent dual value of the commodity, of Karl Marx, *Capital: A Critique of Political Economy*, vol. 1 (London: Penguin Classics, 1990).

46   Edwards, *Currency and Exchange in the Philippines*, 46.

47   The reality, however, was that the military government did not get replaced, but instead coexisted, especially in the non-Christian areas, for almost two more decades. Moreover, the civil colonial government, particularly the judicial, legislative, and executive powers, would take up the moniker Philippine Commission until 1916. See especially Abinales' analysis of the cooperation and conflict between parallel civil and military colonial states in Patricio Abinales, "Progressive-Machine Conflict in Early-Twentieth-Century U.S. Politics and Colonial-State Building in the Philippines," in *The American Colonial State in the Philippines: Global Perspectives*, eds. Julian Go and Ann Foster, 148–181 (Durham, NC: Duke University Press, 2003).

48   "Taft to Secretary of War," August 11, 1901, box 106, folder 808, BIA RG350, NARA.

49   Eventually the Morton Trust also became a reserve bank for Panama, the Dominican Republic, and other Latin American nations that underwent currency reform under the advice of American experts. See Hudson, *Bankers and Empire*, 46.

50   Parrini, "Charles A. Conant, Economic Crises and Foreign Policy, 1896–1903," 47.

51   "Conant to Secretary of War," October 16, 1900, box 106, folder 808, BIA RG350, NARA.

52   Conant would rely heavily on the Spanish imperial monetary debates of the 1890s. Many of the same works, especially those authored by Francisco Godinez, a Spanish economist of the late nineteenth century, are littered throughout the BIA records, especially in folders 808, 1831, and 2325, BIA RG350, NARA; the works of Edwin Kemmerer are in box 199, folder 4, Edwin W. Kemmerer Papers (MC146), Public Policy Papers, Department of Special Collections, Princeton University Library (hereafter EWK MC146, PUL). In addition, there is frequent reference to the British demonetizing of silver in India during 1893, especially in correspondences among Conant, Jenks, G. Bruce Webster, and Edwards. See correspondences between October 1900 and May 1902, mostly box 106, folder 808, BIA RG350, NARA.

53   *Report of the Philippine Commission to the President January 31, 1900* (Washington, DC: U.S. Government Printing Office, 1901), 183–185.

54   *Report of the Philippine Commission*, 308.

55   *Report of the Philippine Commission*, 183–185.

56   *Report of the Philippine Commission*, 306.

57   *Report of the Philippine Commission*, 156–157.

58   Under Spanish colonization, those who were considered of "pure" Spanish blood who were born in the Philippine colony were categorized as Criollos. This was to differentiate them from *Peninsulares*, "pure" Spaniards who were born in the Iberian Peninsula.

59 *Report of the Philippine Commission*, 162.

60 *Report of the Philippine Commission*, 210.

61 It is not clear how much weight was actually given to Legarda's input, especially in regard to the crafting of monetary policies. On one hand, Legarda served on the first Philippine Commission committee on banking and currency in 1901. On the other hand, there are no recorded instances of his individual impact on Conant's thinking. Indeed, none of the significant correspondences or confidential reports concerning currency reform mention Legarda substantially. Moreover, Legarda was never cited in any official reports on the monetary system. I include Legarda's interview, however, to illustrate how Native voices could both contest and corroborate general arguments for or against the institution of a gold standard.

62 *Report of the Philippine Commission*, 177.

63 *Report of the Philippine Commission*, 180.

64 *Report of the Philippine Commission*, 179.

65 *Report of the Philippine Commission*, 178.

66 The history of American exclusionary policies, specifically targeting Chinese labor, is immense. For a brief sample see Sucheng Chan, ed., *Chinese American Transnationalism: The Flow of People, Resources, and Ideas between China and America during the Exclusion Era* (Philadelphia: Temple University Press, 2005); Andrew Gyory, *Closing the Gate: Race, Politics, and the Chinese Exclusion Act* (Chapel Hill: University of North Carolina Press, 1998); Erika Lee, *At America's Gates: Chinese Immigration during the Exclusion Era, 1882–1943* (Chapel Hill: University of North Carolina Press, 2003); and Mai Ngai, *Impossible Subjects: Illegal Aliens and the Making of Modern America* (Princeton, NJ: Princeton University Press, 2004). But for more on how scholars should reframe Chinese exclusion as not merely ignorant xenophobia but instead as part of a logic structured by settler colonial capitalism see Evelyn Nakano Glenn, "Settler Colonialism as Structure: A Framework for U.S. Race and Gender Formation," *Sociology of Race and Ethnicity* 1, no. 1 (2015): 54–74.

67 Although there are many assertions of the Native's racially inherent laziness throughout official reports, see Daland's interview to better understand its connection to anti-Chinese migration in *Report of the Philippine Commission*, 164. This position was eventually supported by notable economic expert, Jeremiah Jenks, who suggested the importation of Chinese and "East Indian" laborers under strict restrictions. "Jenks to Secretary of War," May 6, 1902, box 107, folder 808, BIA RG350, NARA.

68 *Report of the Philippine Commission*, 199–200.

69 *Report of the Philippine Commission*, 216.

70 *Report of the Philippine Commission*, 179.

71 *Report of the Philippine Commission*, 165.

72 *Report of the Philippine Commission*, 169.

73 *Report of the Philippine Commission*, 167.

74 For more on de Los Reyes see William Henry Scott, "A Minority Reaction to American Imperialism: Isabelo de los Reyes," *Philippine Quarterly of Culture and Society* 10, no. 2 (1982): 1–11. For more on Native suspicion of the American

colonial state see the *Report of the Philippine Commission*, 493–495. Also see the second chapter of Melinda Tria Kerkvliet, *Manila Workers' Unions, 1900–1950* (Quezon City, Philippines: New Day Publishers, 1992).

75 Conant, *Special Report on Coinage and Banking*, 15.

76 Conant, *Special Report on Coinage and Banking*, 14, and Rosenberg, *Financial Missionaries to the World*, 16. For an in-depth history of the fate of the gold exchange standard in the Philippine colony see Nagano, "The Philippine Currency System during the American Colonial Period: Transformation from the Gold Exchange Standard to the Dollar Exchange Standard," *International Journal of Asian Studies* 7, no. 1 (2010): 30–34.

77 Conant, *Special Report on Coinage and Banking*, 7.

78 Conant, *Special Report on Coinage and Banking*, 14.

79 Conant, *Special Report on Coinage and Banking*, 8.

80 For more detail on the question of whether to name the new American colonial Philippine monetary unit "dollar" or "peso" can be found in "Magoon to Taft," July 17, 1903, box 106, folder 808, BIA RG350, NARA.

81 Conant, *Special Report on Coinage and Banking*, 21.

82 Conant, *Special Report on Coinage and Banking*, 6.

83 Conant, *Special Report on Coinage and Banking*, 21.

84 Conant, *Special Report on Coinage and Banking*, 8.

85 Conant, *Special Report on Coinage and Banking*, 8

86 "A. M. Townsend of the Hongkong & Shanghai Bank," October 31, 1900, box 106, folder 808, BIA RG350, NARA.

87 "Webster to Secretary of War," October 24, 1900, box 106, folder 808, BIA RG350, NARA.

88 "Paymaster General to Secretary of War," October 17, 1900, box 106, folder 808, BIA RG350, NARA.

89 "Paymaster General to Secretary of War," November 1, 1900, box 106, folder 808, BIA RG350, NARA.

90 Rosenberg cogently summarizes Conant's lobbying strategies in correspondences with Colonel Edwards. See specifically Rosenberg, *Financial Missionaries to the World*, 17.

91 "Press Abstract no. 11, to Be Released March 29, 1902," undated, box 10, folder 808, BIA RG350, NARA.

92 To see more on the public reaction to congressional decisions see correspondences among Conant, the BIA office, and the Philippine Commission: boxes 106 and 107, folders 880 and 3197. BIA RG350, NARA.

93 "An Act Constituting a Gold-Standard Fund in the Insular Treasury," October 10, 1903, no. 938, *Acts of the Philippine Commission* (Washington, DC: U.S. Government Printing Office, 1904), 767–772.

94 "Ide to Secretary of War," May 28, 1903, box 107, folder 808, BIA RG350, NARA.

95 "Director of Mint to Secretary of War," May 20, 1904, box 107, folder 808, BIA RG350, NARA.

96 "Chief Clerk Bureau to Secretary of War," July 1, 1903, box 199, folder 2, EWK MC146, PUL.

97 "Taft Cablegrams," August 6, 1903, box 199, folder 2, EWK MC146, PUL.

98 "Edwards to Taft," August 12, 1903, box 199, folder 2, EWK MC146, PUL.

99 "Edwards Cablegram," September 25, 1903, box 199, folder 2, EWK MC146, PUL.

100 "Whose Fault Is It," *Manila Times*, January 11, 1904, box 203, folder 3, EWK MC146, PUL.

101 "Banker Says Mex Will Go to 2 For 1," *Cable News*, January 19, 1904, box 203, folder 3, EWK MC146, PUL.

102 "Whose Fault Is It."

103 "Bastard Coins Must Go," unknown newspaper, January 1904, box 203, folder 3, EWK MC146, PUL.

104 "All Want Their Mex Exchanged," *Manila Daily Bulletin*, September 1904, box 203, folder 3, EWK MC146, PUL.

105 "'Shoving It,'" *Manila Times*, December 7, 1904, box 203, folder 3, EWK MC146, PUL.

106 "All Want Their Mex Exchanged."

107 Emily Rosenberg, "Foundations of United States International Financial Power: Gold Standard Diplomacy, 1900–1905," *Business History Review* 59, no. 2 (1985): 169–202.

108 Conant, "Currency Problems in the Orient—Discussion," 284.

109 Nagano, "The Philippine Currency System during the American Colonial Period," 35.

110 Fee, *A Woman's Impressions of the Philippines*, 162.

111 Fee, *A Woman's Impressions of the Philippines*, 166.

112 Fee, *A Woman's Impressions of the Philippines*, 166.

3. BAD MONEY

1 "HSBC Head to Hon. Members of the U.S. Commission," January 19, 1904, box 199, folder 4, EWK MC146, PUL.

2 In the Philippine context, the term *peasant* is a fraught category. It is not a clear or precise class stature, like in the European historical context. Economically the Filipino peasant could own a small piece of land, though be heavily indebted or involved in a form of sharecropping. Some who were considered peasants were mere workers, landless or coerced to work large estates. Some did not even work in agriculture as is normatively understood, though their labor and life were socially and economically tied to agricultural industry. Instead *peasant*, in the American colonial Philippines, was to become shorthand for an assemblage of intersecting identities of those dispossessed, exploited, disenfranchised, and excluded from political power. South Asian scholars of Subaltern Studies have had the most rich and generative kinds of analysis of the peasant for my understanding. For a good overview of their work see Vinayak Chaturvedi, ed., *Mapping Subaltern Studies and the Postcolonial* (London: Verso, 2000).

3 Kemmerer often referred to British colonies in his reports and correspondences concerning Philippine currency and banking. For more on British and American imperial rivalry and affinity see Daniel Rodgers, *Atlantic Crossings: Social Politics*

in a Progressive Age (Cambridge, MA: Harvard University Press, 2000), and Stuart Anderson, *Race and Rapprochement: Anglo-Saxonism and Anglo-American Relations, 1895–1904* (Madison, NJ: Fairleigh Dickinson University Press, 1981).

4 Cedric Robinson, *Black Marxism: The Making of the Black Radical Tradition* (Chapel Hill: University of North Carolina Press, 2000).

5 Progressivism was narrated as an antidote for the detrimental social effects of industrial capitalism and the destabilizing force of finance capitalism that exceeded the limits of the politics of Progressivism. If there is one strong element in Kemmerer's thinking that can be linked to Progressivism it is the increased privileging of technocracy and efficiency, especially in reforms of the political system, civil society, and sites of production. For more on these historic trends see Jennifer Karns Alexander, *The Mantra of Efficiency: From Waterwheel to Social Control* (Baltimore, MD: Johns Hopkins University Press, 2008); Samuel Haber, *Efficiency and Uplift: Scientific Management in the Progressive Era, 1890–1920* (Chicago: University of Chicago Press, 1973); Dorothy Ross, *The Origins of American Social Science* (Cambridge: Cambridge University Press, 1991); Stephen Skowronek, *Building a New American State: The Expansion of National Administration Capacities, 1877–1920* (Cambridge: Cambridge University Press, 1982). Some have studied the connections and disconnections between Progressivism and colonialism in the Philippines. See, for example, Patricio Abinales, "Progressive-Machine Conflict in Early-Twentieth-Century U.S. Politics and Colonial-State Building in the Philippines," in *The American Colonial State in the Philippines: Global Perspectives*, eds. Julian Go and Ann Foster (Durham, NC: Duke University Press, 2003), 148–181; and Paul Kramer, "Reflex Actions: Colonialism, Corruption and the Politics of Technocracy in the Early Twentieth Century United States," in *Challenging US Foreign Policy: America and the World in the Long Twentieth Century*, eds. Bevan Sewell and Scott Lucas (New York: Palgrave Macmillan, 2011), 14–35.

6 For more on disavowal through narrativization see Lisa Lowe, *The Intimacies of Four Continents* (Durham, NC: Duke University Press, 2015). For more on the fantasy of white creativity and innovation, rather than land theft, genocide, and enslavement as the basis of U.S. capital accumulation, see Walter Johnson, *The Broken Heart of America: St. Louis and the Violent History of the United States* (New York: Basic Books, 2020).

7 To see more of the crucial way that agricultural production plays a foundational role within this settler colonial narrative of U.S. capitalist superiority see Alyosha Goldstein, "The Ground Not Given: Colonial Dispositions of Land, Race, and Hunger," *Social Text* 36, no. 2 (2018): 83–106.

8 Yoshiko Nagano, "Philippine Currency System during the American Colonial Period: Transformation from the Gold Exchange Standard to the Dollar Exchange Standard," *International Journal of Asian Studies* 7, no. 1 (2010): 33.

9 For more on Kemmerer see Paul Drake, *The Money Doctor in the Andes: The Kemmerer Missions, 1923–1933* (Durham, NC: Duke University Press, 1989). To look specifically at Kemmerer's work in the Philippines, see chapter 1 of Emily Rosenberg, *Financial Missionaries to the World: The Politics and Culture of Dollar*

Diplomacy, 1900–1930 (Durham, NC: Duke University Press, 2004), and chapter 4 of Colin Moore, *American Imperialism and the State, 1893–1921* (Cambridge: Cambridge University Press, 2017).

10 According to Rosenberg, not only were the dominant majority of economists, financial advisors, and bankers identified as male, but notions of the proper management of the capitalist market were largely informed by white bourgeois gender norms. Rosenberg, *Financial Missionaries to the World*, 33.

11 "Edwin W. Kemmerer to Jeremiah Jenks," May 27, 1903, box 199, folder 2, EWK MC146, PUL.

12 "Letter of Job Offer to Kemmerer," May 27, 1903, box 199, folder 2, EWK MC146, PUL.

13 "Ide to Secretary of War," January 23, 1904, box 199, folder 4, EWK MC146, PUL.

14 "J. R. M. Smith to Kemmerer," January 13, 1904, box 199, folder 4, EWK MC146, PUL.

15 "Kemmerer to Jenks," January 14, 1904, box 199, folder 4, EWK MC146, PUL.

16 "HSBC Head to Hon. Members of the U.S. Commission."

17 "J. R. M. Smith to Kemmerer."

18 "HSBC Head to Hon. Members of the U.S. Commission."

19 "Conant to Jenks," March 8, 1904, box 106, folder 808, BIA RG350, NARA.

20 "Jenks to Wright," January 15, 1904, box 199, folder 4, EWK MC146, PUL.

21 "Jenks to Root," January 23, 1904, box 199, folder 4, EWK MC146, PUL.

22 "Kemmerer to Jenks," January 24, 1904, box 199, folder 4, EWK MC146, PUL.

23 "Kemmerer to Jenks," February 16, 1904, box 199, folder 4, EWK MC146, PUL.

24 "Kemmerer to H. Parker Willis," October 26, 1904, box 199, folder 4, EWK MC146, PUL.

25 "Kemmerer to Jenks," January 12, 1905, box 199, folder 4, EWK MC146, PUL.

26 "Kemmerer to Jenks, January 30, 1905, box 199, folder 4, EWK MC146, PUL.

27 "Treasury Bureau, 3rd Indorsement," January 10, 1905, box 201, folder 8, EWK MC146, PUL.

28 "Kemmerer to Jenks," July 18, 1905, box 199, folder 7, EWK MC146, PUL.

29 Anxieties over Chinese smugglers were peppered throughout expert correspondences from 1905 to 1907. See especially box 108, folder 808, BIA RG350, NARA.

30 On the various responses and nervousness over the sudden price increase of silver and on the policy of adjusting the fineness of coins see box 108, folder 808, BIA RG350, NARA.

31 Edwin W. Kemmerer, *Modern Currency Reforms: A History and Discussion of Recent Currency Reforms in India, Puerto Rico, Philippine Islands, Straits Settlements and Mexico* (New York: Macmillan Company, 1916), 365.

32 "Kemmerer to Jenks," January 30, 1905, box 199, folder 7, EWK MC146, PUL.

33 *Report of the Philippine Commission*, vol. 8, pt. 2 (Washington, DC: U.S. Government Printing Office, 1909), 44.

34 "Kemmerer to Henry Ide," July 13, 1904, box 199, folder 7, EWK MC146, PUL.

35 "Division of the Currency, 6th Indorsement," January 5, 1905, box 199, folder 7, EWK MC146, PUL.

36 "Kemmerer to Jenks," January 12, 1905, box 199, folder 7, EWK MC146, PUL.

37 "Kemmerer to Jenks," January 12, 1905, box 199, folder 7, EWK MC146, PUL.

38 "Kemmerer to Frank Branagan," October 31, 1904, box 199, folder 4, EWK MC146, PUL.

39 "Kemmerer to Jenks," January 12, 1905, box 199, folder 7, EWK MC146, PUL.

40 "Executive Order No. 2: The Government of the Philippine Islands," January 13, 1905, box 201, folder 8, EWK MC146, PUL.

41 For more on policies of attraction see Paul Kramer, *The Blood of Government: Race, Empire, the United States, and the Philippines* (Chapel Hill: University of North Carolina Press, 2006), 79.

42 "Kemmerer to Jenks," March 31, 1905, box 199, folder 7, EWK MC146, PUL.

43 "Kemmerer to Henry Ide."

44 Edwin W. Kemmerer, "The Philippine Postal Savings Bank," *Annals of the American Academy of Political and Social Science* 30 (July 1907): 47.

45 Edwin W. Kemmerer, "An Agricultural Bank for the Philippines," *Yale Review* 16 (May 1907): 261.

46 Kemmerer was under the impression that this tour would be paid for by the U.S. colonial state in the Philippines, but he was never reimbursed for his work. He would have to borrow from a friend in the Philippine colonial state, Ben F. Wright, to make it back to the U.S. mainland. See entry by Kemmerer's son, Donald Kemmerer: "Excerpt for Dictionary of American Biography by Donald Kemmerer," June 5, 1990, box 291, folder 3, EWK MC146, PUL.

47 Ben F. Wright, "The Philippine Postal Savings Bank," *University of California Chronicle* 10, no. 4 (1907), box 204, folder 1, EWK MC146, PUL.

48 "Division of Currency, 9th Indorsement," July 12, 1905, box 203, folder 6, EWK MC146, PUL.

49 "Bill Providing for the Establishment of Postal Savings Banks in the Philippines Islands," July 13, 1904, box 199, folder 4, EWK MC146, PUL. This would be enshrined in the first words of the PSB act, which stated that the law would teach "economy and saving among the people of the Philippine Islands." "Public Law: Postal Savings Bank," *Official Gazette*, June 20, 1906, box 203, folder 7, EWK MC146, PUL.

50 "Kemmerer to Winthrop," October 17, 1906. box 203, folder 7, EWK MC146, PUL.

51 William Cameron Forbes, journal, vol. 2; "May 23, 1906," MS Am 1365, Houghton Library, Harvard University (hereafter MS Am 1365, HL), 12–13.

52 Forbes, "May 25, 1906," MS Am 1365, HL, 15.

53 Forbes, "December 16, 1904"; MS Am 1365, HL, 2.

54 Forbes, in a typical imperial American and white supremacist fashion, to prove his point, disavowed the long nineteenth century's modern transformation of both modes of labor and production of capital in the Spanish colonial Philippines. In other words, the Spanish Philippines, long before the arrival of American Empire, had long interacted with the discipline, organization, and promises of capitalist modernity. See Benito Legarda, *After the Galleons: Foreign Trade, Economic Change and Entrepreneurship in the Nineteenth Century Philippines* (Quezon City, Philippines: Ateneo de Manila University Press; Madison: University of Wisconsin Press, 1999), and Josep Fradera, "The Historical Origins of the Philippine Economy: A Survey of Recent Research of the Spanish Colonial Era," *Australian Economic History Review* 44, no. 3 (2004): 307–320.

55 "Postal Savings Bank Thriving," *Manila Times*, October 10, 1906, box 203, folder 7, EWK MC146, PUL.

56 "Wright to Kemmerer," December 10, 1906, box 203, folder 7, EWK MC146, PUL.

57 "The Postal Savings Bank, Press Release for Panay and Negros," undated, most likely 1905 or 1906, box 204, folder 1, EWK MC146, PUL.

58 "Postal Savings Bank, Press Release."

59 Wright, "Philippine Postal Savings Bank."

60 "Statutes of the Monte De Piedad," January 1901, box 198, folder 6, EWK MC146, PUL.

61 "Postal Savings Bank, Press Release."

62 "Wright to Branagan," March 15, 1907, box 198, folder 7, EWK MC146, PUL.

63 "Wright to Branagan."

64 "First Annual Report of Chief of Postal Savings Bank Division," June 30, 1907, box 203, folder 9, EWK MC146, PUL.

65 "Wright to Branagan." For more on education in the American colonial Philippines see Sarah Steinbock-Pratt, *Educating the Empire: American Teachers and Contested Colonization in the Philippines* (Cambridge: Cambridge University Press, 2019).

66 Forbes, journal, "May 25, 1906," MS Am 1365, HL, 15, esp. n. 72.

67 "Postal Savings Bank Contest, Bureau of Education," October 19, 1910, box 203, folder 9, EWK MC146, PUL.

68 "First Annual Report of Chief of Postal Savings Bank Division."

69 Kemmerer, "The Philippine Postal Savings Bank," 45.

70 "Bill Providing for the Establishment of Postal Savings Banks."

71 Kemmerer, "The Philippine Postal Savings Bank," 45.

72 There was a strong American Protestant movement against the maintenance of idleness, especially gambling. See Filomeno V. Aguilar Jr., *Clash of Spirits: The History of Power and Sugar Planter Hegemony on a Visayan Island* (Honolulu: University of Hawai'i Press, 1998).

73 "Postal Savings Bank, Press Release."

74 "Morality and Not Intellectuality the Standard of Self-government," *Manila Times*, December 12, 1906, box 203, folder 3, EWK MC146, PUL.

75 Edwin W. Kemmerer, "Philippine Postal Savings Bank," *American Monthly Review of Reviews* 34 (1906): 468–470.

76 For an in-depth analysis of the 1907 elections see Michael Cullinane, *Ilustrado Politics: Filipino Elite Responses to American Rule, 1898–1908* (Quezon City, Philippines: Ateneo de Manila University Press, 2003), and Ruby Paredes, "Origins of National Politics," in *Philippine Colonial Democracy*, ed. Ruby Paredes (New Haven, CT: Yale University Southeast Asian Studies, 1988).

77 "Wright to Kemmerer," February 23, 1907, box 203, folder 8, EWK MC146, PUL.

78 "Investments for Philippine Banks' Funds Restricted," *Boston Tribune*, April 22, 1907, and "Filipinos and Thrift," *Boston Advertiser*, April 24, 1907, box 203, folder 3, EWK MC146, PUL.

79 Wright, "Philippine Postal Savings Bank."

80 Kemmerer, "The Progress of the Filipino People toward Self-government," *Political Science Quarterly* 23, no. 1 (1908): 66. See Benedict Anderson's take on how

American political innovations created a "cacique democracy" proving that this institution was not as ancient or natural as imperialists such as Kemmerer would like to believe. Benedict R. O'G. Anderson, *The Spectre of Comparisons: Nationalism, Southeast Asia and the World* (New York: Verso, 1998), 200–202.

81 Kemmerer, "Progress of the Filipino People," 71.

82 "Half Month Town," *Manila Times*, April 29, 1907; "Says Filipinos are Improvident," *New York Herald*, April 27, 1907; and "Filipinos and Thrift," *Boston Advertiser*, April 24, 1907; all from box 203, folder 3, EWK MC146, PUL.

83 "Filipino Students Jump on Kemmerer," *Manila Times*, May 4, 1907, box 203, folder 3, EWK MC146, PUL.

84 "Ungrateful Filipinos," *Philadelphia Record*, April 23 1907, box 203, folder 3, EWK MC146, PUL.

85 Kemmerer, "Progress of the Filipino People," 72. For more on the larger historical context of the intricacies of Filipino party politics and the elections of 1907 see Peter W. Stanley, *A Nation in the Making: The Philippines and the United States, 1899–1921* (Cambridge, MA: Harvard University Press, 1974); Bonifacio S. Salamanca, *Filipino Reaction to American Rule, 1901–1913* (Hamden, CT: Shoe String Press, 1968); Michael Cullinane, "Playing the Game: The Rise of Sergio Osmena, 1898–1907," in *Philippine Colonial Democracy*, ed. Ruby R. Paredes (New Haven, CT: Yale University Southeast Asian Studies, 1988); Frank Jenista, Jr. "Conflict in the Philippine Legislature: The Commission and the Assembly from 1907 to 1913," in *Compadre Colonialism: Studies on the Philippines under American Rule*, ed. Norman G. Owen (Ann Arbor: University of Michigan, 1971).

86 "Kemmerer to Jenks," September 15, 1904, box 203, folder 3, EWK MC146, PUL.

87 "General Order, October 22nd," 1904, box 199, folder 4, EWK MC146, PUL; and "Public Announcement (by Local Business)," November 26, 1903, box 199, folder 3, EWK MC146, PUL.

88 "Kemmerer to Jenks," September 15, 1904, box 199, folder 7, EWK MC146, PUL.

89 "Kemmerer to Jenks," September 15, 1904, box 199, folder 7, EWK MC146, PUL.

90 "Free trade" was simply a way to lock the Philippines into exporting what was needed by U.S. settler capitalists, without protecting Philippine commodities, and forcing higher valued U.S. commodities into the Philippines, again without the ability to set tariffs on U.S. imports into the colony. For more on the nominal free trade see Frank Golay, *Face of Empire: United States–Philippines Relations, 1898–1946* (Quezon City, Philippines: Ateneo de Manila University Press; Madison: University of Wisconsin Press, 1998), 129.

91 "Good Profit on Coinage," October 1, 1910, box 544, folder 9342, BIA RG350, NARA.

92 "Conant to McIntyre," June 15, 1911, box 544, folder 9342, BIA RG350, NARA.

93 "Proposed Changes in the Monetary Law of the Philippine Islands," October 27, 1914, box 202, folder 3, EWK MC146, PUL.

94 "Conant to McIntyre," October 5, 1910, box 544, folder 9342, BIA RG350, NARA; and "Conant to Edwards," December 9, 1910, box 544, folder 9342, BIA RG350, NARA.

95 "Insular Bureau Memorandum," October 12, 1910, box 544, folder 9342, BIA RG350, NARA.

96 "Proposed Changes in the Monetary Law."

97 "Forbes to Stimson," December 21, 1911, box 544, folder 9342, BIA RG350, NARA.

98 "Bureau of Treasury, 2nd Indorsement," March 19, 1912, box 544, folder 9342, BIA RG350, NARA.

99 Arturo Corpuz, *The Colonial Iron Horse: Railroads and Regional Development in the Philippines, 1875–1935* (Quezon City: University of the Philippines Press, 1999), 111–119.

100 "Proposed Changes in the Monetary Law."

101 "Wm. A Jones to Quezon," June 20, 1912, box 544, folder 9342, BIA RG350, NARA.

4. AN ORGY OF MISMANAGEMENT

1 Leonard Wood and Cameron Forbes, *Report of the Special Mission on Investigation to the Philippine Islands of the Secretary of War* (Washington, DC: U.S. Government Printing Office, 1921), 38 (hereafter, *Wood-Forbes Report*).

2 *Wood-Forbes Report*, 38.

3 For more on the entanglement between material imperial institutions and ideological market institutions in colonial zones see Emily Rosenberg, *Financial Missionaries to the World: The Politics and Culture of Dollar Diplomacy, 1900–1930* (Durham, NC: Duke University Press, 2003), and Peter Hudson, *Bankers and Empire: How Wall Street Colonized the Caribbean* (Chicago: University of Chicago Press, 2017).

4 For more on the United States' newfound role in the global political economy see Ron Chernow, *The House of Morgan: An American Banking Dynasty and the Rise of Modern Finance* (New York: Grove Press, 1990); Edwin Burrows and Mike Wallace, *Gotham: The History of New York City to 1898* (London: Oxford University Press, 1999); Jeff Friedman, "Sectoral Conflict and Foreign Economic Policy, 1914–1940," *International Organization* 42, no. 1 (1988): 59–90; and Emily Rosenberg, *Spreading the American Dream: American Economic and Cultural Expansion, 1890–1945* (New York: Hill and Wang, 1982).

5 There indeed remained limitations and tensions within the United States' global rise in economic power. For more see J. Lawrence Broz, *The International Origins of the Federal Reserve* (Ithaca, NY: Cornell University Press, 1997); James Livingston, *Origins of the Federal Reserve System: Money, Class, and Corporate Capitalism, 1890–1913* (Ithaca, NY: Cornell University, 1896), and Chernow, *House of Morgan*.

6 For more sustained analysis of the various historical reasons for the Federal Reserve System see Broz, *International Origins of the Federal Reserve*; Livingston, *Origins of the Federal Reserve System*; Roger Lowenstein, *America's Bank: The Epic Struggle to Create the Federal Reserve* (New York: Penguin Books, 2015); and Allan Meltzer, *A History of the Federal Reserve*, vol. 1, *1913–1951* (Chicago: University of Chicago Press, 2003).

7 For more on Wilson and how his logic of self-determination was greatly shaped by racial paternalist ideologies see chapter 2 of Adam Ewing, *The Age of Garvey: How a Jamaican Activist Created a Mass Movement and Changed Global Black Politics* (Princeton, NJ: Princeton University Press, 2014).

8   Erez Manela asserts that Wilsonian language helped created the conditions for certain kinds of anti-imperial nationalisms. Although true, Wilsonianism was simultaneously a language of antiradicalism as well, and in many ways offered nationalist elites a set of concepts to suppress and domesticate demands for absolute decolonization. Erez Manela, *The Wilsonian Moment: Self-Determination and the International Origins of Anticolonial Nationalism* (Oxford: Oxford University Press, 2007). For more on the contradictions of Wilsonian anti-imperialism see Ewing, *Age of Garvey*, and Mary Renda, *Taking Haiti: Military Occupation and the Culture of U.S. Imperialism, 1915–1940* (Chapel Hill: University of North Carolina Press, 2001).

9   "Bandholtz to McIntyre," January 24, 1913; microfilm edition, reel 5, Harry H. Bandholtz Papers, Bentley Historical Library, University of Michigan.

10 The literature on land consolidation and accumulation in the eighteenth- and nineteenth-century Philippines is substantial. For the more successful studies see Filomeno V. Aguilar Jr., *Clash of Spirits: The History of Power and Sugar Planter Hegemony on a Visayan Island* (Honolulu: University of Hawai'i Press, 1998); Ed. C. de Jesus, *The Tobacco Monopoly in the Philippines: Bureaucratic Enterprise and Social Change, 1766–1880* (Quezon City, Philippines: Ateneo de Manila Press, 1998); Josep Fradera, "The Historical Origins of the Philippine Economy: A Survey of Recent Research of the Spanish Colonial Era," *Australian Economic History Review* 44, no. 3 (2004): 307–420; Benito J. Legarda, *After the Galleons: Foreign Trade, Economic Change and Entrepreneurship in the Nineteenth Century Philippines* (Quezon City, Philippines: Ateneo de Manila University Press, 1999); Norman G. Owen, *Prosperity without Progress: Manila Hemp and Material Life in the Colonial Philippines* (Berkeley: University of California Press, 1984); and Jim Richardson and Jonathan Fast, *Roots of Dependency: Political and Economic Revolution in 19th Century Philippines* (Quezon City, Philippines: Foundation for Nationalist Studies, 1979).

11 "Congreso Agricola de Filipinas," September 27, 1915, box 297, folder 6769, BIA RG350, NARA.

12 There is much on the very public bank and forth between Filipino lawmakers and leaders on the national necessity for an agricultural bank, see especially box 675, folder 6769, BIA RG350, NARA.

13 Yoshiko Nagano, "The Agricultural Bank of the Philippine Government, 1908–1916," *Journal of Southeast Asian Studies* 28, no. 2 (1997): 319.

14 Emilio Aguinaldo, "For an Agricultural Loan Bank," August 28, 1915, box 617, folder 6769, BIA RG350, NARA.

15 H. Parker Willis, "The Philippine National Bank," *Journal of Political Economy* 25, no, 5 (1917): 417.

16 "Following Correspondence from Manila and London," Associated Press, New York, January 25, 1916; box 661, folder 6769, BIA RG350, NARA.

17 "McIntyre to Harrison," October 30, 1915, box 661, folder 6769, BIA RG350, NARA.

18 Henderson Martin, "The Insular Bank of the Philippines," September 14, 1915, box 661, folder 6769a, BIA RG350, NARA.

19 Willis was not alone in making this connection between the Philippine colonial economic experts and the Federal Reserve. Indeed, noted Philippine expert, Edwin Kemmerer, was tapped by Governor Benjamin Strong of Federal Reserve

Bank of New York to write a book on the Federal Reserve for the general public in 1919. It was popular enough to have myriad reprintings, going into a fifth reprint in less than five years. Edwin Kemmerer, *The ABC of the Federal Reserve System* (Princeton, NJ: Princeton University Press, 1919).

20 There are frequent allusions to the freelance investigative work by H. Parker Willis in the correspondences between Kemmerer and Jenks from August to October 1904. For example, see box 199, folder 4, EWK MC146, PUL. And for an example of Willis's early work on the economic conditions of the Philippine colony see H. Parker Willis, "The Economic Situation in the Philippines," *Journal of Political Economy* 13, no. 2 (1905): 145–172, and *Our Philippine Problem: A Study of American Colonial Policy* (New York: Henry Holt, 1905).

21 Willis, "Philippine National Bank," 416–417.

22 "Insular Bank Bill," December 14, 1915, box 661, folder 6769, BIA RG350, NARA. "McIntyre to Willis," December 31, 1915, box 661, folder 6769, BIA RG350, NARA.

23 Peter W. Stanley, *A Nation in the Making: The Philippines and the United States, 1899–1921* (Cambridge, MA: Harvard University Press, 1974), 236–237.

24 "Remarks of H. P. Willis at Meeting of Manila Merchant's Association," June 22, 1916, Henry Parker Willis papers; box 17, folder 16, Rare Book and Manuscript Library, Columbia University.

25 Francis Coates, "Investigation of the Currency Reserve Fund and the Gold Standard Fund of the Philippine Treasury," March 3, 1921, box 668, folder 6769, BIA RG350, NARA.

26 H. Parker Willis, "The New Philippine Bank and Our Trade with the Islands," *The Nation's Business,* November 1916, box 675, folder 6769a, BIA RG350, NARA.

27 Willis, "Philippine National Bank," 417.

28 For more on Willis after leaving the Philippine colony see chapter 4 of Yoshiko Nagano, *State and Finance in the Philippines, 1898–1941: The Mismanagement of an American Colony* (Quezon City, Philippines: Ateneo de Manila University Press; Singapore: National University Press, 2015).

29 Coates, "Investigation of the Currency Reserve Fund.".

30 "Willis to the War Department," August 9, 1916, box 662, folder 6769, BIA RG350, NARA.

31 Coates, "Investigation of the Currency Reserve Fund."

32 Stanley, *Nation in the Making,* 240.

33 Stanley, *Nation in the Making,* 38–40.

34 "The Effects of the Present Crisis Will Be Felt until 1923," *El Ideal,* Manila, June 29, 1921, box 675, folder 6769a, BIA RG350, NARA.

35 Jack C. Lane, "Wood, Leonard," in *American National Biography,* modified February 2000, https://doi.org/10.1093/anb/9780198606697.article.0600730.

36 *Wood-Forbes Report,* 8.

37 *Wood-Forbes Report,* 19.

38 "The Debt of the Philippine Islands–The Banking Situation," *New York Times,* July 6, 1923, box 675, folder 6769a, BIA RG350, NARA.

39 Frederick Gilman Hoyt, "The Wood-Forbes Mission to the Philippines, 1921" (PhD diss. Claremont Graduate School and University Center, 1963), 301–304.

40 "Philippines in Chaos; Big Harding Task," *Washington Tribune*, February 26, 1921, box 675, folder 6769a, BIA RG350, NARA.

41 "The First Arrest in the Bank Case," *El Comercio*, June 25, 1921, box 675, folder 6769a, BIA RG350, NARA.

42 "F. Harrison Makes Disclosure about P. National Bank," *Philippine Herald*, July 16, 1924, box 675, folder 6769a, BIA RG350, NARA.

43 "Philippines in Chaos; Big Harding Task."

44 At the time, both the Wood administration and conservative Philippine newspapers blamed Concepción as the sole cause of crisis, and in the discipline of history, Stanley—for English language readers—in *Nation in the Making* is most famous for reproducing this narrative. In heterogeneous ways, many subsequent histories have inherited Stanley's analysis of Concepción and the PNB. See, for example, Patricio N. Abinales and Donna J. Amoroso, *State and Society in the Philippines* (New York: Rowman and Littlefield, 2005); David Ekbladh, *The Great American Mission: Modernization and the Construction of an American World Order* (Princeton, NJ: Princeton University Press, 2011); Paul Hutchcroft, *Booty Capitalism: The Politics of Banking in the Philippines* (Ithaca, NY: Cornell University Press, 1998); Alfred McCoy, *Policing America's Empire: The United States, the Philippines, and Rise of the Surveillance State* (Madison: University of Wisconsin, 2009).

45 "The First Arrest in the Bank Case," *El Comercio*, June 25, 1921, box 675, folder 6769a, BIA RG350, NARA.

46 Coates, "Investigation of the Currency Reserve Fund." As others have shown, the assessment of racialized people's ability to perform and comprehend modernity provided a constantly malleable gauge by which colonialism could be continued indefinitely. This constantly malleable gauge could, in turn, ensure that Filipino authority over an autonomous economy would always be constantly displaced into some distant horizon. Paul Kramer refers to this imperial and colonial strategy of measurement and deferment of colonial subjects as "colonial calibration." In this he is not alone. Similarly, others in different works, such as Warwick Anderson refer to the measuring of "capacity," while Dipesh Chakrabarty describes it as "the waiting room." Warwick Anderson, *Colonial Pathologies: American Tropical Medicine, Race, and Hygiene in the Philippines* (Durham, NC: Duke University Press, 2006); Dipesh Chakrabarty, *Provincializing Europe: Postcolonial Thought and Historical Difference* (Princeton, NJ: Princeton University Press, 2000); and Paul Kramer, *The Blood of Government: Race, Empire, the United States and the Philippines* (Chapel Hill: University of North Carolina Press, 2006).

47 Coates, "Investigation of the Currency Reserve Fund."

48 Coates, "Investigation of the Currency Reserve Fund."

49 Underlines are contained in the original. Coates, "Investigation of the Currency Reserve Fund."

50 "Philippines in Chaos; Big Harding Task."

51 "Venancio Concepción, Ex-president of the National Bank, Indicted," *La Vanguardia*, Manila, June 24, 1921, box 675, folder 6769a, BIA RG350, NARA.

52 "We Now Have a Case of Malfeasance in the National Branch Bank," *La Revolución*, Cebu, May 28, 1921, box 675, folder 6769a, BIA RG350, NARA.

53 "The Conduct of General Concepción as President of the National Bank," *El Ideal*, June 20, 1921, box 675, folder 6769a, BIA RG350, NARA.

54 "Concepción to Willis," June 5, 1919; "Concepción to Willis," June 17, 1919; and "Willis to Concepción," June 20, 1919; all from box 667, folder 6769, BIA RG350, NARA.

55 "Willis to Walcutt," June 19, 1919, box 667, folder 6769, BIA RG350, NARA.

56 Nagano, *State and Finance in the Philippines*, 171–180.

57 Yoshiko Nagano, "The Philippine Currency System during the American Colonial Period: Transformation from the Gold Exchange Standard to the Dollar Exchange Standard," *International Journal of Asian Studies* 7, no. 1 (2010): 31–34.

58 "Deveyra to Kemmerer," December 12, 1917, box 200, folder 3, EWK MC146, PUL. "Yeater to Walcutt," April 20, 1919, box 667, folder 6769, BIA RG350, NARA.

59 Nagano, "Philippine Currency System," 35–42.

60 By 1920 approximately 85 percent of Philippine exports were directed toward the United States, while almost 60 percent of Philippine imports came from the United States. O. D. Corpuz, *An Economic History of the Philippines* (Quezon City: University of the Philippines Press, 1997), 243.

61 George F. Luthringer, *The Gold-Exchange Standard in the Philippines* (Princeton, NJ: Princeton University Press, 1934), 114.

62 "The Philippine National Bank," *Manila Times*, June 9, 1923, box 675, folder 6769a, BIA RG350, NARA.

63 See the set of documents within system 6769, BIA RG350, NARA.

64 Nagano, *State and Finance in the Philippines*, 128–137.

65 "Philippine National Bank," *Manila Times*.

66 "Gen. Wood Gives Out Rejected Message Condemns National Bank," *New York Times*, August 19, 1923, box 675, folder 6769a, BIA RG350, NARA.

67 "Philippines in Chaos; Big Harding Task."

68 "The National Bank Will Soon Be Able to Render the Services Expected of It," *El Ideal*, Manila, September 14, 1921, box 675, folder 6769a, BIA RG350, NARA.

69 "Philippine National Bank," *Manila Times*.

70 "Conversion of the National Bank into a Purely Agricultural Bank," *El Ideal*, Manila, March 18, 1922, box 675, folder 6769a, BIA RG350, NARA.

71 Nagano, *State and Finance in the Philippines*, 182.

72 "Gen. Wood Gives Out Rejected Message."

73 "Protest Publicity on Filipino Bank," *Washington Post*, August 20, 1923, box 675, folder 6769a, BIA RG350, NARA.

74 "An Orgy of Mismanagement: The Story of the PNB," *Far Eastern Review*, September 1923, box 675, folder 6769a, BIA RG350, NARA.

75 "An Orgy of Mismanagement."

76 "The Trend of Events in the Philippines: The High Cost of Altruism" *Far Eastern Review*, September 1923, box 675, folder 6769a, BIA RG350, NARA.

77 "McIntyre to Coates," April 5, 1921, box 670, folder 6769, BIA RG350, NARA.

78 "Memorandum for the Secretary of War," February 28, 1923, box 672, folder 6769, BIA RG350, NARA.

79 "Wright to McIntyre," January 30, 1923, box 672, folder 6769, BIA RG350, NARA.

80 Ben F. Wright, "Report on the Philippine National Bank: A Revaluation of the Bank's Assets," May 14, 1921, box 672, folder 6769, BIA RG350, NARA.

81 Wright, "Report on the Philippine National Bank."

82 "PNB Views of a Filipino on the Governor General's Powers," *New York Times*, April 10, 1921, 11, box 675, folder 6769, BIA RG350, NARA.

83 "Leonard Wood to Frank McIntyre," April 6, 1923, box 675, folder 6769, BIA RG350, NARA.

84 "The National Bank Grants a Loan to the Bank of the Islands of 6,000,000 Pesos in Place of Helping the Farmers." *El Ideal*, November 16, 1921, box 675, folder 6769a, BIA RG350, NARA.

85 "Alegre Accuses Americans: Maintains That They Are Principal Defrauders of the Bank," *El Debate*, April 27, 1923, box 675, folder 6769a, BIA RG350, NARA.

86 *Bagong Lipang Kalabaw* was a revival of a magazine *Lipang Kalabaw* previously published during the first decade of American rule. Both incarnations were headed by Lope K. Santos. For more see Alfred W. McCoy and Alfredo R. Roces, *Philippine Cartoons: Political Caricature of the American Era, 1900–1941* (Quezon City, Philippines: Vera-Reyes, 1985).

87 "De Veyra to Kemmerer," February 15, 1918, box 200, folder 3, EWK MC146, PUL.

88 "Ang Mga Esperto sa Bangko Nasyonal at ang Lehistura Pilipina" [The Experts at the National Bank and the Philippine Legislature], *Bagong Lipang Kalabaw*, November 18, 1922, 1. All Tagalog translations are my own.

89 "Mga Mangingisda sa Malabong Ilog ng Bangko Nasyonal ng Pilipinas" [The Fishermen at the Murky River of the Philippine National Bank], *Bagong Lipang Kalabaw*, November 11, 1922, front cover.

90 "Isang Bagong Samson" [A Brand New Samson], *Bagong Lipang Kalabaw*, August 15, 1923, front cover.

91 "Pinipilit Igiba ang Bangko Nasyonal" [Forced Destruction of the National Bank], *Bagong Lipang Kalabaw*, August 15, 1923, 1.

92 "The Governor General and Filipino Leaders Have Diametrically Opposed Views on the PNB," *Philippine Press Bureau*, June 29, 1923, box 675, folder 6769a, BIA RG350, NARA.

93 Camilo Osias, "A Year of Governor Wood's Administration," in *Governor-General Wood and the Filipino Cause*, ed. Manuel Quezon and Camilo Osias (Manila: Manila Book, 1924), 93.

94 Osias, "A Year of Governor Wood's Administration," 98.

95 Osias, "The Historic National Issue," *Governor-General Wood and the Filipino Cause*, 197.

96 "Manila Bank Reorganizes," *New York Times*, November 9, 1924, box 675, folder 6769a, BIA RG350, NARA.

97 "Proposed Bank Bill Worse than Disease," *Manila Bulletin*, October 18, 1924, box 675, folder 6769a, BIA RG350, NARA.

98 "Bank Officials to Show Wright Report Wrong in Conclusions," *Philippine Herald*, December 10, 1925, box 675, folder 6769a, BIA RG350, NARA.

99 "Shake-up of National Bank Recommended," *Manila Bulletin*, October 21, 1925, box 675, folder 6769a, BIA RG350, NARA.

100 "New Quo Warranto Suit to Decide Control of National Bank Impends," *Manila Bulletin*, January 18, 1927, box 675, folder 6769a, BIA RG350, NARA.

101 "Hints of Mismanagement in Philippine National Draw Official Answer," *Manila Bulletin*, March 5, 1927, box 675, folder 6769a, BIA RG350, NARA.

102 "Emphasizing Nation in 'National,'" *Philippine Herald*, May 8, 1928, box 675, folder 6769a, BIA RG350, NARA.

103 "Californian Named Auditor for Bank," *Manila Times*, May 8, 1928, box 675, folder 6769a, BIA RG350, NARA.

104 "American Majority of Bank Believed Injurious to Filipinos," *Philippine Herald*, May 19, 1927, box 675, folder 6769a, BIA RG350, NARA.

105 "Wright to Kemmerer," July 29, 1927, box 200, folder 6, EWK MC146, PUL.

106 "Majority of Bank's Directors May Be Eventually Americans," *Philippine Herald*, May 19, 1927, box 675, folder 6769a, BIA RG350, NARA.

107 "Wright to Kemmerer," July 22, 1929, box 200, folder 6, EWK MC146, PUL.

108 "Wright to Kemmerer," July 22, 1929. Despite their friendship it is interesting that Kemmerer eventually agreed to be hired as an advisor to the Philippine colonial state even after Wright's resignation. See, for instance, "Schwulst to Kemmerer," August 15, 1929, box 200, folder 6, EWK MC146, PUL.

109 Corpuz, *Economic History of the Philippines*, 243.

110 *Independence for the Philippine Islands: Hearings before the Committee on Territories and Insular Affairs* (Washington, DC: U.S. Government Printing Office, 1932), xxvii.

5. UNDER COMMON WEALTH

1 Sergio Osmeña, *The Commonwealth: A Year of Accomplishments (1938–39)* (Manila, Bureau of Printing, 1939), 15.

2 Leonard Wood and Cameron Forbes, *Report of the Special Mission on Investigation to the Philippine Islands of the Secretary of War* (Washington, DC: U.S. Government Printing Office, 1921).

3 Osmeña, *Commonwealth*, 15.

4 For more on the refusal of monetary policymakers to cooperate see Barry Eichengreen, *Golden Fetters: The Gold Standard and the Great Depression, 1919–1939* (New York: Oxford University Press, 1992); Charles Kindleberger, *The World in Depression, 1929–1939* (Berkeley: University of California Press, 1976); and Peter Temin, *Lessons from the Great Depression* (Cambridge, MA: MIT Press, 1989).

5 Emily Rosenberg, *Financial Missionaries to the World: The Politics and Culture of Dollar Diplomacy, 1900–1930* (Cambridge, MA: Harvard University Press, 1999), 242.

6 Rosenberg, *Financial Missionaries to the World*, 243.

7 Feliks Mlynarski, "The Reform of the Gold-Exchange Standard: Selected Documents Submitted to the Gold Delegation of the Financial Committee, Sept. 8, 1930," in *Selected Documents Submitted to the Gold Delegation of the Financial Committee* (Geneva: League of Nations, 1930); Procopio Bumagat Victoriano, "The Gold Exchange Standard of the Philippine Islands, India, the Dutch East Indies, the Straits Settlements and Some European Countries" (MBA thesis, University of

Washington, 1933); and Alan M. Taylor, Maurice Obstfeld, and Jay C. Shambaugh, "Monetary Sovereignty, Exchange Rates and Capital Controls: The Trilemma in the Inter-war Period," *IMF Staff Papers*, 51 (2004): 75–108.

8 For more on radical and revolutionary movements against colonial and racial capitalism see the chapter "Brussels" in Vijay Prashad, *The Darker Nations: A People's History of the Third World* (New York: The New Press, 2007), and chapter 9 in Cedric Robinson, *Black Marxism: The Making of the Black Radical Tradition* (Chapel Hill: University of North Carolina Press, 2000).

9 See chapters 4 and 5 especially of Rick Baldoz, *The Third Asiatic Invasion: Empire and Migration in Filipino America, 1898–1946* (New York: New York University Press, 2011).

10 On race and commodities in the American colonial Philippines see chapter 6 in Paul A. Kramer, *The Blood of Government: Race, Empire, the United States, and the Philippines*, (Chapel Hill: The University of North Carolina Press, 2006).

11 U.S. cartels specializing in sugar and fats and oils fumed over what they believed to be an unjust trade relation for Americans. Cartels wanted an immediate end to free trade for Philippine imports. As a result, the Agricultural Adjustment Act of 1934, the Revenue Act of 1934, and the Cordage Act of 1935 all introduced, in various ways, additional restrictions and taxes on Philippine products at nearly the same moment of the Commonwealth's founding. Any attempt to amend the asymmetrical process of decolonization was continuously sidestepped or parried by Congress. For more on this process see chapter 11 in Frank Golay, *Face of Empire: United States-Philippines Relations, 1898–1946* (Quezon City, Philippines: Ateneo de Manila University Press; Madison: University of Wisconsin Press, 1998).

12 Harry Hawes, "The Philippine Independence Act," *Annals of the American Academy of Political and Social Science* 168 (1933): 144.

13 O. D. Corpuz, *An Economic History of the Philippines* (Quezon City: University of the Philippines Press, 1997), 243.

14 *National Economic Protectionism Association* (Manila: NEPA, 1935), 3.

15 *National Economic Protectionism Association*, 3.

16 Isidro Marfori, "The Commonwealth and NEPA," *Manila Times*, November 14, 1936, box 13, folder 10, Joseph Ralston Hayden Papers, Bentley Historical Library, University of Michigan (hereafter Hayden, BHL, UM).

17 Corpuz, *Economic History of the Philippines*, 256–260.

18 Golay, *Face of Empire*, 215.

19 *Independence for the Philippine Islands: Hearings before the Committee on Territories and Insular Affairs* (Washington, DC: U.S. Government Printing Office, 1932), 135.

20 *Independence for the Philippine Islands*, 95.

21 *Independence for the Philippine Islands*, 85.

22 *Independence for the Philippine Islands*, 108.

23 *Independence for the Philippine Islands*, 125.

24 *Independence for the Philippine Islands*, 13.

25 *Independence for the Philippine Islands*, 78.

26 *Independence for the Philippine Islands*, 22, 47.

27 *Independence for the Philippine Islands*, 110.

28 *Independence for the Philippine Islands*, 111–112.

29 Corpuz, *Economic History of the Philippines*, 253.

30 "Gives Figures Showing P.I. Currency Is Most Stable," *Philippines Herald*, August 22, 1935, box 15, folder 15, Hayden, BHL, UM.

31 "Talk of Change in Money System," *Philippines Herald*, August 15, 1934, box 15, folder 15, Hayden, BHL, UM.

32 P. A. Santiago, "Thorough Economic Planning Is Needed," *Manila Times*, January 5, 1936, box 13, folder 10, Hayden, BHL, UM.

33 Some of the most prominent and public of these "Native" economic experts include the following. Miguel Cuaderno, who was educated as a lawyer, served as a former assistant general manager of the PNB and later as secretary of Finance, would go on to receive training with bankers at the Federal Reserve in preparation to serve as first governor of the Central Bank of the Philippines. Vicente Singson Encarnacion, who served as a senator of the Philippine Assembly, president of several Philippine corporations, and was instrumental in drafting budget for the Commonwealth Constitution. Jaime Hernandez, who trained and educated as a lawyer and a public accountant, served as auditor general of the Bureau of Audits and later as secretary of Finance. Rafael Corpus, who trained as a lawyer and began his career in the colonial state as director of Bureau of Lands then moved on to become secretary of Agriculture and Natural Resources; served as first Filipino president of the PNB after the resignation of Wilson, acting manager of the Sugar Centrals Board, and then eventually chairman of the Board of the Central Bank of the Philippines. Jose Avelino, who was educated as a lawyer; served as secretary of Labor and as secretary of Public Works and Transportation and eventually president of the senate in the independent Philippine Republic. Andres Castillo, who was one of the first Filipinos to earn a PhD in Economics; served as second governor of the Central Bank of the Philippines. Biographical information was collected from various sources including several issues of the *Philippine Yearbook*; Zoilo M. Galang, *Leaders of the Philippines: Inspiring Biographies of Successful Men and Women of the Philippines* (Manila: National Publishing Company, 1932); Franz Weissblatt, ed., *Who's Who: A Biographical Dictionary of Notable Living Men of the Philippines*, vol. 2, *1940–1941* (Manila: Ramon Roces, 1940).

34 Andres V. Castillo, "How We Are Solving Our Economic and Financial Problems," *Philippine Yearbook*, November 1936, 46.

35 Castillo, "How We Are Solving," 46.

36 Tirso Garcia "Annual Report of Bank Commissioner of the Philippines, 1934," box 361, folder 1988, BIA RG350, NARA.

37 Executive Order 6102 was signed on April 3, 1933, and the subsequent Gold Reserve Act was passed on January 30, 1934. Tirso Garcia "Annual Report of Bank Commissioner of the Philippines, 1935," box 361, folder 1988, BIA RG350, NARA.

38 The Treasury ended up profiting almost three billion U.S. dollars. For more on the institutional plans for anticipated profits, see the *Hearings before the Committee on Coinage, Weights, and Measures House of Representatives: Gold Reserve Act of 1934* (Washington, DC: United States Government Printing Office, 1934).

39 Yoshiko Nagano, "The Philippine Currency System during the American Colonial Period: Transformation from the Gold Exchange Standard to the Dollar Exchange Standard," *International Journal of Asian Studies* 7, no. 1 (2010): 44–45.

40 "Press Release: Approval by the President of the United States on March 16th of Act No. 4199," March 21, 1935, box 16, folder 3, Hayden, BHL, UM.

41 "Devaluation in Dollar Brings Immense Gain," *Manila Bulletin*, April, 14, 1934, box 15, folder 21, Hayden, BHL, UM.

42 For more on the tense correspondences over the "devaluation profit" see Golay, *Face of Empire*, 329–330.

43 Golay, *Face of Empire*, 517.

44 Garcia "Annual Report of Bank Commissioner of the Philippines, 1935."

45 Jaime Hernandez, "The Present Financial Structure of the Commonwealth Government," *Philippine Yearbook*, November 1936, 37.

46 Hernandez, "Present Financial Structure," 37.

47 Jose L. Celeste, "For a Planned Monetary System," *Philippine Herald Yearbook*, September 29, 1934, 123.

48 Celeste, "For a Planned Monetary System," 123.

49 Celeste, "For a Planned Monetary System," 123.

50 Hernandez, "Present Financial Structure," 37.

51 Celeste, "For a Planned Monetary System," 123.

52 During the mid-1920s, the Philippine monetary system shifted to a dollar-exchange standard rather than a gold-exchange standard. For a more detailed account of this shift in standard see Nagano, "Philippine Currency System," 39.

53 Vicente Singson Encarnacion, "A Central Bank and Economic Development in the Philippines," *Philippine Herald Yearbook*, September 29, 1934, 147.

54 Encarnacion, "Central Bank and Economic Development," 148.

55 These two conferences were the 1920 International Financial Conference in Brussels and the 1934 International Economic Conference in London. Encarnacion, "Central Bank and Economic Development," 148.

56 "Cablegram from Governor General Murphy," January 17, 1934, box 875, folder 17128, BIA RG350, NARA.

57 "Dern to Secretary of War," October 11, 1933, box 875, folder 17128, BIA RG350, NARA.

58 "Secretary of Treasury to Secretary of War," November 3, 1933, box 875, folder 17128, BIA RG350, NARA.

59 "Sabater to the Governor General," October 24, 1934, box 876, folder 17128, BIA RG350, NARA.

60 Many of the gold mining companies would target land in Muslim-dominated areas of the archipelago. Jose Yasay, "Mindanao Has Its Own Gold Rush," *Graphic*, November 2, 1933, 12.

61 "Some Go Up and Some Go Down," *Graphic*, October 5, 1933, 16.

62 Castillo, "How We Are Solving," 46.

63 "Soliven Discusses P.I. Currency Plan," *Manila Times*, February 2, 1937, box 15, folder 15, Hayden, BHL, UM.

64 "Cuaderno Scouts Talk on Independent Currency," *Tribune*, September 10, 1937, box 15, folder 15, Hayden, BHL, UM.

65 Daniel Doeppers, "The Philippines in the Great Depression: A Geography of Pain," in *Weathering the Storm: The Economies of Southeast Asia in the 1930s Depression*, eds. Peter Boomgaard and Ian Brown (Singapore: Institute of Southeast Asian Studies, Singapore, 2000), 54.

66 Smaller-denomination coins, however, remained constant in local markets. W. G. Wolters, "Uneven Impact and Regional Responses: The Philippines in the 1930s Depression" in *Weathering the Storm*, 89.

67 Theodore Roosevelt Jr. quote is in Doeppers, "Philippines in the Great Depression," 68.

68 Benedict J. Kerkvliet, *Huk Rebellion: A Study of Peasant Revolt in the Philippines* (Quezon City, Philippines: New Day Publishers, 1979), and David Sturtevant, *Popular Uprisings in the Philippines, 1840–1940* (Ithaca, NY: Cornell University Press, 1976).

69 Wolters, "Uneven Impact and Regional Responses," 89.

70 "Davis to Kemmerer," January 5, 1932; "Kemmerer to Davis," February 7, 1930; both from box 200, folder 6, EWK MC146, PUL.

71 Several official reports had a range from 50 to 200 percent interest rates. Wolters, "Uneven Impact and Regional Responses," 99.

72 Newspapers consistently reported on usury in the early 1930s. See especially the Hayden collection: box 16, folder 5, Hayden, BHL, UM.

73 Garcia "Annual Report of Bank Commissioner of the Philippines, 1935."

74 "New Government Banks Created in Philippines," April 5 1940, box 361; folder 1988, BIA RG350, NARA.

75 Wolters, "Uneven Impact and Regional Responses," 102.

76 "Message of Manuel L. Quezon to the National Assembly, Delivered June 16, 1936;" reel 3, Manuel Quezon Papers, BHL, UM.

77 Kerkvliet, *Huk Rebellion*, 38.

78 Wolters, "Uneven Impact and Regional Responses," 104.

79 Kerkvliet, *Huk Rebellion*, 27.

80 Kerkvliet, *Huk Rebellion*, 31.

81 Kerkvliet, *Huk Rebellion*, 29.

82 Kerkvliet, *Huk Rebellion*, 31.

83 Kerkvliet, *Huk Rebellion*, 36.

84 Newspapers were especially prone to speculate on connections between peasant labor strikes and the PKP. See especially Hayden's meticulous collection of press clippings in box 25, folder 18, Hayden, BHL, UM.

85 See box 25, folder 18, Hayden, BHL, UM.

86 This logic of blending together political "extremes" such as fascism with communism is on display in the "Bolsheviki" files of the BIA. Box 1295, file 28342, BIA RG350, NARA.

87 Crisanto Evangelista, *Nasyonalismo Proteksiyonismo vs. Internasyonalismo Radikal* (Manila: Katipunan ng mga Anak-Pawis sa Pilipinas, 1928), 22.

88 Evangelista, *Nasyonalismo Proteksiyonismo vs. Internasyonalismo Radikal*, 17.

89 Evangelista, *Nasyonalismo Proteksiyonismo vs. Internasyonalismo Radikal*, 22.

90 Evangelista, *Nasyonalismo Proteksiyonismo vs. Internasyonalismo Radikal*, 21.

91 "Communist Seeds Sprouting in North Warns T. Confesor," *Manila Herald*, January 19, 1931; "Red Flags Displayed as House to Canvass Is Made," *Manila Times*, March 19, 1931; both from box 25, folder 18, Hayden, BHL, UM.

92 "Earnshaw Urges Passage of Law Banning Red Flag," *Manila Herald*, January 26, 1931, box 25, folder 18, Hayden, BHL, UM.

93 "319 Are Jailed as Election Nears; Forecasts Made," *Manila Bulletin*, June 1, 1931; "A Philippine Hyde Park," *Manila Bulletin*, January 26, 1931; both from box 25, folder 18, Hayden, BHL, UM.

94 William Pomeroy, *The Philippines: Colonialism, Collaboration, and Resistance* (New York: International Publishers, 1992), 74.

95 Jim Richardson, *Komunista: The Genesis of the Philippine Communist Party, 1902–1935* (Quezon City, Philippines: Ateneo de Manila University, 2011), 250.

96 Patricio N. Abinales and Donna J. Amoroso, *State and Society in the Philippines* (New York: Roman and Littlefield, 2005), 149.

97 Motoe Terami-Wada, "The Sakdal Movement, 1930–34," *Philippine Studies* 36, no. 2 (1988): 132.

98 Abinales and Amoroso, *State and Society in the Philippines*, 148.

99 Sturtevant, *Popular Uprisings in the Philippines*, 223–225.

100 "Sakdal Uprising Report," 11, box 25, folder 29, Hayden, BHL, UM.

101 "Sakdal Uprising Report," 11.

102 "Sakdal Uprising Report," 5.

103 "Common Sense: A Filipino's View," *Manila Bulletin*, October 21, 1937, box 25, folder 18, Hayden, BHL, UM.

104 "Quezon Sets Labor on New Course as 100,000 Parade City," *Manila Bulletin*, June 6, 1939; "Quezon Asks 'Social Peace' from 10,000 Pampangans at Rice Fete," *Manila Bulletin*, July, 20, 1939; both from box 25, folder 18, Hayden, BHL, UM.

105 "Quezon Places Soldiers over Tenant Towns," *Manila Bulletin*, May 10, 1939, box 25, folder 18, Hayden, BHL, UM.

106 "Social Justice Likened to New Deal by Dr. Romulo in College Address," *Manila Bulletin*, March 31, 1938, box 25, folder 18, Hayden, BHL, UM.

107 "Social Justice, Minimum Wage Given Impetus," *Manila Bulletin*, October 15, 1937, box 25, folder 18, Hayden, BHL, UM.

108 Osmeña, *Commonwealth*, 9.

109 *Labor Bulletin*, vol. 1, no. 7, November 1938, box 1330, folder 28842, BIA RG350, NARA.

110 Shirley Jenkins, *American Economic Policy toward the Philippines* (Stanford, CA: Stanford University Press, 1954), 40–41.

111 "Jobless Total 1,500,000 Here," *Manila Bulletin*, August 4, 1938, box 25, folder 18, Hayden, BHL, UM.

112 "Communists in Pampanga Demand Expropriation of Land for Peasants," *Manila Bulletin*, July 31, 1939, box 25, folder 21, Hayden, BHL, UM.

113 Luis Taruc, *Born of the People* (New York: International Publishers, 1953), 46.

114 Sturtevant, *Popular Uprisings in the Philippines*, 244–245.

115 "Landowners Band Together," *Manila Bulletin*, December 18, 1939, box 25, folder 18, Hayden, BHL, UM.

116 "Text of President Quezon's Message," *Manila Bulletin*, February 1, 1941, box 24, folder 1, Hayden, BHL, UM.

117 "Text of President Quezon's Message."

CONCLUSION

Epigraphs: Miguel Cuaderno, *Guideposts to Economic Stability and Progress; a Selection of the Speeches and Articles of Miguel Cuaderno, Sr., Governor of the Central Bank of the Philippines* (Manila: Central Bank of the Philippines 1955), 176; Luis Taruc, *Born of the People* (New York: International Publishers, 1953), 267.

1 Cuaderno, *Guideposts to Economic Stability and Progress,* 176.

2 Vijay Prashad, *The Darker Nations: A People's History of the Third World* (New York: The New Press, 2007) and *The Poorer Nations: A Possible History of the Global South* (London: Verso, 2012).

Bibliography

ARCHIVES AND ORIGINAL COLLECTIONS

Bentley Historical Library, University of Michigan, Ann Arbor
  Dean C. Worcester Papers
  Frank Murphy Papers
  Joseph Ralston Hayden Papers

Butler Library, Columbia University, New York
  Henry Parker Willis Papers

Filipinas Heritage Library, Makati, Philippines

Houghton Library, Harvard University, Cambridge, MA
  William Cameron Forbes Papers

Lopez Memorial Museum, Ortigas, Philippines

Mudd Manuscript Library, Princeton University, Princeton, NJ
  Edwin W. Kemmerer Papers

National Archives and Records Administration, College Park, MD
  Bureau of Insular Affairs Collection, RG350, War Department

National Archives of the Philippines and National Library of the Philippines, Manila
  Manuel Quezon Papers
  Philippine Insurgent Records

Newberry Library, Chicago
  Edward E. Ayer Collection

Rizal Library, Ateneo de Manila University, Quezon City, Philippines
  American Historical Collection
  Trinidad H. Pardo de Tavera Collection
University Library, University of the Philippines-Diliman, Quezon City

NEWSPAPERS AND PERIODICALS

Ang Bayan
Ang Freeman
Bagong Lipang Kalabaw
Cable News
El Comercio
El Debate
Far Eastern Review
Graphic
Manila Bulletin
Manila Daily Bulletin
Manila Times
New York Times
Philippine Daily Inquirer
Philippine Free Press
Philippine Herald
Philippine Political Science Review
Philippine Review
Philippine Herald Yearbook
Philippine Star
Philippine Yearbook
La Politica de España en Filipinas
El Tiempo

GOVERNMENT PRIMARY SOURCES

Acts of the Philippine Commission. Washington, DC: U.S. Government Printing Office, 1904.
Annual Report of the High Commissioner to the President of the United States. Manila: Bureau of Printing, 1936.
Annual Reports of the Chief of Division of Currency. Washington, DC: U.S. Government Printing Office, 1904–1905.
Annual Reports of the Governor General of the Philippine Islands. Washington, DC: U.S. Government Printing Office, 1917–1934.
Annual Reports of the President of the Commonwealth to the President of the United States. Manila: Bureau of Printing, 1936–1940.
Annual Reports of the Treasurer of the Philippine Islands. Manila: Bureau of Printing, 1910–1924.
Annual Reports of the United States Philippine Commission to the Secretary of War. Washington, DC: U.S. Government Printing Office, 1900–1916.

Census of the Philippine Islands. 4 vols. Washington, DC: U.S. Bureau of the Census, 1905.

Central Bank of the Philippines: January 3, 1949–January 3, 1974. Manila: Central Bank of the Philippines, 1974.

Certain Economic Questions in the Spanish and Dutch Colonies in the Orient. Washington, DC: U.S. Government Printing Office, 1902.

Commission on International Exchange. *Gold Standard in International Trade: Report on the Introduction of the Gold-Exchange Standard into China, the Philippine Islands, Panama, and Other Silver-Using Countries and on the Stability of Exchange.* Washington, DC: U.S. Government Printing Office, 1904.

Guevara, Sulpicio, ed. *The Laws of the First Philippine Republic (The Laws of Malolos) 1898–1899.* Manila: National Historical Institute, 1972.

Hearings before the Committee on Coinage, Weights, and Measures House of Representatives: Gold Reserve Act of 1934. Washington, DC: U.S. Government Printing Office, 1934.

Independence for the Philippine Islands: Hearings before the Committee on Territories and Insular Affairs. Washington, DC: U.S. Government Printing Office, 1932.

Memorandum for Secretary of War on Currency and Exchange in the Philippines. Washington, DC: U.S. Government Printing Office, 1900.

National Economic Protectionism Association. Manila: NEPA, 1935.

Report of the Philippine Commission to the President January 31, 1900. Washington, DC: U.S. Government Printing Office, 1901.

Report of the Philippine Commission, volume 8, part 2. Washington, DC: U.S. Government Printing Office, 1909.

Report on the Agricultural Bank of Egypt to the Secretary of War. Washington, DC: U.S. Government Printing Office, 1906.

Report on Coinage and Banking in the Philippine Islands. Washington, DC: U.S. Government Printing Office, 1901.

Reports of the Taft Philippine Commission. Washington, DC: U.S. Government Printing Office, 1901.

Selected Documents Submitted to the Gold Delegation of the Financial Committee. Geneva: League of Nations, 1930.

Wood, Leonard, and Cameron Forbes. *Report of the Special Mission on Investigation to the Philippine Islands of the Secretary of War.* Washington, DC: U.S. Government Printing Office, 1921.

SUPPLEMENTAL PRIMARY SOURCES

Alvarez, Santiago V. *Katipunan at ang Paghihimagsik* (The Katipunan and the Revolution: Memoirs of a General). Translated by Paula Carolina Malay. Quezon City, Philippines: Ateneo de Manila University Press, 1992.

Biosca, Francisco Aguilar y. *Legislacion Sobre Moneda.* 1893. Reprinted in *Barrilla: The Central Bank Money Museum Quarterly* 6, no. 2 (1979): 60–64.

Brown, John Clifford. *Gentleman Soldier: John Clifford Brown and the Philippine-American War.* College Station: Texas A&M University Press, 2004.

Conant, Charles A. "Can New Openings Be Found for Capital," *Atlantic Monthly* 84 (1899): 600–608.

Conant, Charles A. "Crises and Their Management." *Yale Review* 9 (1901): 374–398.

Conant, Charles A. "The Currency of the Philippine Islands." *Annals of the American Academy of Political Science* 20 (1902): 44–59.

Conant, Charles A. "Currency Problems in the Orient—Discussion." *American Economic Association* 4, no. 1 (1903): 280–295.

Conant, Charles A. "The Economic Basis of 'Imperialism.'" *North American Review* 167, no. 502 (1898): 326–340.

Conant, Charles A. "Recent Economic Tendencies." *Atlantic Monthly* 85 (1900): 736–748.

Conant, Charles A. *A Special Report on Coinage and Banking in the Philippine Islands.* Washington, DC: U.S. Government Printing Office, 1901.

Cuaderno, Miguel. *Guideposts to Economic Stability and Progress; a Selection of the Speeches and Articles of Miguel Cuaderno, Sr., Governor of the Central Bank of the Philippines.* Manila: Central Bank of the Philippines, 1955.

de Viana, Augusto V. *The I-stories: The Philippine Revolution and the Filipino American War as Told by Its Eyewitnesses and Participants.* Manila: University of Santo Tomas Publishing House, 2006.

Evangelista, Crisanto. *Nasyonalismo Proteksiyonismo vs. Internasyonalismo Radikal.* Manila: Katipunan ng mga Anak-Pawis sa Pilipinas, 1928.

Fee, Mary H. *A Woman's Impressions of the Philippines.* Chicago: A. C. McClurg, 1910.

Galang, Zoilo M. *Leaders of the Philippines: Inspiring Biographies of Successful Men and Women of the Philippines.* Manila: National Publishing Company, 1932.

Gates, John. *Schoolbooks and Krags: The United States Army in the Philippines, 1898–1902.* Westport, CT: Greenwood Press, 1973.

Gatewood, Willard B., Jr. *"Smoked Yankees" and the Struggle for Empire: Letters from Negro Soldiers, 1898–1902.* Fayetteville: University of Arkansas Press, 1987.

Godinez, Francisco. "Papel Moneda en Filipinas." In *La Solidaridad,* vol. 6, 307–310.

Godinez, Francisco *Regularizar la Situacón Monetaria en las Islas Filipinas.* Madrid: Imprenta de Luis Aguado, 1894.

Hawes, Harry. "The Philippine Independence Act." *Annals of the American Academy of Political and Social Science* 168, no. 1 (1933): 142–145.

Jenks, Jeremiah. "The Agricultural Bank for the Philippine Islands." *Annals of the American Academy of Political and Social Science* 30, no. 1 (1907): 38–44.

Jenks, Jeremiah. "Currency Problems in the Orient." *American Economic Association* 4, no. 1 (1903): 269–279.

Jenks, Jeremiah. ed. "Essays in Colonial Finance by Members of the American Economic Association." *Publications of the American Economic Association* 1, no. 3 (1900): 1–20.

Kemmerer, Edwin W. *The ABC of the Federal Reserve System.* Princeton, NJ: Princeton University Press, 1919.

Kemmerer, Edwin W. "An Agricultural Bank for the Philippines." *Yale Review* 16 (May 1907): 262–279.

Kemmerer, Edwin W. "Agricultural Credit in the United States." *American Economic Review* 2, no. 4 (1912): 852–872.

Kemmerer, Edwin W. *Modern Currency Reforms: A History and Discussion of Recent Currency Reforms in India, Puerto Rico, Philippine Islands, Straits Settlements and Mexico*. New York: Macmillan Company, 1916.

Kemmerer, Edwin W. "Philippine Postal Savings Bank." *American Monthly Review of Reviews* 34 (July 1906): 468–470.

Kemmerer, Edwin W. "The Philippine Postal Savings Bank." *Annals of the American Academy of Political and Social Science* 30, no. 1 (July 1907): 45–51.

Kemmerer, Edwin W. *Postal Savings: An Historical and Critical Study of the Postal Savings Bank System of the United States*. Princeton, NJ: Princeton University Press, 1917.

Kemmerer, Edwin W. "The Progress of the Filipino People toward Self-government." *Political Science Quarterly* 23, no. 1 (1908): 47–74.

Kemmerer, Edwin W. "Six Years of Postal Savings in the United States." *American Economic Review* 7, no. 1 (1917): 46–90.

Lewis, Peter. *Foot Soldier in an Occupation Force: The Letters of Peter Lewis, 1898–1902*. Manila: Linguistics Office, De La Salle University, 1999.

Lininger, Clarence. *The Best War at the Time*. New York: R. Speller, 1964.

Luthringer, George F. *The Gold-Exchange Standard in the Philippines*. Princeton, NJ: Princeton University Press, 1934.

Mabini, Apolinario. *The Letters of Apolinario Mabini*. Manila: National Historical Institute, 1999.

Osmeña, Sergio. *The Commonwealth: A Year of Accomplishments (1938–39)*. Manila: Bureau of Printing, 1939.

Quezon, Manuel, and Camilo Osias, eds. *Governor-General Wood and the Filipino Cause*. Manila: Manila Book, 1924.

Rizal, Jose. *El Filibusterismo*. Translated by Ma. Soledad Lacson-Locsin. 1891. Reprint, Makati: The Bookmark, 2004.

Sancianco y Goson, Gregorio. *The Progress of the Philippines: Economic, Administrative and Political Studies*. Translated by Encarnacion Alzona. 1881. Reprint, Manila: National Historical Institute, 1975.

La Solidaridad. Translated by Guadalupe Forés-Ganzon and Luis Mañeru. Manila: Fundacion Santiago, 1996.

Taruc, Luis. *Born of the People*. New York: International Publishers, 1953.

Victoriano, Procopio Bumagat. "The Gold Exchange Standard of the Philippine Islands, India, the Dutch East Indies, the Straits Settlements and Some European Countries." MBA thesis, University of Washington, 1933.

Weissblatt, Franz. *Who's Who: A Biographical Dictionary of Notable Living Men of the Philippines*. Vol. 2, *1940–1941*. Manila: Ramon Roces, 1940.

Willis, Henry Parker. "The Economic Situation in the Philippines" *Journal of Political Economy* 13, no. 2 (1905): 145–172.

Willis, Henry Parker. *Our Philippine Problem: A Study of American Colonial Policy*. New York: Henry Holt, 1905.

Willis, Henry Parker. "The Philippine National Bank." *Journal of Political Economy* 25, no. 5 (1917): 409–441.

Abinales, Patricio. "Progressive-Machine Conflict in Early-Twentieth-Century U.S. Politics and Colonial-State Building in the Philippines." In *The American Colonial State in the Philippines: Global Perspectives*, edited by Julian Go and Ann Foster, 148–181. Durham, NC: Duke University Press, 2003.

Abinales, Patricio N., and Donna J. Amoroso. *State and Society in the Philippines*. New York: Rowman and Littlefield, 2005.

Abu-Lughod, Janet. *Before European Hegemony: The World System A.D. 1250–1350*. Oxford: Oxford University Press, 1989.

Agoncillo, Teodoro. *The Revolt of the Masses: The Story of Bonifacio and the Katipunan*. Quezon City: University of the Philippines Press, 2002.

Agoncillo, Teodoro. ed. *The Revolutionists: Aguinaldo, Bonifacio, Jacinto*. Manila: National Historical Institute, 1993.

Agoncillo, Teodoro. *The Writings and Trial of Andres Bonifacio*. Manila: A. J. Villegas and the University of the Philippines, 1963.

Aguilar, Filomeno V., Jr. *Clash of Spirits: The History of Power and Sugar Planter Hegemony on a Visayan Island*. Honolulu: University of Hawai'i Press, 1998.

Alexander, Jennifer Karns. *The Mantra of Efficiency: From Waterwheel to Social Control*. Baltimore, MD: Johns Hopkins University Press, 2008.

Ali, Omar H. *In the Lion's Mouth: Black Populism in the New South, 1886–1900*. Oxford: University of Mississippi Press, 2010.

Anderson, Benedict. *Under Three Flags: Anarchism and the Anti-Colonial Imagination*. New York: Verso, 2005.

Anderson, Benedict R. O'G. *Imagined Communities: Reflections on the Origin and Spread of Nationalism*. New York: Verso, 2006.

Anderson, Benedict R. O'G. *The Spectre of Comparisons: Nationalism, Southeast Asia and the World*. New York: Verso, 1998.

Anderson, Stuart. *Race and Rapprochement: Anglo-Saxonism and Anglo-American Relations, 1895–1904*. Madison, NJ: Fairleigh Dickinson University, 1981.

Anderson, Warwick. *Colonial Pathologies: American Tropical Medicine, Race, and Hygiene in the Philippines*. Durham, NC: Duke University Press, 2006.

Arrighi, Giovanni. "Hegemony Unraveling 1." *New Left Review* 32 (March–April 2005): 23–80.

Arrighi, Giovanni. "Hegemony Unraveling 2." *New Left Review* 33 (May–June 2005): 83–116.

Baldoz, Rick. *The Third Asiatic Invasion: Empire and Migration in Filipino America, 1898–1946*. New York: New York University Press, 2011.

Barker, Joanne. *Critically Sovereign: Indigenous Gender, Sexuality, and Feminist Studies*. Durham, NC: Duke University Press, 2017.

Bickers, Robert, and R. G. Tiedemann, eds. *The Boxers, China, and the World*. Lanham, MD: Rowman and Littlefield, 2007.

Blackhawk, Ned. *Violence over the Land: Indians and Empires in the Early American West*. Cambridge, MA: Harvard University Press, 2006.

Broz, J. Lawrence. *The International Origins of the Federal Reserve*. Ithaca, NY: Cornell University Press, 1997.

Burrows, Edwin, and Mike Wallace. *Gotham: The History of New York City to 1898*. London: Oxford University Press, 1999.

Byrd, Jodi. *The Transit of Empire: Indigenous Critiques of Colonialism*. Minneapolis: University of Minnesota Press, 2011.

Byrd, Jodi A., Alyosha Goldstein, Jodi Melamed, and Chandan Reddy. "Predatory Value: Economies of Dispossession and Disturbed Relationalities." *Social Text* 135, no. 36.2 (2018): 1–18.

Chakrabarty, Dipesh. *Provincializing Europe: Postcolonial Thought and Historical Difference*. Princeton, NJ: Princeton University Press, 2000.

Chan, Sucheng, ed. *Chinese American Transnationalism: The Flow of People, Resources, and Ideas between China and America during the Exclusion Era*. Philadelphia: Temple University Press, 2005.

Chaturvedi, Vinayak, ed. *Mapping Subaltern Studies and the Postcolonial*. London: Verso, 2000.

Cheah, Pheng. *Spectral Nationality: Passages of Freedom from Kant to Postcolonial Literatures of Liberation*. New York: Columbia University Press, 2003.

Cheng, Lucie, and Edna Bonacich. *Labor Immigration under Capitalism: Asian Workers in the United States before World War II*. Berkeley: University of California Press, 1984.

Chernow, Ron. *The House of Morgan: An American Banking Dynasty and the Rise of Modern Finance*. New York: Grove Press, 1990.

Chu, Richard. *The Chinese and Chinese Mestizos of Manila: Family, Identity, and Culture 1860s to 1930s*. Leiden: E. J. Brill, 2010.

Chu, Richard T. *Chinese Merchants of Binondo in the Nineteenth Century*. Manila: University of Santo Tomas Publishing House, 2010.

Clarke, Steven V. O. *Central Bank Cooperation: 1924–31*. New York: Federal Reserve Bank of New York, 1967.

Clutario, Genevieve. "The Appearance of Filipina Nationalism: Body, Nation, Empire." PhD diss., University of Illinois at Urbana-Champaign, 2014.

Cohen, Cathy. "Punks, Bulldaggers, and Welfare Queens: The Radical Potential of Queer Politics?" GLQ 3, no. 4 (1997): 437–465.

Cohen, Paul A. *History in Three Keys: The Boxers as Event, Experience, and Myth*. New York: Columbia University Press, 1997.

Collins, Patricia Hill. *Black Feminist Thought: Knowledge, Consciousness, and the Politics of Empowerment*. New York: Routledge, 1991.

Combahee River Collective, The. *The Combahee River Collective Statement: Black Feminist Organizing in the Seventies and Eighties*. Albany, NY: Kitchen Table: Women of Color Press, 1986.

Cooper, Melinda. *Life as Surplus: Biotechnology and Capitalism in the Neoliberal Era*. Seattle: University of Washington Press, 2008.

Corpuz, Arturo. *The Colonial Iron Horse: Railroads and Regional Development in the Philippines, 1875–1935*. Quezon City: University of the Philippines Press, 1999.

Corpuz, Onofre D. *American Colonial Bureaucracy in the Philippines*. Quezon City: University of the Philippines, 1957.

Corpuz, Onofre D. *An Economic History of the Philippines*. Quezon City: University of the Philippines Press, 1997.

Coulthard, Glen. *Red Skin, White Masks: Rejecting the Colonial Politics of Recognition*. Minneapolis: University of Minnesota Press, 2014.

Crenshaw, Kimberle. "Demarginalizing the Intersection of Race and Sex: A Black Feminist Critique of Antidiscrimination Doctrine, Feminist Theory and Antiracist Politics." *University of Chicago Legal Forum* 1, no. 8 (1989): 139–167.

Crenshaw, Kimberle. "Mapping the Margins: Intersectionality, Identity Politics, and Violence against Women of Color." *Stanford Law Review* 43, no. 6 (1991): 1241–1299.

Cullinane, Michael. *Ilustrado Politics: Filipino Elite Responses to American Rule, 1898–1908*. Quezon City, Philippines: Ateneo de Manila University Press, 2003.

Cullinane, Michael. "Playing the Game: The Rise of Sergio Osmena, 1898–1907." In *Philippine Colonial Democracy*, edited by Ruby R. Paredes, 70–113. New Haven, CT: Yale University Southeast Asian Studies, 1988.

Day, Iyko. *Alien Capital: Asian Racialization and the Logic of Settler Colonial Capitalism*. Durham, NC: Duke University Press, 2016.

de Jesus, Ed. C. *The Tobacco Monopoly in the Philippines: Bureaucratic Enterprise and Social Change, 1766–1880*. Quezon City, Philippines: Ateneo de Manila Press, 1998.

de la Cruz, Deirdre. *Mother Figured: Marian Apparitions and the Making of a Filipino Universal*. Chicago: University of Chicago Press, 2015.

Diokno, Maria Serena. "The Political Aspect of the Monetary Crisis in the 1880s." *Kasarinlan* 14, no. 1 (1998): 21–36.

Doeppers, Daniel F. *Manila, 1900–1941: Social Change in a Late Colonial Metropolis*. New Haven, CT: Yale University Southeast Asia Studies, 1984.

Doeppers, Daniel F. "Mortgage Loans and Lending Institutions in Pre-War Manila." *Philippine Studies* 31, no. 3 (1983): 189–215.

Doeppers, Daniel F. "The Philippines in the Great Depression: A Geography of Pain." In *Weathering the Storm: The Economies of Southeast Asia in the 1930s Depression*, edited by Peter Boomgaard and Ian Brown, 53–82. Singapore: Institute of Southeast Asian Studies, Singapore, 2000.

Drake, Paul. *The Money Doctor in the Andes: The Kemmerer Missions, 1923–1933*. Durham, NC: Duke University Press, 1989.

Du Bois, W. E. B. *Black Reconstruction in America*. 1935. Reprint, New York: The Free Press, 1998.

Du Bois, W. E. B. *The Souls of Black Folk*. 1903. Reprint, New Haven, CT: Yale University Press, 2015.

Edwards, Clarence R. *Memorandum for Secretary of War on Currency and Exchange in the Philippines*. Washington, DC: U.S. Government Printing Office, 1900.

Eichengreen, Barry. *Golden Fetters: The Gold Standard and the Great Depression, 1919–1939*. New York: Oxford University Press, 1992.

Ekbladh, David. *The Great American Mission: Modernization and the Construction of an American World Order*. Princeton, NJ: Princeton University Press, 2011.

Elliott, John H. *Empires of the Atlantic World: Britain and Spain in America 1492–1830*. New Haven, CT: Yale University Press, 2006.

Esherick, Joseph. *The Origins of the Boxer Uprising*. Berkeley: University of California Press, 1987.

Estes, Nick. *Our History Is the Future: Standing Rock versus the Dakota Access Pipeline, and the Long Tradition of Indigenous Resistance*. Brooklyn, NY: Verso, 2019.

Ewing, Adam. *The Age of Garvey: How a Jamaican Activist Created a Mass Movement and Changed Global Black Politics*. Princeton, NJ: Princeton University Press, 2014.

Fanon, Frantz. *The Wretched of the Earth*. New York: Grove Press, 2004.

Foster, Ann L. *Projection of Power: The United States and Europe in Colonial Southeast, 1919–1941*. Durham, NC: Duke University Press, 2010.

Foucault, Michel. *The Birth of Biopolitics: Lectures at the College de France, 1978–1979*. New York: Palgrave Macmillan, 2008.

Fradera, Josep. "The Historical Origins of the Philippine Economy: A Survey of Recent Research of the Spanish Colonial Era." *Australian Economic History Review* 44, no. 3 (2004): 307–420.

Fradera, Josep. "Reading Imperial Transitions: Spanish Contraction, British Expansion, and American Irruption." In *Colonial Crucible: Empire in the Making of the Modern American State*, edited by Alfred McCoy and Francisco Scarano, 34–62. Madison: University of Wisconsin Press, 2009.

Frank, Andre Gunder. *ReOrient: Global Economy in the Asian Age*. Berkeley: University of California Press, 1998.

Friedman, Jeff. "Sectoral Conflict and Foreign Economic Policy, 1914–1940." *International Organization* 42, no. 1 (1988): 59–90.

Fry, Joseph A. "From Open Door to World Systems: Economic Interpretations of Late Nineteenth Century American Foreign Relations." *Pacific Historical Review* 65, no. 2 (1996): 277–303.

Gilmore, Ruth Wilson. *Golden Gulag: Prisons, Surplus, Crisis, and Opposition in Globalizing California*. Berkeley: University of California Press, 2007.

Gindin, Sam, and Leo Panitch. *The Making of Global Capitalism: The Political Economy of American Empire*. London: Verso, 2013.

Glenn, Evelyn Nakano. "Settler Colonialism as Structure: A Framework for U.S. Race and Gender Formation." *Sociology of Race and Ethnicity* 1, no. 1 (2005): 54–74.

Go, Julian, and Ann Foster, eds. *The American Colonial State in the Philippines: Global Perspectives*. Durham, NC: Duke University Press, 2003.

Golay, Frank. *Face of Empire: United States–Philippine Relations, 1898–1946*. Quezon City, Philippines: Ateneo de Manila University Press; Madison: University of Wisconsin Press, 1998.

Goldstein, Alyosha. "The Ground Not Given: Colonial Dispositions of Land, Race, and Hunger." *Social Text* 36, no. 2 (2018): 83–106.

Guerrero, Milagros. "Luzon at War: Contradictions in Philippine Society, 1898–1902." PhD diss., University of Michigan, 1977.

Gyory, Andrew. *Closing the Gate: Race, Politics, and the Chinese Exclusion Act*. Chapel Hill: University of North Carolina Press, 1998.

Haber, Samuel. *Efficiency and Uplift: Scientific Management in the Progressive Era, 1890–1920*. Chicago: University of Chicago Press, 1973.

Harvey, David. *The New Imperialism*. Oxford: Oxford University Press, 2003.

Hau, Caroline. "'The Chinese Question': A Marxist Interpretation." In *Marxism in the Philippines: Continuing Engagements*, edited by Teresa Tadem, 156–187. Manila: Anvil Publishing and University of the Philippines Third World Studies Center, 2010.

Hau, Caroline. *The Chinese Question: Ethnicity, Nation, and Region in and beyond the Philippines*. Singapore: National University of Singapore Press, 2014.

Hau, Caroline. *Necessary Fictions: Philippine Literature and the Nation, 1946–1980*. Quezon City, Philippines: Ateneo De Manila University Press, 2000.

Hau, Caroline. *On the Subject of the Nation: Filipino Writings from the Margins, 1981–2004*. Quezon City, Philippines: Ateneo De Manila University Press, 2004.

Hilferding, Rudolf. *Finance Capital: A Study of the Latest Phase of Capitalist Development*. 1910. Reprint, London: Routledge and Kegan Paul, 1981.

Hoyt, Frederick Gilman. "The Wood-Forbes Mission to the Philippines, 1921." PhD diss., Claremont Graduate School and University Center, 1963.

Hudson, Michael. *Super Imperialism: The Origins and Fundamentals of U.S. World Dominance*. London: Pluto Press, 1972.

Hudson, Peter. *Bankers and Empire: How Wall Street Colonized the Caribbean*. Chicago: University of Chicago Press, 2017.

Hudson, Peter. "Racial Capitalism and the Black Proletariat." *Boston Review: Forum 1* (Winter 2017): 59–66.

Hutchcroft, Paul. *Booty Capitalism: The Politics of Banking in the Philippines*. Ithaca, NY: Cornell University Press, 1998.

Ileto, Reynaldo. *Pasyon and Revolution: Popular Movements in the Philippines, 1840–1910*. Quezon City, Philippines: Ateneo de Manila University Press, 1998.

Jacobsen, Matthew Frye. *Whiteness of a Different Color: European Immigrants and the Alchemy of Race*. Cambridge, MA: Harvard University Press, 1998.

James, C. L. R. *The Black Jacobins: Toussaint L'Ouverture and the San Domingo Revolution*. New York: Vintage Books, 1989.

Jenista, Frank, Jr. "Conflict in the Philippine Legislature: The Commission and the Assembly from 1907 to 1913." In *Compadre Colonialism: Studies on the Philippines under American Rule*, edited Norman G. Owen, 73–102. Ann Arbor: University of Michigan, 1971.

Jenkins, Destin, and Justin Leroy, eds. *Histories of Racial Capitalism*. New York: Columbia University Press, 2021.

Jenkins, Shirley. *American Economic Policy toward the Philippines*. Stanford, CA: Stanford University Press, 1954.

Johnson, Walter. *The Broken Heart of America: St. Louis and the Violent History of the United States*. New York: Basic Books, 2020.

Johnson, Walter. "To Remake the World: Slavery, Racial Capitalism, and Justice." *Boston Review*. February 20, 2018. https://bostonreview.net/forum/walter-johnson-to-remake-the-world.

Johnson, Walter. *River of Dark Dreams: Slavery and Empire in the Cotton Kingdom*. Cambridge, MA: Harvard University Press, 2013.

Karuka, Manu. *Empire's Tracks: Indigenous Nations, Chinese Workers, and the Transcontinental Railroad.* Berkeley: University of California Press, 2019.

Karuka, Manu [also Manu Vimalassery]. "The Wealth of the Natives: Toward a Critique of Settler Colonial Political Economy." *Settler Colonial Studies* 3, nos. 3–4 (2013): 295–310.

Kerkvliet, Benedict J. *The Huk Rebellion: A Study of Peasant Revolt in the Philippines.* Quezon City, Philippines: New Day Publishers, 1979.

Kerkvliet, Melinda. *Manila Workers' Unions, 1900–1950.* Quezon City, Philippines: New Day Publishers, 1992.

Kindleberger, Charles. *The World in Depression, 1929–1939.* Berkeley: University of California Press, 1976.

Kramer, Paul A. *The Blood of Government: Race, Empire, the United States, and the Philippines.* Chapel Hill: The University of North Carolina Press, 2006.

Kramer, Paul A. "Empires, Exceptions, and Anglo-Saxons: Race and Rule between the British and United States Empires, 1880–1910." *Journal of American History* 88, no. 4 (2002): 1315–1353.

Kramer, Paul A. "How Not to Write the History of U.S. Empire." *Diplomatic History* 42, no. 4 (2018): 911–931.

Kramer, Paul A. "Power and Connection: Imperial Histories of the United States in the World," *American Historical Review* 116, no. 5 (2011): 1348–1391.

Kramer, Paul A. "Reflex Actions: Colonialism, Corruption and the Politics of Technocracy in the Early Twentieth Century United States." In *Challenging US Foreign Policy: America and the World in the Long Twentieth Century*, edited by Bevan Sewell and Scott Lucas, 14–35. New York: Palgrave Macmillan, 2011.

LaFeber, Walter. *The New Empire: An Interpretation of American Expansion, 1860–1898.* Ithaca, NY: Cornell University Press, 1963.

Lee, Erika. *At America's Gates: Chinese Immigration during the Exclusion Era, 1882–1943.* Chapel Hill: University of North Carolina Press, 2003.

Legarda, Angelita Ganzon. *Piloncitos to Pesos: A Brief History of Coinage in the Philippines.* Manila: Bancom Development, 1976.

Legarda, Benito J. *After the Galleons: Foreign Trade, Economic Change and Entrepreneurship in the Nineteenth Century Philippines.* Quezon City, Philippines: Ateneo de Manila University Press; Madison: University of Wisconsin Press,1999.

Lenin, V. I. *Imperialism, the Highest Stage of Capitalism.* 1916. Reprint, Moscow: Foreign Languages Publishing House, 1961.

Livingston, James. *Origins of the Federal Reserve System: Money, Class, and Corporate Capitalism, 1890–1913.* Ithaca, NY: Cornell University Press, 1896.

Lorde, Audre. *Sister Outsider: Essays and Speeches.* Trumansburg, NY: Crossing Press, 1984.

Lowe, Lisa. *The Intimacies of Four Continents.* Durham, NC: Duke University Press, 2015.

Lowenstein, Roger. *America's Bank: The Epic Struggle to Create the Federal Reserve.* New York: Penguin Books, 2015.

Lumba, Allan E. S. "Empire, Expansion, and Its Consequences." In *A Companion to the Gilded Age and Progressive Era*, edited by Christopher Nichols and Nancy Unger, 399–409. Oxford: Wiley-Blackwell, 2017.

Lumba, Allan E. S. "Imperial Standards: Colonial Currencies, Racial Capacities, and Economic Knowledge during the Philippine American War." *Diplomatic History* 39, no. 4 (September 2015): 603–628.

Lumba, Allan E. S. "Philippine Colonial Money and the Futures of Spanish Empire." In *The Cultural History of Money and Credit: A Global Perspective*, edited by Thomas Luckett, Chia Yin Hsu, and Erika Vause, 97–111. Lanham, MD: Lexington Books, 2016.

Majul, Cesar Adib. *The Political and Constitutional Ideas of the Philippine Revolution.* Quezon City: University of the Philippines Press, 1967.

Manela, Erez. *The Wilsonian Moment: Self-Determination and the International Origins of Anticolonial Nationalism.* Oxford: Oxford University Press, 2007.

Marx, Karl. *Capital: A Critique of Political Economy.* Vol. 1. London: Penguin Classics, 1990.

McCormick, Thomas, and Walter LaFeber, eds. *Behind the Throne: Servants of Power to Imperial Presidents, 1898–1968.* Madison: The University of Wisconsin Press, 1993.

McCoy, Alfred. *Policing America's Empire: The United States, the Philippines, and the Rise of the Surveillance State.* Madison: University of Wisconsin Press, 2009.

McCoy, Alfred, and Francisco Scarano, eds. *Colonial Crucible: Empire in the Making of the Modern American State.* Madison: University of Wisconsin Press, 2009.

McCoy, Alfred W., and Alfredo R. Roces. *Philippine Cartoons: Political Caricature of the American Era, 1900–1941.* Quezon City, Philippines: Vera-Reyes, 1985.

Melamed, Jodi. "Racial Capitalism." *Critical Ethnic Studies* 1, no. 1 (2015): 76–85.

Melamed, Jodi. *Represent and Destroy: Rationalizing Violence in the New Racial Capitalism.* Minneapolis: University of Minnesota Press, 2011.

Meltzer, Allan. *A History of the Federal Reserve.* Chicago: University of Chicago Press, 2003.

Mendoza, Victor. *Metroimperial Intimacies: Fantasy, Racial-Sexual Governance, and the Philippines in U.S. Imperialism, 1899–1913.* Durham, NC: Duke University Press, 2015.

Michaels, Walter Benn. *The Gold Standard and the Logic of Naturalism: American Literature at the Turn of the Century.* Berkeley: University of California Press, 1987.

Mintz, Sidney W. *Sweetness and Power: The Place of Sugar in Modern History.* New York: Penguin Books, 1986.

Mitchell, Timothy. *Rule of Experts: Egypt, Techno-Politics, Modernity.* Berkeley: University of California Press, 2002.

Mitchell, Timothy. "The Stage of Modernity." In *Questions of Modernity*, edited by Timothy Mitchell, 1–34. Minneapolis: University of Minnesota Press, 2000.

Mojares, Resil B. *Brains of the Nation: Pedro Paterno, T.H. Pardo de Tavera, Isabelo de los Reyes, and the Production of Modern Knowledge.* Quezon City, Philippines: Ateneo de Manila University Press, 2006.

Moore, Colin. *American Imperialism and the State, 1893–1921.* Cambridge: Cambridge University Press, 2017.

Murray, John. "Chinese-Filipino Wage Differentials in Early-Twentieth-Century Manila." *Journal of Economic History* 62, no. 3 (2002): 773–791.

Nagano, Yoshiko. "The Agricultural Bank of the Philippine Government, 1908–1916." *Journal of Southeast Asian Studies* 28, no. 2 (1997): 301–323.

Nagano, Yoshiko. "The Philippine Currency System during the American Colonial Period: Transformation from the Gold Exchange Standard to the Dollar Exchange Standard." *International Journal of Asian Studies* 7, no. 1 (2010): 29–50.

Nagano, Yoshiko. *The Philippine National Bank: The American Colonial State and Finance, 1898–1941*. Quezon City, Philippines: Ateneo de Manila University Press; Singapore: National University Press, 2015.

Nagano, Yoshiko. *State and Finance in the Philippines, 1898–1941: The Mismanagement of an American Colony*. Quezon City, Philippines: Ateneo de Manila University Press; Singapore: National University Press, 2015.

Ngai, Mai. *Impossible Subjects: Illegal Aliens and the Making of Modern America*. Princeton, NJ: Princeton University Press, 2004.

Owen, Norman G. *Prosperity without Progress: Manila Hemp and Material Life in the Colonial Philippines*. Berkeley: University of California Press, 1984.

Palyi, Melchior. *The Twilight of Gold, 1914–1936*. Chicago: Henry Regency Company, 1972.

Paredes, Ruby, ed. "Origins of National Politics." In *Philippine Colonial Democracy*, 41–69. New Haven, CT: Yale University Southeast Asian Studies, 1988.

Parrini, Carl. "Charles A. Conant, Economic Crises and Foreign Policy, 1896–1903." In *Behind the Throne: Servants of Power to Imperial Presidents, 1898–1968*, edited by Thomas J. McCormick and Walter LaFeber, 35–66. Madison: The University of Wisconsin Press, 1993.

Parrini, Carl. *Heir to Empire: United States Economic Diplomacy, 1916–1923*. Pittsburgh: University of Pittsburgh Press, 1969.

Parrini, Carl, and Martin Sklar. "New Thinking about the Market, 1896–1904: Some American Economists on Investment and the Theory of Surplus Capital." *Journal of Economic History* 43, no. 3 (1983): 559–578.

Polanyi, Karl. *The Great Transformation: The Political and Economic Origins of Our Time*. Boston: Beacon Press, 2001.

Pomeroy, William. *The Philippines: Colonialism, Collaboration, and Resistance*. New York: International Publishers, 1992.

Prashad, Vijay. *The Darker Nations: A People's History of the Third World*. New York: The New Press, 2007.

Prashad, Vijay. *The Karma of Brown Folk*. Minneapolis: University of Minnesota Press, 2000.

Prashad, Vijay. *The Poorer Nations: A Possible History of the Global South*. London: Verso, 2012.

Rafael, Vicente L. *Contracting Colonialism: Translation and Christian Conversion in Tagalog Society under Early Spanish Rule*. Durham, NC: Duke University Press, 1992.

Rafael, Vicente L. *The Promise of the Foreign: Nationalism and the Technics of Translation in the Spanish Philippines*. Durham, NC: Duke University Press, 2005.

Rafael, Vicente L. "Welcoming What Comes: Sovereignty and Revolution in the Colonial Philippines." *Comparative Studies in Society and History* 52, no. 1 (2010): 157–179.

Rafael, Vicente L. *White Love and Other Events in Filipino History*. Durham, NC: Duke University Press, 2000.

Renda, Mary. *Taking Haiti: Military Occupation and the Culture of U.S. Imperialism, 1915–1940*. Chapel Hill: University of North Carolina Press, 2001.

Richardson, Jim. *Komunista: The Genesis of the Philippine Communist Party, 1902–1935*. Quezon City, Philippines: Ateneo de Manila University, 2011.

Richardson, Jim, and Jonathan Fast. *Roots of Dependency: Political and Economic Revolution in 19th Century Philippines*. Quezon City, Philippines: Foundation for Nationalist Studies, 1979.

Ritter, Gretchen. *Goldbugs and Greenbacks: The Antimonopoly Tradition and the Politics of Finance in America*. Cambridge: Cambridge University Press, 1999.

Robinson, Cedric. *Black Marxism: The Making of the Black Radical Tradition*. Chapel Hill: University of North Carolina Press, 2000.

Rodgers, Daniel T. *Atlantic Crossings: Social Politics in a Progressive Age*. Cambridge, MA: Harvard University Press, 2000.

Rodney, Walter. *How Europe Underdeveloped Africa*. London: Verso, 2018.

Roediger, David. *The Wages of Whiteness: Race and the Making of the American Working Class*. London: Verso, 1991.

Rosenberg, Emily. *Financial Missionaries to the World: The Politics and Culture of Dollar Diplomacy, 1900–1930*. Durham, NC: Duke University Press, 2004.

Rosenberg, Emily. "Foundations of United States International Financial Power: Gold Standard Diplomacy, 1900–1905." *Business History Review* 59, no. 2 (1985): 169–202.

Rosenberg, Emily. *Spreading the American Dream: American Economic and Cultural Expansion, 1890–1945*. New York: Hill and Wang, 1982.

Ross, Dorothy. *The Origins of American Social Science*. Cambridge: Cambridge University Press, 1991.

Rothbard, Murray N. *A History of Money and Banking in the United States: The Colonial Era to World War II*. Auburn, AL: Ludwig von Mises Institute, 2002.

Salamanca, Bonifacio S. *Filipino Reaction to American Rule, 1901–1913*. Hamden, CT: Shoe String Press, 1968.

Schmitt, Carl. *The Concept of the Political*. Chicago: University of Chicago Press, 1996.

Schmitt, Carl. *Political Theology: Four Chapters on the Concept of Sovereignty*. Cambridge, MA: MIT Press, 1985.

Scott, William Henry. "A Minority Reaction to American Imperialism: Isabelo de los Reyes." *Philippine Quarterly of Culture and Society* 10, no. 2 (1982): 1–11.

Sexton, Jay. *The Monroe Doctrine: Empire and Nation in Nineteenth-Century America*. New York: Hill and Wang, 2011.

Shafer, Neil. *A Guide Book of Philippine Paper Money*. Racine, WI: Whitman, 1964.

Silbey, David. *The Boxer Rebellion and the Great Game in China*. New York: Hill and Wang, 2012.

Simpson, Audra. "Sovereignty, Sympathy, and Indigeneity." In *Ethnographies of U.S. Empire*, edited by John Collins and Carole McGranahan, 72–89. Durham, NC: Duke University Press, 2018.

Sklansky, Jeffrey. *Sovereign of the Market: The Money Question in Early America*. Chicago: University of Chicago Press, 2017.

Sklar, Marin J. *The Corporate Reconstruction of American Capitalism, 1890–1916*. Cambridge: Cambridge University Press, 1988.

Skowronek, Stephen. *Building a New American State: The Expansion of National Administration Capacities, 1877–1920*. Cambridge: Cambridge University Press, 1982.

Stanley, Peter W. *A Nation in the Making: The Philippines and the United States, 1899–1921*. Cambridge, MA: Harvard University Press, 1974.

Steinbock-Pratt, Sarah. *Educating the Empire: American Teachers and Contested Colonization in the Philippines.* Cambridge: Cambridge University Press, 2019.

Stoddard, Lothrop. *The Rising Tide of Color: Against White World Supremacy.* New York: Charles Scribner's Sons, 1920).

Sturtevant, David. *Popular Uprisings in the Philippines, 1840–1940.* Ithaca, NY: Cornell University Press, 1976.

Tadiar, Neferti. *Fantasy-Production: Sexual Economies and Other Philippine Consequences for the New World Order.* Quezon City, Philippines: Ateneo de Manila University Press, 2004.

Tadiar, Neferti. *Things Fall Away: Philippine Historical Experience and the Makings of Globalization.* Durham, NC: Duke University Press, 2009.

Taylor, Alan M., Maurice Obstfeld, and Jay C. Shambaugh. "Monetary Sovereignty, Exchange Rates and Capital Controls: The Trilemma in the Inter-war Period." IMF *Staff Papers* 51 (2004): 75–108.

Taylor, John R. M. *The Philippine Insurrection against the United States.* Vol 3. Pasay, Philippines: Eugenio Lopez Foundation, 1971.

Temin, Peter. *Lessons from the Great Depression.* Cambridge, MA: MIT Press, 1989.

Terami-Wada, Motoe "The Sakdal Movement, 1930–34." *Philippine Studies* 36, no. 2 (1988): 131–150.

Thornton, John. *Africa and Africans in the Making of the Atlantic World, 1400–1800.* Cambridge: Cambridge University Press, 1998.

Trask, Haunani-Kay. *From a Native Daughter: Colonialism and Sovereignty in Hawai'i.* Honolulu: University of Hawai'i Press, 1999.

Veeser, Cyrus. *A World Safe for Capitalism: Dollar Diplomacy and America's Rise to Global Power.* New York: Columbia University Press, 2002.

Wallerstein, Immanuel. *The Capitalist World-Economy.* New York: Maison des Sciences de l'Homme; Cambridge: Cambridge University Press, 1979.

Wickberg, Edgar. *The Chinese in Philippine Life 1850–1898.* Quezon City, Philippines: Ateneo De Manila University Press, 2000.

Wilderson, Frank, III. *Red, White and Black: Cinema and the Structure of U.S. Antagonisms.* Durham, NC: Duke University Press, 2010.

Williams, Eric. *Capitalism and Slavery.* Chapel Hill: University of North Carolina Press, 1994.

Williams, William Appleman. *The Tragedy of American Diplomacy.* New York: W. W. Norton, 1972.

Wilson, Andrew R. *Ambition and Identity: Chinese Merchant Elites in Colonial Manila, 1880–1916.* Honolulu: University of Hawai'i Press, 2004.

Wolfe, Patrick. "Land, Labor, and Difference: Elementary Structures of Race." *American Historical Review* 106, no. 3 (2001): 866–905.

Wolfe, Patrick. *Settler Colonialism and the Transformation of Anthropology.* London: Cassell, 1999.

Wolters, Willem G. "Flooded with Foreign Coins: Spanish and American Administrators Dealing with Currency Problems in the Philippines 1890–1905." *Journal of the Humanities and Social Sciences of Southeast Asia and Oceania* 157, no. 3 (2001): 511–538.

Wolters, Willem G. "From Silver Currency to the Gold Standard in the Philippine Islands." *Philippine Studies* 51, no. 3 (2003): 375–404.

Wolters, Willem G. "How Were Labourers Paid in the Philippine Islands during the 19th Century?" In *Wages and Currency: Global Comparisons from Antiquity to the Twentieth Century*, edited by Jan Lucassen, 139–168. Bern, Switzerland: Peter Lang AG, 2007.

Wolters, Willem G. "Uneven Impact and Regional Responses: The Philippines in the 1930s Depression." In *Weathering the Storm: The Economies of Southeast Asia in the 1930s Depression*, edited by Peter Boomgaard and Ian Brown, 83–108. Singapore: Institute of Southeast Asian Studies, Singapore, 2000.

Index

Baldoz, Rick, 123

Banco Español Filipino, 18, 23, 50, 54

Bangko Sentral ng Pilipinas. *See* Central Bank of the Philippines

Banking Holiday, 130

banking under American rule, 6–7, 10, 47, 49–51, 63, 69–70, 75, 79–80, 82–86, 92–93; banker resistance, 67, 72–74. *See also* Philippine National Bank (PNB)

Bankruptcy, 31, 76, 104

Barnes, Charles Ilderton, 53–54

bimetallic currency systems, 17–18, 20–21, 42, 58

Biosca, Francisco Aguilar y, 12–13

bonds, 30–32, 34, 91, 98, 100, 108–9, 130; Liberty Loan, 107

Boxer Rebellion (China), 49–50, 167n37

Bretton Woods system, 153

Bryan, William Jennings, 42

Bureau of Audits (Philippines), 185n33

Bureau of Education (Philippines), 83–84

Bureau of Insular Affairs (BIA, U.S.), 61, 90–91, 99, 104–5, 107–10

Bureau of Posts (Philippines), 83–84

Bureau of Treasury (Philippines), 108

Cabinet Crisis (1923), 110

capitalist crisis, 2, 11, 129–30

capitalists, Filipino, 34–35, 97–98, 109, 116, 120, 124–26, 143. *See also* Filipino elites

Caribbean, 15, 28–29, 96. *See also individual countries*

Casa de Moneda de Manila, 17

Castillo, Andres V., 129, 135–36, 185n33

Catholicism, 26, 161n20

cedulas, 25, 28, 33

Celeste, Jose, 132–33

centimos de pesos, 17

Central Bank of the Philippines, 4, 129, 136, 148–49, 185n33

central banks, 4, 96, 108, 130, 133–37, 147–49, 185n33

Certificate Redemption Fund, 90

Chartered Bank of India, Australia, and China, 18, 50

Chase National Bank, 128

China, 15, 16, 65, 77, 107. *See also* Boxer Rebellion (China)

Chinese population, 21–23, 34; currency usage, 49, 73; financial practices, suspicion of, 76–77; policing and surveillance of, 57, 68, 75, 73, 79, 135; racism toward, 56–57, 64, 169nn66–67

Christianity, 13, 16, 26, 77, 91, 145, 151, 162n46, 168n47. *See also* Catholicism; Protestantism

class, 35–38, 137–40, 142–45, 149. *See also* peasants

Coates, Francis, 105–6, 108–10, 112–13

coffee, 16

coins, 24, 33, 40, 52, 58, 61, 66–67, 72, 89–90, 93, 187n66; access to, 99–100; copper, 16–17, 48–49, 75, 77–78; counterfeiting of, 7, 17, 22–23, 59–60, 64–65, 77; gold, 17–18, 20–21, 46, 54–56; Malay, 14; minting of, 15, 17, 21, 33, 63, 100; silver, 21, 23, 50, 59–60, 63, 76, 100; unofficial, 76–78; valuation of, 30, 51, 54–55. *See also* "bad money,"; currency; Mexican coins; pesos (Filipino)

colonial calibration, 180n46

colonial pedagogy, 67–68, 73–75, 80–84

Commission of International Exchange (CIE, U.S.), 43, 65, 71

communism, 122, 140–41, 148. *See also* anticommunism

Communist Party of the Philippines. *See* Partido Komunista ng Pilipinas (PKP)

Conant, Charles, 41, 43–46, 52–53, 71, 74, 81, 166n13, 166n15, 166n21, 168n52; currency reform, 55, 57–66, 89–90, 92, 108, 169n61

Concepción, Venancio, 101–2, 105–7, 180n44

conditional decolonization. *See* decolonization, conditional

consumerism, 54, 56, 124

copper coins, 16–17, 48–49, 75, 77–78

Cornell University, 71, 86

Corpus, Rafael, 112, 116, 185n33

corruption, 7, 35, 70, 86, 104, 106

counter-decolonization, 3, 66, 75, 97, 145; and banking, 10, 79–80, 82–86, 92–93; Commonwealth tactics, 121, 145–46; and currency reform, 62, 68, 72, 77–79, 89, 92–93; and military campaigns, 66, 69, 87–88; and monetary authority, 3–6, 68, 71, 150–52; and the PNB, 95, 99, 103–6, 109, 117; and self-governance, 11, 84–87 counterfeiting, 7, 17, 22–23, 59–60, 64–65, 77

countersovereignty, 3, 156n7

credit, 6–7, 83, 95, 99–100, 107, 115, 126–27, 133–4, 137, 145; agricultural, 42, 69, 95, 98, 109, 138–39, 144; foreign, 9–10, 30–32, 121; and Chinese merchants, 22; and counter-decolonization, 89. *See also* loans

credit networks, 22, 138, 144

Criollos population, 13, 19–20, 54, 161n24, 168n58

criticism of American colonial rule, 58, 87, 114–15, 147

Cuaderno, Miguel, 136–37, 147–50, 185n33

cuartillas, 17

Cuba, 3, 29, 47, 65, 103

currency: autonomous, 129–34, 136; and counter-decolonization, 62, 68, 72, 77–79, 89, 92–93; in the Malolos Republic, 30, 32–33; precolonial, 14–15; under Spanish rule, 12, 15–18, 20–21. *See also* American colonial currency; "bad money,"; Conant, Charles; exchange rates

Currency Reserve Fund (CRF), 90, 107–8, 144

currency reserves, 7, 104, 106–8

Daland, William A., 55, 57

debt, 4, 9, 63, 84, 88, 102, 122, 142; and Chinese merchants, 22; national, 31–32, 104, 126; personal, 137–39, 143, 145, 152, 171n2; imperial, 129–32, 136; and sovereignty, 6. *See also* credit; loans

decolonization, conditional, 14, 27, 93, 140; and capitalism, 125, 127, 143, 149–50; economic experts, 128–29; legacy of, 153–54; and Malolos Republic, 9, 29, 32, 35, 38; and monetary authority, 137, 152; movement for, 1–2, 120–21, 126–28; and the PNB, 95, 117–18; under Wilson administration, 97

decolonization, unconditional, 8, 14, 27; movements for, 38, 140–43, 146, 153–54; and racial capitalism, 7, 150, 152; threat of, 19, 38, 87, 97, 121, 126, 149–50

de los Reyes, Isabelo, 58

del Pilar, Marcelo, 25–27

del Rosario, Arcadio, 34

democracy, 85, 87, 104, 120, 127, 133–34, 153; cacique, 175–76n80

Democratic Party (U.S.), 42, 94–97, 165n6

devaluation (currency), 121, 129–32, 136

dispossession, 5, 70, 138, 142, 171n2

Division of Currency, 71, 79, 89, 98

dollar (U.S.), 44, 58–62, 101, 153; dollar diplomacy, 121; and Mexican dollar, 46, 48, 50, 52, 67, 73–75; and Philippine monetary system, 6, 11, 69, 128–33, 136–37, 147, 150–51. *See also* gold standard system

dollar/peso (Mexican), 25, 28, 76–77; counterfeiting of, 22–23; and Philippine peso, 59–60, 63; role in Philippines economy, 15–18, 40; silver vs. gold politics, 20–21, 54–55; and U.S. dollar, 46, 48, 50, 52, 67, 73–75. *See also* Mexican coins

Du Bois, W. E. B., 2, 165n6

Dutch East Indies, 16, 53

economic experts: American, 2, 4–7, 9–10, 41–42, 63, 70–71, 93, 96, 108, 113; criticism of, 64, 112–14, 116; Filipino, 8, 120, 124, 128–29, 131, 135–37, 185n33; importance of, 26–27, 42–44, 51–52, 65, 150; international, 134

economic imperialism, 2, 5–6, 9, 41–46, 61, 65–66, 70–71, 96, 151, 172n6

economic nationalism, 120, 122–25, 132, 153

education of Filipinos by American authorities, 67–68, 73–75, 80–84

Edwards, Clarence, 90

embezzlement, 76

Encarnacion, Vicente Singson, 130, 133–34, 185n33

Enlightenment, 19

Evangelista, Crisanto, 140–41

exchange rates, 7, 12, 20, 46–47, 50–51, 56, 61, 63, 72, 74, 137

Executive Order 6102 (U.S.), 130, 134, 185n37

experts, economic. *See* economic experts

exports, 16, 69, 98, 101, 117–18, 123–24, 137–38, 181n60

Fanon, Frantz, 5, 38, 157–58n16

Far Eastern Review, 110

farming. *See* agriculture

fascism, 122, 140. *See also* authoritarianism; Nazism

Feced, Jose and Pablo, 20

Federal Reserve Act (1913), 99

Fee, Mary, 40–41, 66

interest, 31, 82–83, 89, 91–92; rates, 5, 32, 138, 187n71

interimperialism, 2, 11, 43, 65, 151

internationalism, 132, 134, 140–42

interstate cooperation, 121–22, 153

Islam, 14, 16, 186n60

Japan, 1, 16, 60, 105, 124, 142

Japanese occupation of the Philippines, 124, 131, 138, 141–42, 144, 146, 148, 153

Java, 53, 127

Jenks, Jeremiah, 71–74, 77, 81, 90, 168n52, 169n67, 179n20

Jones, H. D. C., 55, 57

Kalipunang Pambansa ng mga Magsasaka sa Pilipinas. *See* National Association of Peasants in the Philippines

Karuka, Manu, 3, 156n7

Katipunan, 28–29, 87, 163n60

Kawal ng Kapayapaan (Soldiers of Peace), 144

Kemmerer, Edwin, 71–78, 90, 117, 171n3, 172n5, 174n46, 175–76n80, 178–79nn19–20, 183n108; on banking policy, 79–81, 84, 98, 138; on colonial currency, 88; on self-governance, 84–87

Kramer, Paul, 7, 159n23, 180n46

labor market, 35–38, 123, 140, 144

labor organizations, 139–40, 144

La Política de España en Filipinas (journal), 20–21

La Solidaridad (newspaper), 25–26

Latin America, 16, 71, 76, 96, 168n49

League of Nations, 121

Legarda, Benito, 55–57, 169n61

literacy, 48–49, 59, 113

loans, 6–7, 43–44, 96, 100; agricultural, 42, 69, 98; and economic crises, 107–8, 138; and infrastructure, 88, 91; national (under Malolos Republic), 30–32, 34; and the PNB, 95, 102, 104–6, 111, 145; from the Postal Savings Bank, 82–83

loyalists (to Spanish colonial rule), 9, 20–21, 23–24

Luzon, 16, 33, 35, 37, 77, 91, 137–38, 144

Mabini, Apolinario, 31

MacArthur, Arthur, 49–52

Malaysia, 14, 16, 141

Malolos Republic, 9, 29–39, 57–58, 69, 131

Manela, Erez, 178n8

Manila, 1, 15, 28, 30, 53, 57–58, 67–68, 92, 139–42, 153; banks in, 47, 50, 63, 72, 74, 81–82, 88; as financial center of the Philippines, 18, 20, 22, 48, 50, 63, 72, 77, 81, 91; strikes in, 37

Manila Customs House, 32

Mariana Islands, 3, 29

market, laws of, 5, 51–52, 74, 132

market knowledge, 3, 5, 7, 9–10, 41–44, 54, 65, 105, 150; of Filipinos, 8, 54, 64, 68, 73, 75, 79, 97, 106, 129. *See also* economic experts

Martin, Henderson, 99

Marx, Karl, 51

Marxism, 122, 157–58n16

McIntyre, Frank, 99, 109–12

McKinley, William, 42, 44, 50, 52, 69, 96, 166n13

Mcleod, John T., 54

Mestizo population, 7, 13–14, 16, 18–21, 24–25, 28, 33, 55–56, 85; bankers, 72, 75; Chinese mestizo population, 34, 57, 161n24

methodology of book, 8–11

Mexican coins, 16–18, 20–23, 25, 28, 40, 48, 50, 52, 54–55, 59–60; circulation after American colonial currency adopted, 63, 72–77. *See also* dollar/peso (Mexican)

Mexico, 3, 15, 21, 65

migrants: Chinese, 21, 56–57; Filipino, 120, 122–23, 125

migration, 56–57, 123, 125

militarism, 11, 122, 137

military (Spanish), 14, 28

military (U.S.), 6, 29, 32, 37, 39, 45–53, 63, 68–69, 79, 91–92, 143, 150–52; expenditure, 66, 77–78, 87–89, 107; U.S. Army, 61, 94, 103; U.S. Navy, 28

Mindanao, 141

minting of coins, 15, 17, 21, 33, 62–63, 100

monetary authority, definition, 3–4

monetary system, autonomous, 128–37, 147

monetary unification, 21, 23

moneychangers, 41, 47, 50, 64, 76

"Money Question," 42, 165nn7–8

monometallic currency systems, 17

Monroe Doctrine, 3

Monte de Piedad, 18

morality, 18, 50, 57, 85, 111, 116
Morton Trust Company, 53, 168n49
Murphy, Frank, 124, 130

Nacionalista Party (Philippines), 116
Nagano, Yoshiko, 107, 170n76, 179n28, 186n52
National Association of Peasants in the Philippines, 139
National Development Company, 124–25
National Economic Council, 124–25
National Economic Protectionism Association
(NEPA), 124
nationalism, 8, 11, 27–28, 36, 58, 95, 112, 129,
145, 151, 178n8; economic, 98–99, 114,
120, 122–25, 132, 134, 153; and internationalism, 140–41; and un/conditional
decolonization, 14, 120, 152
National Land Settlement Administration,
145
Native Filipinos: and banking and savings,
80–87, 93, 152; and capitalism, 111–12,
124–25, 151; currency usage, 48–49, 55–
56, 59–61, 63–64, 73–75, 93; education of,
67–68, 73–75, 80–84; precolonial, 14–15;
policing of, 75, 77–79; and race, 7, 22,
53–57, 84; self-governance of, 4, 6, 84–87,
91, 104–6, 120, 135, 146, 151–52; uprisings
and opposition to authority, 18–19, 28,
36–37, 39; wages paid to, 54–55, 77.
See also Philippine American War (1899)
natural laws of economics, 3–4, 26, 43–45,
128, 132
Nazism, 122, 140
nepotism, 72, 106, 114
Netherlands, 141. See also Dutch East Indies
New Spain. See Mexico
newspapers, 64, 106, 109–10, 113–14, 140,
187n72, 187n84; anticommunist, 140,
187n84; critical of American authorities,
63, 86–87, 104–5, 142; pro-American,
46–47, 50, 104, 108
New York City, 62, 69, 88, 96, 101, 106–7
Nolting, William, 81–82

onzas, 17
Open Door thesis, 165n6, 166n21
Osias, Camilo, 115
Osmeña, Sergio, 97–98, 101, 112–13, 117,
119–20, 124, 130

paper currency, 23–25, 32–33, 90, 100
Parrini, Carl, 156n7, 165n7, 166n13
Partido Komunista ng Pilipinas (PKP), 140–41,
187n84
Partido Sakdalista (Sakdal Party), 142. See also
Sakdalista movement
paternalism, 4, 6, 60–61, 70–71, 75, 78, 81–82,
95; and banking, 83, 85, 90, 111–12; and
decolonization, 120, 125, 127–28, 143, 145,
152; of Wilson administration, 96–97; of
Wood regime, 103–6, 113
patriotism, 30, 34–35, 124
Payne-Aldrich Tariff Act (1907), 89
peasants, 7, 25, 171n2; collective action of,
139–40, 142; and finances, 22, 82, 88, 100,
137–38, 145; rebellion of, 11, 19, 28, 69, 92,
97–98, 144, 153, 187n84
pedagogy, colonial, 67–68, 73–75, 80–84
pensionados, 86
People's Homesite Corporation, 145
pesos (Filipino), 17, 59–60, 62–65, 76, 100,
130, 132. See also American colonial currency; Conant, Charles
Philadelphia Record (newspaper), 86–87
Philippine (Las Filipinas), origins of word,
160n3
Philippine American War (1899), 9–10, 29–31,
41, 39–41, 46, 57, 93, 99, 101, 166–67n24;
insurgencies after, 62, 68–69, 87–88, 97,
151–52; war tax, 33–35
Philippine Chamber of Commerce, 109
Philippine Coinage Act (1903), 61–62
Philippine Commission, 52–57, 62, 85, 87,
168n47, 169n61
Philippine Commission for Independence, 126
Philippine Commonwealth, 11, 119, 121, 124,
141, 184n11, 185n33; and imperial debt,
131, 136; monetary system, 129, 131–38;
opposition to, 142–43, 146, 153; status of,
127–28, 145
Philippine Independence Mission, 1
Philippine Legislature, 100, 114–15; Philippine
Assembly, 85, 87, 91, 93, 185n33
Philippine National Bank (PNB), 10, 95,
98–102, 151; and anti-Filipinization,
103–6; crisis of, 94, 102, 104–9, 111–18,
152; and Wood regime, 109–17
Philippine National University, 115, 132
Philippine Revolution (1896), 151

policing, 28, 75–76, 80, 91, 120, 134, 136, 150; of Chinese population, 57, 68, 73, 75, 79, 135; of economics, 7, 10, 66, 68, 152; of Native population, 68, 77–79; of radical organizations, 140–43. *See also* surveillance

politics of recognition, 7, 37–38

Portugal, 15, 141

Postal Savings Bank (PSB), 79–86, 92, 108, 111, 174n49

postcolonialism, 2, 7, 11, 133, 148–50, 153–54

poverty, 28, 53, 81, 86, 137–39, 143–44, 149

Prashad, Vijay, 154, 184n8

progressive conservatism, 143–44

Progressivism, 70–71, 172n5

protectionism, 120, 122–25, 129, 140–41. *See also* tariffs

Protestantism, 175n72

Puerto Rico, 3, 29, 80

Quezon, Manuel, 92, 97, 99, 114, 116–17, 124, 128, 130, 139, 142; social justice campaign, 143–45

racial capitalism, 2–9, 13–14, 19–20, 35, 38, 42, 65–66, 70–71, 127, 149–50, 157n14; crisis of, 11, 44, 120–24, 129

racial hierarchies, 2, 5–6, 56, 75, 122, 128, 143, 149–50, 166n15; and monetary systems, 53–55, 89; under Spanish rule, 9, 13–14, 19, 23–24, 28; and taxation, 33–34

racial paternalism. *See* paternalism

racism, 5, 140, 145; toward Chinese population, 21–23, 56–57, 64, 135, 169nn66–67; toward Filipino migrants, 122–23, 125; toward Indio population, 23–25; institutional, 7, 123, 125; toward Native Filipinos, 53–54, 56, 84. *See also* Filipinization: opposition to; Nazism; slavery; white supremacy

radicalism, 19, 120, 139–45, 148, 150; and currency, 59–60, 67, 73, 129; Philippine radical tradition, 11, 121–22, 153; and violence, 38

Rafael, Vicente, 6, 160n3, 163n63

railroads, 7, 35–37, 91

Ramos, Benigno, 142

reactionary logics, 3, 11, 59, 70, 120, 122, 124, 131, 140–41, 144–46

reales, 17

reparations, 131

Republican Party (U.S.), 42, 94–97, 103–5

retail, 30, 37, 41, 46–48, 59, 67, 138; Chinese retailers, 7, 49, 57, 68; Native retailers, 49, 55, 57

Retana, Wenceslao, 20

rice crisis, 138–39

Rizal, Jose, 20, 22

Robinson, Cedric, 157n14, 184n8

Roosevelt, Franklin D., 122, 130, 134

Roosevelt, Theodore, 62, 69

Roosevelt, Theodore, Jr., 137

Root, Elihu, 53

Rosenberg, Emily, 173n10, 173n10

Rothbard, Murray N., 165n9

Roxas, Manuel, 1–3, 114–16, 127

rural communities, 69–70, 82, 97–98, 137–40, 142, 144–45. *See also* Agricultural Bank

Russian Revolution (1917–1923), 140

Sakdal (newspaper), 142

Sakdalista movement, 140–44

salapi, 14, 16

Sancianco, Gregorio, 33

saving, 7, 18, 47, 69, 93, 135, 174n49; and self-governance, 79–87, 152. *See also* Postal Savings Bank (PSB)

securitization, 72, 80, 90–92, 97, 100, 109; of capitalism, 29, 124–25, 134, 149–51; of colonialism, 41, 69, 126; through market knowledge, 3; of racial hierarchies, 5–7, 9, 120

seigniorage, 6–7, 53, 62, 89

self-determination, 97, 124, 147–48, 150, 154

self-governance, 2, 11, 103–4; Native Filipino capacity for, 4, 6, 37, 84–87, 97, 105–6, 125–27, 151–52. *See also* decolonization, conditional; Philippine Commonwealth; postcolonialism

Seven Years War, 15

Silver Certificate Fund, 62, 107

silver coins, 17–18, 20–21, 23, 46–50, 54–63, 76, 100. *See also* bimetallic currency systems; Mexican coins

silver standard system, 18, 20–21, 26, 40–42, 46–65, 76, 100, 107, 109; British demonetization of, 168n52; "free silver" movement, 42

"white love," 6

whiteness, 40, 53–55, 80, 84, 122; and banking, 68, 72, 75, 106–7, 116, 152, 173n10; as category, 166n15; and the Democratic Party, 42, 165n6; and racial capitalism, 5–7, 9, 41, 44–45, 65, 70, 157n16, 172n6; and self-determination, 96–97; white paternalism, 6, 10

white supremacy, 2–4, 13, 61, 70, 96–97, 122–23, 142, 151, 155n2, 174n54; and economic experts, 41, 44–45, 103, 113, 152

Willis, Henry Parker, 99–102, 105, 107, 178n19, 179n20

Wilson, E. R., 109, 111–13, 185n33

Wilson, Woodrow, 96–97, 103–4, 178n8

Wisconsin school (diplomatic history), 156n8, 165n7

Wood, Leonard, 94–95, 102–4, 107–11, 180n44; Filipino challenges to Wood regime, 112–18

Wood-Forbes Report, 94, 103–6, 119

worker organizations, 139–40, 144

World War I (Great War), 94, 96, 98, 121–22; financial crisis, 102–3, 107–8, 152

World War II, 123, 144, 146, 148–49, 153

Wright, Ben F., 81–87, 108, 110–12, 114–17, 174n46, 183n108

Wright, Luke, 78